Stranger in the Family

Stranger in the Family

A Guide to Living with the Emotionally Disturbed

by Claire Burch

The Bobbs-Merrill Company, Inc.
Indianapolis / New York

The Bobbs-Merrill Company, Inc.
Publishers: Indianapolis / New York

Library of Congress catalog card number 76-173211
Designed by Martin Stephen Moskof, Inc./Mitchell Zetlin
Manufactured in the United States of America

For Laura and Emily and Elizabeth and for Bradley Burch

Acknowledgments

The author wishes to express her gratitude to Marshall Bellovin whose research and writing during the earlier development of this book made it possible to continue at a time when a personal tragedy had literally stopped progress.

She also wishes to express gratitude to literary agent Phoebe Larmore for her loving patience, to Robert L. Robinson, public information officer of the American Psychiatric Association for his enormously helpful advice and guidance, to the numerous psychiatrists and mental health personnel, both conventional and radical, who gave freely of their time and energy during interviews, and to her children and family for their understanding during the hundreds of hours that went into preparing the manuscript.

And finally to editor Sonia Robbins for allowing the spirit of the book to emerge: the single premise that every human being in emotional pain has a right to dignified treatment which respects his individuality.

Table of Contents

Preface

STRANGER IN THE FAMILY: A Guide to Living with the Emotionally Disturbed may help thousands of American families troubled by emotional disturbance in their midst. It may also help many mentally ill persons themselves to understand what form their treatment may take.

It is a timely book, coming as it does when the main thrust of modern treatment of the mentally ill is away from long-term stays in mental hospitals and toward the treatment of the mentally ill person in his own community. In most cases families are being asked to cope with their sick member while he or she is undergoing some form of treatment or rehabilitation. Indeed, they are not only asked to "cope," they are asked to *help,* and it is difficult for many families to do either. It is for these families in trouble that the author offers so much and with a broader scope and perspective than we have seen before.

Relatives of those in emotional trouble can learn from this book how to live more calmly and comfortably with an individual who might be identified in psychiatric terminology as "schizophrenic," "paranoid," "manic-depressive," "phobic," "addicted," "brain damaged," "mentally retarded," or what will you. (It is not the names that should matter to the family, but rather the behavior that disrupts interpersonal relationships, as the author so clearly explains.) Virtually the entire range of troublesome situations that arise in coping with a mentally ill person are described in this book, and so far as possible sensible advice is rendered as to how to deal with them. It is anything but an itemization of discrete "nursing tips," however. Rather, it helps the anguished relative to understand how his own attitudes, values, and thought processes affect the therapeutic situation for better or worse.

The winds of change blow vigorously in our society. Since 1954, changing policies and attitudes toward the mentally ill, together with the advent of the psychotropic drugs, have greatly reduced the number of patients confined in public mental hospitals and the length of time they stay there. Had the annual rate of increase in the number of patients hospitalized in the early fifties continued to this day, there would now be upward of 800,000 patients in public mental hospitals. Instead, the figure hovers around 350,000, and it goes down every year. Some states make more rapid progress than others in reducing their public mental hospital patient population. In Massachusetts, for example, the patient census is down fifty percent since 1955. At the Boston State Hospital, where this writer was superintendent for many years, there has been a 72 percent decrease in number of patients since 1953! California has actually closed one of its public mental hospitals, and at least two other states are about to do the same.

Nevertheless, public mental hospitals continue to be an essential and important component of the national armamentarium for combating mental illness. While some of them, unfortunately, continue to suffer from lack of public support, most of them are giving excellent care to patients as part of a network or continuum of community services. For most patients the duration of stay in them is now measured in days and weeks rather than months and years. The old image of the public mental hospital as a "warehouse" for the forgotten mentally ill has long since ceased to reflect the reality.

Understandably, as a professional, this writer would put some things differently than does the author. For example, we would like to see some of the remarkable advances in medicine, psychiatry, and behavioral science described a little more fully —as for example the discovery of the relationship between rubella early in pregnancy and mental deficiency; new knowledge of inborn errors of metabolism; the mapping of areas of the brain related to functioning, the exciting development of the science of genetics, and various other biomedical and biochemical advances. It is true, as the author points out, that we have a long way to go before all of the mysteries of the origins of the mental illnesses are uncovered, but truly remarkable advances have been made.

We would also take a much harder line than does the author by way of disabusing the public of the notion purveyed by some that mental illness is a "myth." Syphilis of the brain is no myth, nor were the conquest of pellagra and the elimination of the triad of symptoms associated with it—diarrhea, dementia, and death. Toxic deliria, caused by septic infections, has all but disappeared. The delirium associated with alcoholism and drugs is very much with us, but the process is reversible if managed early enough. These forms of mental disorder are no myths and manifestly these illnesses call for diagnosis, evaluation and treatment by a physician.

Be that as it may, the author is eminently fair in presenting to her readers the potentialities and the limitations of the range of professionals who administer to the mentally ill today.

Perhaps the greatest virtue of the book is that it is written by a poet and an artist and, moreover, by one who herself has suffered the turmoil of emotional disturbance in her family. She has thus experienced the initial bitterness that so naturally attends the onset of tragedy. But the bitterness, anxiety, and frustration have receded as she has transferred her energy into articulating the painful, but successful, learning experience she endured for the benefit of others.

Throughout the book she fervently pleads with the troubled family never to give up hope. But she also cautions them repeatedly against false expectations. Her poetic and heartfelt plea is a simple one addressed to all humans; namely, that they consciously aspire to ever greater tolerance of those who are "different" in an effort to lessen the gulf that exists between them and us so that the "different ones" who can function outside of a protected setting can be free to live in our world, accepted on their own terms, as people "different but equal." Psychiatrists know that when families sincerely make such an effort in behalf of one of their own it usually works, and we vigorously endorse her plea.

Walter E. Barton, M.D.
Medical Director
American Psychiatric Association

Stranger in the Family

Chapter 1
What Is Emotional Disturbance?

You are the friend or relative of a person who is emotionally disturbed and you are starting to read a book which tells you how it is possible to best live with that person, maybe even help him. If your husband, brother, wife, sister, parent, child, friend or lover has been having emotional problems for a very long time you will be at this point thoroughly confused, so confused in fact that you may be in great emotional pain yourself. Your feeling will reflect the jungle of conflicting attitudes and opinions that have been expressed to you by authorities from the time you first tried to get help, the jungle of conflicting attitudes in the community in which you and the "patient" live, and the jungle of conflicting attitudes in yourself which have come about because there is so little agreement about what "crazy" is, what makes it come about, and who is really suffering from it.

Up to now you may have been told at various times that your relative's inability to function in the way that the majority of people do in this culture was caused by constitutional weakness, metabolic or chemical inbalance, or poor heredity. If so, as a loving friend or family member you are clearly the nurse or caretaker taking steps to protect, discipline, reeducate or simply watch over him.

Suppose, however, you have also been told or have read at various times that your relative may be emotionally disturbed because he was unconsciously rejected by his mother or father in infancy, or because his marriage partner or the family in which he grew may have laid on him their own confusion, mystification, or unexpressed goals (thus putting him into a double bind), or even because he is having a reaction to the warped values of the society in which he lives. These statements will have alternately confused and upset you, made you feel frightened and angry, and interfered with your ability to help the person you love.

Let us suppose for a moment that in varying degrees all these statements may be true. If they are, doesn't that make you feel unable to cope with the role you have assigned yourself out of concern?

Not necessarily, for you can help yourself become more aware of the way all of us push each other's buttons without succumbing to paralyzing guilt, if you understand exactly *why* you are *not guilty.*

Out of the tower of babel which makes up theories of emotional disturbance in our time, one clear pattern can be finally observed. This pattern will help you live with your relative, falling neither into the simplistic trap of blaming everything on a physical situation over which you can have no control, nor the opposite trap of assuming that because you may sometimes play a role in aggravating your relative's symptoms, you are at fault, should blame yourself, or should feel that you are not the person to help.

The pattern is this: some people come into this world more sensitive to pain and conflict stimuli than others. For assorted reasons, constitutional, biochemical, whatever, their reactions as they proceed through life are such that traumas which can be accepted by some of us cause trouble in them. Maybe their perceptions in some areas are expanded in the way that a person's perceptions are expanded when he is on an LSD or mescaline trip; maybe their perceptions are distorted in a similar way. Whatever the cause, if your relative is one of these especially sensitive people, he will be caused excessive pain by the ordinary kinds of mistakes every family makes in the process of raising children; he will be caused excessive pain by the ordinary injustices of the world in which he lives.

If your relative is disturbed and clearly organic causes like brain tumor, hardening of the arteries of the brain, diet deficiency illness, etc., have been ruled out, chances are that he is one of those extraordinarily sensitive people and has been so from birth. Without blaming yourself, therefore, you can recognize that some of the events which may happen in your family can trigger or worsen his symptoms, and learn to probe these events or interactions in the way that will be described in this book, neither taking on guilt nor ignoring your possible role in the ups and downs of his disturbance. When you understand that there is no blame attached to the possibility that your goals for him may have been experienced by him as pressures or that your lack of goals may have been experienced by him as absence of confidence, you will begin to truly help, for you will be dealing with him where *he* is at, and that courageous understanding will open previously closed doors.

Not only will this awareness help you deal specifically with the problems of functioning he faces, but it will help you not to view each instance of emotional disturbance as a tragedy but more a situation in which this supersensitive person can be guided to an awareness of the pitfalls and by the same token the positives (these qualities can lead to art and sometimes do) of his nature.

Bob, a seventeen-year-old boy with clear eyes and neat brown hair, stands at the window of his ward at the State Hospital, waiting for his mother to arrive for a visit. Since he was a small child he has been excessively aggressive, hitting and beating up other children, disturbing classes, constantly demanding attention. Years of treatment with only small signs of improvement have drained his parents of emotional and financial resources, so that they now feel it necessary to hospitalize him, for their own and their other children's sake as well as Bob's. The hospital staff describes him as follows:

> . . . the patient has a marked thought disorder involving gross tangentiality, flight of ideas and loosening of association. He also has some self-referential and delusional thinking leading to paranoid fears. His affect is somewhat flat, though he is emotionally very labile, being capable of laughing and crying within a short space of time. His speech is extremely rapid. Interpretation of proverbs are moderately concrete. He is fully oriented in time, space and with regard to person, and there is no significant memory loss.

Bob's mother is still baffled and gnawed by guilt, never quite sure that her son's behavior is not somehow her fault. The doctor's diagnosis has left her as much in the dark about the meaning of Bob's trouble as in her first years of running from doctor to doctor for help. And Bob, hunched over the phonograph in the dayroom listening to a Beatles' record, finds his condition even more mystifying, for he has been told that he is ill, but what he actually experiences is rage, frustration, anxiety, and having been labeled right out of his former world, his own room and books, his chance to "be with the other boys."

What is wrong? What is this "emotional disturbance" and why has it happened? We can deal with someone who is ill or disturbed without knowing exactly what caused his condition, but our own feelings of health and confidence will be strengthened if we know something about what we are dealing with.

There are many professional theories about the causes of emotional disturbances or illnesses. For Dr. Lauretta Bender there is a "maturational lag," a predisposition to illness. Dr. Heath of Tulane University postulates biochemical causes. Heredity is responsible, according to Dr. Kallman. Drs. Hoffer and Osmond suggest hormonal difficulties which cause changes in the senses. Numerous psychological theories stress imperfect nurturing, unloving handling or some kind of environmental trauma. Dr. Bruno Bettelheim, who writes that "love is not enough," describes children emotionally crippled by their parents' unconscious wish for these children "not to be." Some social scientists lay mental illness at the door of poverty and corruption. And Dr. Ronald Laing suggests that "mentally ill" is simply a label given to those whose style of alienation differs from the alienation of the majority. Any one or two or more of these conceptions may be correct, but knowing what they are may not be so helpful when someone close to you suddenly begins to act in a bizarre manner and is called "mentally ill."

As the reader of this book, you are probably a parent, child, or spouse of someone who has been labeled mentally or emotionally ill or disturbed. Your relative may be hospitalized, as Bob is, or living at home. Whatever the circumstances of your particular situation, this chapter will try to give you some solid ground in what may often be misty territory.

It is easier for us to say what mental or emotional illness is *not* than to say what it is. It is not a disease like measles, proven to exist by characteristic physical signs.

Emotional illness exists in a broad frame of reference, the prevailing values of the world into which the patient is born.

The trouble it causes is comparative rather than absolute, and any opinion about its severity is as reflective of the person describing it as of the condition.

It probably has multiple causes, any of which can trigger a course of events in which disappointment leads to frustration and frustration leads to a succeeding disappointment.

It can be considered a "special strategy that a person invents in order to live in an unlivable situation."

Mental illness has been called a "myth" by Dr. Thomas Szasz. It can more simply be seen as a communication or language problem. So far I have used the terms "mental illness," "emotional illness," and "emotional disturbance" interchangeably. Each term means something different to everyone who uses it. Dr. Karl Menninger calls this situation the Tower of Babel in reverse. "We are not all using different words for the same thing, but we are using the same word for different things." In one sense we use these three terms to refer to a condition where behavior is different from what we consider as being normal. But the ways in which this behavior is different vary so widely that we are really not talking about the same thing at all.

You may know someone who surprised you greatly by announcing that she had been seeing an analyst four times a week for the past three years. Nothing in her behavior would have led you to call her mentally ill. At the other extreme is the young man described at the beginning of this chapter whose behavior was so displaced from the norm that he had to be hospitalized. Both these people can be considered emotionally disturbed, but the difference depends as much upon the theory invoked as on their outward behavior.

It is not simply a set of symptoms that defines a person as emotionally disturbed. We all know the image of a man seemingly mad who, viewed from another perspective, would be the only sane man in a mad world. However, society is based on a set of values and though we cannot say it is *better* to navigate bomber planes than sit crosslegged in the woods involved in fantasy, we admit that the person who is so different from the prevailing norm is in big trouble, will likely as not be unhappy, and may turn in bewilderment or rage to behavior that eventually makes his difference damaging.

Once a person has been identified as a patient and a label given to his disturbance, a predictable series of events begins. People "watch out" for his symptoms, interpret them as a sign of malignancy, and force him either to change or become resigned to being thought ill. Before this labeling, his symptoms could have been interpreted by those around him as "bad moods," "general orneriness," or "weak character," and anger rather than concern would be the usual response.

Mental illness is a condition in which other people have examined the patient and called his problem mental illness. Behavior may be privately disturbing to a person but not classified as an emotional problem until someone tells the patient his feelings are "different from the normal, that what he is feeling is not what most people experience in that situation." A soldier shaking and urinating in fear under direct fire is not considered mentally disturbed; he can see many of his comrades similarly agitated. The same soldier experiencing these symptoms during a USO show back at the base would be classified as sick because he is now *out of step* with the people around him.

One way we can look at the situation is to see positive as well as negative mental health problems. Dr. Gerald Caplan has said that psychiatry can be helpful even to those classified as "well" and for this reason we include under the scope of disturbance what are called "transient situational reactions." These include social injustice of all kinds, dire poverty, deprivation of human rights, a degraded self-image as a result of prejudice, early loss of a beloved relative, incurable physical illness, earthquake, hurricane . . . war!

Pressures these problems cause can hardly be dismissed by generalizing; the tenth child of itinerant migrant workers is rarely received in the same way as is the tenth child of well-to-do parents who plan for him and are able to provide for him materially as well as emotionally. All emotional disturbances have a social and economic side. This is a positive mental health problem in that "deviant" behavior under some circumstances is acceptable under others. Every social worker knows that a child who will not "make it" in one foster home will in another. The child's inner difficulties may still be there, but his outer world is important also.

Another aspect of this side of the problem was observed by the famous nineteenth-century psychiatrist Janet who said, half jokingly, "If a patient is poor he is committed to a public hospital as psychotic; if he can afford the luxury of a private sanatarium, he is put there with a diagnosis of neurasthenia; if he is wealthy enough to be isolated in his own home under constant watch of nurses and physicians, he is simply an indisposed eccentric."

Negative mental health problems are what we usually call "illnesses." The people in whom they occur may or may not become patients, depending on the severity of their discomfort, how obvious it is to others, how much they want help, and whether or not help is available. What is called the medical model, in which one kind of behavior is called "schizophrenia," another "personality disorder," a third "psychoneurosis," has some limited value both in imposing a certain amount of order on what would otherwise be a chaotic situation and in providing some attempt at communication among doctors, patients, and families.

When a close relative or friend is classified as ill or disturbed, you can be with that person in a way that is helpful and non-hurting even if you do not know what his trouble really "is." You cannot, nor should you try it, be a therapist. You need not know the causes of symptoms to learn to accept all the emotions a person experiences. When symptoms seem to you especially self-destructive, remember that you too are entitled to your honest reactions. Progress is often made with a warm-hearted nurse, an involved parent, a gentle volunteer, with another human being who is there and responsive.

"People help people," says Dr. Milton Greenblatt, "even patients help patients." Whatever the cause, expectations or prognosis, your attitude of hopefulness can sometimes accomplish as much as professional goal-oriented therapy.

Only when confronted with "professional" failure does the mysterious and elusive nature of what is often called mental illness become so troublesome and haunting. Overwhelmed perhaps by the pain of living with a chronic sufferer you may feel a compulsion to grasp at the reasons for his torture in a way that is less vague, less contradictory, that has some "rules." On a day when your son or daughter says (after three years of major tranquilizers, five years of therapy, two courses of shock treatment and a year in a therapeutic facility), "They are back. They are putting poison in my food because they want to kill me," you will probably beg for The Answer.

Beyond this need for concrete cause-and-effect, cure, and answers, you may begin to look at the hairline differences between the emotionally disturbed and "sane" people such as author Anais Nin who at age twelve wrote in her literary diary, "There is one thing that troubles me. I feel different from everybody. I notice no child in my class of my age that thinks as I do. They are all alike, they are in accord. I know their thoughts, their ambitions. And I make comparisons. I am altogether different. Instead of being like brothers to me they are strangers. My desires, my dreams, my ambitions, my opinions, are different. Why am I not like everybody?"

Dr. Karl Menninger suggests that the labeled patient is not so different from you and me. "We think of the patient, not as one afflicted with a certain disease which [we] must name and then battle with and attempt to dispel, but rather as a human being, one somewhat isolated from his fellows, whose relationships have become mutually unsatisfactory and disturbing; to this he has reacted in various ways, all intended to salvage the situation and ensure survival, even at the cost of social acceptance. . . . Suppose that instead of putting so much emphasis on different *kinds* of illness we tried to think of all mental illness as being essentially the same in quality and differing, rather, quantitatively. This is what we mean when we say that we all have mental illness of differing degree at different times, and that sometimes some of us are much worse or much better. If one moves along a scale of well-being we can say that some people are relatively healthy, some are relatively sick, and that the latter are either mildly, moderately, or extremely sick. This behavior would vary of course depending upon the culture in which one lives, and the duration of the particular episode of maladjustment."

If mental health and illness are simply poles of a continuum, what can we say about mental health? At different times, in different places, we learn that:

> Health is a state of complete physical, mental, and social well being, and not merely the absence of disease or infirmity.
>
> Mental health is a condition which permits the optimum development, physical, intellectual, and emotional, of the individual as far as this is compatible with that of other individuals.
>
> A good society is one which allows this development of its members while at the same time ensuring its own development and being tolerant toward other societies.
>
> The healthy mind can meet with ease all normal environmental situations and the healthy minded person has the capacity to live harmoniously in a changing situation.
>
> There can be various levels of mental health accenting the possibility that the individual has a personal system of values in which mental health represents a value related to the values of the society as a whole.
>
> There are occasions and situations in which, from the point of view of mental health, rebellion or non-conformity may be far more important than social adaptation. It is clear that no single act should be taken out of context and no single criterion of behavior used in judgment of mental health.
>
> It would appear that in a changing society people who

do not change are in more danger of being in mental ill health than those who do.

A new goal may make unhealthy what has previously been regarded by society as mentally healthy. A judgment on the mental health of people must take account of the existence of ambitions within the group.

Dr. Lynn Gillis defines mentally healthy people simply:

> They feel comfortable about themselves; they experience emotions freely but are not bowled over by them—by fears, anger, love, jealousy, guilt, worries—and they take life's disappointments in their stride. They neither under- nor over-estimate themselves, they accept their shortcomings and have respect for themselves. They get pleasure from easy everyday things, have a tolerant and easy-going attitude and can laugh at themselves. Mentally healthy people feel right about others. They are able to give and receive love, certainly the greatest boon of all, and are able to have satisfying and lasting personal relationships. They respect the many differences they find in people, and have a sense of considerateness and responsibility toward them. Finally, they are able to meet the demands of life. In doing so they make the fullest use of their own capacities and put their best efforts into what they are doing. They set realistic goals for themselves, shaping their environment whenever possible and adjusting to it whenever necessary. They are able to think for themselves, accept their responsibilities and make their own decisions.

If the above statements constitute mental health you may realize that now and then you are exchangeable with the "patient," for no one exists in this world without sometimes experiencing the opposite of these praiseworthy emotions and ambitions. Like the patient, you will be bowled over by emotion, unable to take disappointments, fail to respect yourself, experience dissatisfaction, be unable to give and receive love. At such moments you will have some sense of the torment that hovers *most* of the time over the emotionally disturbed, to such an extent that they become disabled. You may understand then what Dr. Dana Farnsworth means when he says that people become ill because they have not learned how to manage their emotional and intellectual and physical resources.

If you have lived with an identified patient for many years you will probably agree with the idea that the absence of mental disease is not a sufficient yardstick for mental health. You may also find it helpful to realize that mental health is not the same for everyone. The genius, the moron, and the average man each has his own type of mental health.

Those who work closely with even the most severely disturbed know that your encounters with them may benefit you both. Fountain House is a rehabilitation center in New York where patients out of hospitals or chronically ill with emotional problems are given counseling and job training. If you sit in the waiting room of Fountain House you may find yourself in conversation with a young man who says he can remember events back to the time he spent in his mother's womb. When asked for details he gives authentic-sounding descriptions of his intrauterine existence.

If you acknowledge that his unusual description makes him "special," he may glow with friendliness and pride, for he is on a voyage where you cannot follow. Who is to say that if you only stand by without running in terror from his "thought disorder," you will not be broadened by his view?

Medical model descriptions, though necessary to the psychiatrist so that he can preserve some coherence in communication, are artificial in the sense that they pull, from the high narrow bridge along which we all walk, those people who draw attention to themselves by their lack of resemblance to the majority. How "sick" they would be in other circumstances, in other "rooms," hearing other voices, is impossible to tell in retrospect. You cannot snap their picture, take their histories, without a sense of concern, for sometimes their voyage is yours.

Chapter 2
Learning to Roll with the Problem

A forty-five-year-old man gets up to go to work in the morning. He pulls himself out of bed, reaches for the last cigarette of the pack he has smoked between 2 a.m. and dawn, and both his hands tremble so violently that the cigarette falls to the floor. "I can't make it," he says, starting to perspire in the same way he has every morning for a month. "I just can't pull myself together to face it. Put me away."

By "it" he means life, his job, responsibilities, family activities he has faced with unremitting effort and even some enjoyment for nearly twenty years. Now, for no reason that seems apparent, he is in the grip of a deathly depression, choked with anxiety about every detail of his day, so panicked to go about his previous routine that he would rather be placed in a mental hospital than have to look at his real feelings, decide what is the matter, and take some constructive action.

Looking at him you cannot know whether his drawn yellow face, the hollows under his eyes, and his weak fluttering movements are caused by the gradual onset of a psychotic illness, the painful result of a long neurotic conflict, or a difficult realistic situation which he has not revealed.

A mother, aged fifty-six, has just been discharged from a state hospital where she has spent seven years. She has had what the doctors called "hebephrenic schizophrenia," a form of illness in which much of her conversation consisted of foolish aimless phrases and her expressions seemed so vague and silly as to barely suggest the person she was before. Now a stabilizing dose of a strong tranquilizer has enabled her to sound normal, conceal some of her symptoms and handle others in a less disturbed way. Since her daughter has been told that she is well enough to leave, the young woman's conscience suggests that she should take her home. The mother cannot yet live alone or in a strange environment; she needs continuing support and help.

A nineteen-year-old girl has suffered from severe epilepsy all her life. Years ago tests determined that she also had minimal brain damage; recent retesting confirms this and the recommendation is that she be given vocational training so that she can manage to partially support herself in a sheltered workshop situation. Her mother has five younger children, the vocational training center is near an aunt's home and the aunt is asked to care for her niece for the next two years.

Accepting Mental Illness in the Family

It is never easy to accept the situation created by physically caused mental illness or emotional disturbance in your own family. Suppose your aged father, who has functioned well for most of his life, begins wetting the bed and displaying other symptoms of disturbance and senility. Normal aging brings problems of its own; if added to these is what the doctors may diagnose as a senile psychosis (probably a result of hardening of the arteries of the brain), the family will have to face a decision that is always difficult. Suppose the elderly man is now unable to cope with even his small retirement activities. His speech is slurred and sometimes rapid, vague references to the past becoming mixed with events of the present so that time seems fragmented. Recently he refuses to eat most of the food that has been prepared for him, saying that it probably is poisoned. A long-term organic psychosis in which there is progressive deterioration of brain tissue is very painful to accept. A realistic plan for the future must take many factors into account: prognosis with or without home care, family structure, what kind of community assistance is available, how strong the individual family members are.

Accepting the situation requires a measure of understanding of the *choices* that are available. Often there are multiple choices, any of which can lead to a healthy outcome if made freely and according to the capabilities of the particular family involved. What can sabotage those choices is irrational guilt, the kind that comes when a husband, wife, parent or child suddenly feels responsible in some measure for the present condition of his family member. This is the strongest deterrent to accepting the situation in a constructive way. Decisions involving sick people don't have to be made in a tragic miasma of pain and depression; they can be explored, the alternatives considered and the final choice recognized as never so final that it is irreversible.

You Shouldn't Accept the Situation as a Serious Problem Too Soon

Perhaps the most constructive way to accept emotional disturbance in the family is to refuse to accept it initially. By this is meant only the use of every preventive and persuasive power that families have to see if that part of the illness that may relate to outside pressure or realistic conditions can be helped.

Some people break down because of constitutional handicaps that exist in them from infancy, lags in maturing which make coping with the ordinary pains and annoyances of life an impossibility. Other people break down because a combination of constitutional sensitivity and unusual hard knocks in their environment are too much to take. Others break down because their outside trials and tribulations are all too real and extraordinary.

If a member of your family is slipping into a depression after some crisis such as loss of a child, involvement in a disaster, despair over attaining a desired job or marital relationship, you can lose that family member into a protracted psychotic illness by accepting the situation too soon. His doctor will treat the symptoms; it is your job to make yourself aware as quickly as possible of what his breakdown represents. What is he fleeing from; what in his present life, or memories, or view of the future, does he find so intolerable, so chilling that he must begin to slide into a slow-speaking shambling grey world?

Only a loving relative or another truly dedicated person can at such transition or prepsychotic moments almost literally grab hold of the patient and say, "Don't go, don't go! We *hear* you. We know what you suffer and will try to change what can be changed and mourn with you over what can't."

You should never accept the situation of a relative being seriously emotionally disturbed until you have exhausted all possibilities that what appears an insolvable problem to him is in reality unsolvable (there just *is* no alternative to his tension-producing job, he really *is* too old to change from driving a car to truck farming, there really *is* no way to raise the illegitimate child she still wants, there really *isn't* any way to save a marriage that has run a painful stormy course for many years).

You should first give the potential patient every opportunity to recover by the simplest possible means; rest, sympathetic attention, support and reassurance. You should never assume his complaints are crazy without first seeing, with an open mind, if there is any possibility of real justification for them. It may be helpful to see that he has a physical checkup to rule out organic illness or exhaustion, which may cause similar symptoms.

Except where there is danger of violence to others or himself, a wait-and-see period at home or while he is still able to function will sometimes bring out material that shows him to be wanting to *escape* into a hospital situation. If it is badly run or understaffed, occasionally hospitalization will only postpone uncovering his real problem.

With these cautions in mind, assume now that the man who finds it hard to get out of bed in the morning to face his job has been given the correct drug, encouraged to express his feelings, told that if his job is unbearable he will be helped to change. None of these measures have worked; despite his efforts to get hold of himself, he shows fatigue and apathy, loss of sleep, appetite and weight. As his depression deepens the tone of his muscles and skin lessens, he looks sad, feels heavy and slow. Routine tasks cheerfully executed before seem to become great burdens. He quits his job, stays at home, loses interest in his environment, hobbies, food and sex. Endlessly and painfully his thoughts circle around a very few subjects, his own inadequacy, his past sins, and the hopeless future. The slightest mistake made years ago reemerges as a grossly distorted haunting memory.

It is likely that he is now in the grip of a depression which you can care for at home only by accepting the situation as it has hardened into fact, no longer spending most of your time and effort trying to pull him up. A full-blown psychotic depression can be alleviated by special drugs, by special therapy and other means, but often it will have to run its course, which can go from months to years.

Accepting the situation of emotional disturbance in the family is, like the disturbance itself, a constantly changing position. The parent who totally conceals his child's disturbance on principle and the parent who presents it as an excuse for every bit of deviant behavior are both making the mistake of not suiting the degree of acceptance to the stage of the difficulty.

Accepting the situation does not preclude continued acceptance of the person who is disturbed, for the disturbance is not the patient. Family feeling or real feeling by any responsible person continues to exert a pull upwards against the illness that is sometimes an important determination in being able to accept a possibly permanent problem.

A terminal cancer patient remarked to his visitor, "Emotional disturbance is a luxury. You can't even *think* about such problems until you are reasonably sure you will continue to have a body in which they will develop."

Conditioned as we are to think about emotional disturbances as hopeless and mysterious, it is a cheerful note to realize that any disturbance which occurs in a physically healthy body is at least subject to eventual change. Except in cases where irreversible brain damage already exists, such problems can change. Maybe this is small comfort to those who have been told that the illness of a friend or relative is serious, possibly recurrent, in many cases representing a lifelong anxiety and watchfulness. Yet accepting the situation involves this point, for in it lies strength.

Emotional Disturbance Is Not a Death Sentence

A very tiny proportion of emotional disturbance leads to total debilitation and death. In this sense, there is always room for hope. What kind of hope? In accepting the situation, you must be careful about holding on to hope of a type that is unrealistic according to previous expectations. If this happens, hope can be a hindrance that leads to incorrect or harmful decisions, rather than the encouraging spur that it should be.

Sometimes you find it hard to accept the situation of emotional disturbance in your family for the reasons that the community stigmatizes the patient. There is an unpleasant quality to many of the responses of the disturbed person that baffles and antagonizes the person who is trying to help. In general, patients with a physical ailment will respond with some measure of gratitude to efforts at care. This gratitude provides a reward for the person in charge and makes it more likely that he will continue to want to help. People with psychotic and even neurotic problems are likely to vent anger or hatred or be indifferent to those who devote their day to selfless help. Therefore, an important incentive is often missing for the person who has to care for an emotionally ill relative. How can you keep doing what you do when he doesn't at least act grateful? Appreciation may not be forthcoming until his illness is gone, if ever.

Nevertheless, we are only human. Nobody short of a saint can give the devoted vigilant care that is needed by these patients, without compensation of some kind. Accepting the situation implies that some satisfactions will have to come to the person in charge. What these satisfactions can be depend to a great extent on personal needs and desires; they can be *anything,* but you must not expect them to proceed from the patient.

Evaluating the Situation

The kinds of trouble people get into emotionally are hard to classify and even harder to evaluate. Psychiatric labels can hurt; diagnosis can, in our present stage of community misunderstanding and suspicion, stigmatize the patient right out of his job, his friendships, even his marriage. Therefore, it is vital to find someone who can give you an accurate picture of what the situation actually is, without causing you to become so overwhelmed by the label or the name of the illness that you lose your sense of proportion.

It may help to look at the situation from the point of view of Samuel Butler, a novelist rather than a psychiatrist, who wrote, "All of our lives long, every day and every hour, we are engaged in the process of accommodating our changed and unchanged selves to changed and unchanged surroundings; living, in fact, is nothing else than this process of accommodation; when we fail in it a little we are stupid, when we fail flagrantly we are mad, when we suspend it temporarily we sleep, when we give up the attempt altogether we die. In quiet, uneventful lives the changes internal and external are so small that there is little or no strain in the process of fusion and accommodation; in other lives there is great strain, but there is also great fusing and accommodating power; in others great strain with little accommodating power. A life will be successful or not, according as the power of accommodation is equal or unequal to the strain of fusing and adjusting internal and external changes."

Viewed this way, it is hardly a disgrace to have an emotional problem, for sometimes these problems arise when highly endowed people make efforts so strong that even they cannot cope with their extraordinary demands upon themselves.

Arranging for Expert Advice

When you consult an expert for diagnosis and guidance, remember that in living with and caring about a family member you may have accumulated valuable insights that count for something in the psychological testing he will undergo. Don't be afraid to trust some of your own observations. Even when the situation has been so clearly confirmed by doctors that you cannot doubt it exists, you might remember that your own attitude will always have to loom large in deciding how it should be handled. Suppose, as has been discussed, the diagnosis is senile psychosis. Sure Grandpa is senile, certainly he wets the bed, talks wildly, and has difficulty remembering where he has put his glasses, his dentures, and his pipe. But the question of whether or not his illness should be accepted at home, in a nursing home, or in a state hospital is yours to answer; no amount of psychiatric dynamic explanation of his actions can replace unique self-knowledge. How much of Grandpa's company and illness can you take? How destructive will his presence be to the family? How will guilt about his exile to a state hospital affect your life and work? The choice of where treatment should take place should always take into consideration your actual relationship with the patient.

Are You Unconsciously Keeping the Patient from Improving?

Many individuals avoid depression by unconsciously keeping another person dependent upon them. It may not be obvious that this is the case; an alcoholic wife or husband or seriously disturbed child may seem to exist as a great burden for which the caretaking member of the family appears to sacrifice himself. The situation only becomes clear when the responsibility is somehow removed (death or treatment can do it). At that point the responsible person loses an object that is a convenient target for anger and depression, at the same time dependent on and part of himself.

This kind of complicated situation where the left hand does not know what the right hand is doing is not something you can work on directly in yourself. If it exists, treatment is needed for the caretaking person as well as the identified patient.

What usually happens is that the patient in the family by his real problem (and more often than not it *is* real, troublesome, and a source of quite conscious despair) provides an outlet rolled up into one neat package for all your negative feelings. You may therefore use the patient as an excuse to keep from having to face actions that are frightening and about which you have little real confidence.

> Mrs. William S. has had an unhappy marriage for at least nine of the eighteen years she has been married to Mr. S. Their six-year-old autistic (withdrawn, non-speaking) child Peter is a constant management problem; they have not been able to find a satisfactory day school and he requires

almost constant physical care. Falling into bed exhausted at the end of each day, Mrs. S. daydreams of taking a stand against her husband's unreasonable demands, getting a separation or a divorce. "If only I didn't have Peter to worry about," she muses, "I could fix myself up, get a job and step into some kind of new life, and pull out of this morass." What she fails to realize is that Peter is actually *needed,* for her promise to herself masks deep fear, almost total panic that were she to march off tomorrow she would not make it in that new life, that underneath she is simply not acceptable.

Dr. Don Jackson describes a situation in which change in the "patient" causes changes in the other family members. In one of his cases a husband called the psychiatrist to let him know that his wife, who has been hospitalized many times for depression, was planning to commit suicide. The doctor answered that there was little cause for concern, that the wife had actually shown improvement in her condition. The husband shot himself to death the day after the telephone call.

This need to embrace the patient's illness as the sponge that sops up family problems can be limited to one member of the family or spread like an epidemic. Dr. Boszormenyi-Nagy describes a patient who, after having spent many years in a psychotic state, started to show clear signs of improvement. This improvement produced or at least definitely coincided with a rash of anxiety in the other family members. In one family therapy session the mother explained, "Susan, you may have improved with the help of these doctors, but I know that deep down you will always harbor the same old resentments toward me that you used to have before." Naturally, the doctor points out, this statement elicited a feeling of despair in the easily discouraged patient, at the same time that it led to the collapse of her efforts at better behavior. Yet in this family nearly every member, for their own neurotic reasons, found it necessary to maintain young Susan as the patient, lest it become necessary to face certain conclusions about their own problems.

Often a problem of emotional disturbance in the family really exists, but people in charge of the patient create even more complications and unhappiness than are inherent in the situation itself. You may find yourself adding impediments to your moment-to-moment life with the person who has been labeled sick. This tendency not to make the best of things but to search out the most painful parts of every action can effectively prevent you from really accepting the situation by making it so bad that *nobody* could be expected to accept it.

Can You Roll with the Problem?

What can and cannot be accepted in a situation depends entirely on the individual makeup of the person living with the patient. This should be assessed with total honesty in a joint meeting between patient, friend or relative in charge, and doctor.

How to accept specific problems involved in caring for a friend or relative plagued by major emotional disturbance or even neurosis will be discussed in greater detail in later chapters. There you will find guides to day-to-day existence charted out by explorers *who have been there,* doctors, nurses and ordinary people who have spent much of their lives living with illness in many constructive and imaginative ways. As these chapters suggest, diagnosis need not be a signal for gloom or pessimism. Within the limits of the actual accepted difficulty, some reasonably pleasant life is often possible.

Suppose, however, that you have followed with the best will in the world the suggestions made by the doctor, the appropriate section of this book, and your own deeply involved urge to help. If, despite these efforts, made not blindly but with an acceptance of objective evaluation, the situation is getting worse, what is to be done then? You see your depressed mother flounder further and further inside the personal abyss across which you shout daily. You observe your aged father who had been diagnosed as suffering from a chronic brain syndrome become less and less coherent, unable to maintain any control over his body functions, confused and mischievous in a way that is dangerous to the others at home. You see your emotionally disturbed child start acting out in a way that is not responsive to reassurance, disciplinary measures or sedation, setting fires or becoming sexualyl promiscuous to the point where other people are harmed.

Less obvious than these signs, suppose you simply find

yourself at a low ebb, unable for some reason (a temporary personal situation or just cumulative exhaustion) to handle the kinds of difficulty that you had handled before. What was possible for a while seems overwhelming; you find your equilibrium all but gone.

In all these situations, you must face and deal with the possibility that hospitalization (hopefully temporary) may be necessary. Forward-looking community mental health centers recognize the tremendous need for partial hospitalization of all kinds to ease living arrangements that almost work except for stress. In an ideal community setting, a relative caring for a patient could explain that he needs temporary relief from the responsibility. Day hospitals would be available where the patient could go for a structured therapeutic eight hours, and return home to sleep. Night hospitals would be available where the patient who is making a gradual adjustment could be put up for an overnight lodging. Part-time hospitals would be available where the patient could divide his time between such an unpressured and organized environment and the increasing pressures of his family and the outside world, thereby giving patient and family hours of intermission and respite. Unfortunately such arrangements exist only in a few communities. Understandably, families often give up in exhaustion, when a little relief of this nature would save the situation.

Let us assume that community facilities for partial hospitalization are not available or have been attempted without success. In this case you must learn to face hospitalization with the same pragmatic approach, recognizing it as a possibility that may have value in this situation.

If Hospitalization Is Necessary

Freud once said, "Psychoanalysis is the process whereby we learn to give up neurotic suffering for just ordinary day-to-day misery." Bearing in mind that unfortunately this is more than a joke, sometimes you may have to face the fact that all your care is not enough. Perhaps you are just too tired to shoulder the whole responsibility for a while. Or perhaps it is beyond what you can ever hope to provide at home.

If you have tried to maintain your relative, adjusting family schedules, making special arrangements for outside help and advice, and it has not worked out, this is not time to feel like a failure. Certainly your efforts, though they may not have eliminated the problem, will have helped the patient to know that he is wanted, that an incentive exists for him to get better. Even as you pack his suitcase for the hospital, don't forget that he is a little better off, maybe much better off, than if you hadn't tried.

Only children and neurotics believe themselves to be all-powerful. You are not. Some emotional illnesses respond totally to sensitive handling at home, others don't. Some problems tend to disappear, only to appear again at a time when energy is at a low ebb. When this happens, learn to shrug, and hospitalize the patient for as long as is necessary for you to regain your strength to help him begin to function again outside.

For as Long as Is Necessary

These words of course spell the difference between justice and injustice. Occasionally there are facts to be taken into consideration that have nothing to do with the patient's condition, only the world in which he lives.

> Carolyn W. is divorced. She has two young sons and a seventeen-year-old daughter with a history of emotional difficulties since she was three. Annie's problems are a difficult, disorganized personality that is cumulatively trying to everyone around her, and anxiety that takes the form of a constant barrage of pressured, worrying questions. These symptoms have through the years been resistant to careful constant handling, extra measures of love and attention, drug therapy, and psychotherapy. The other children have suffered, Mrs. W. has suffered, and in her own way Annie has suffered, for she is in no way retarded and is in every way painfully aware of her own differences from other people.
>
> Annie has been hospitalized briefly twice before, both times when Mrs. W. was at a low ebb, both times with not too good results. Each time the goal was to help her to return home as quickly as possible; each time Mrs. W. mentally prepared herself to resuming the task of guiding Annie through her perilous encounters with other people.

This time Mrs. W.'s position has changed, both in life and in her thinking. Now, in order to have a balanced existence without extreme deprivation, she would have to work. With Annie at home, life was sharply limited, Mrs. W.'s days revolving (despite all the resistance she could muster) around her daughter's extraordinary needs. In a going marriage there are contentments and joys, apart from child care, built into the situation at home. Without them, Mrs. W. is caught in a net of uninterrupted burden, and, still in tune with her own nature, she realizes that the job she was once able to do can no longer be done by her.

Home care may be feasible under one set of circumstances and impossible in another. When caring for the patient makes it impossible to provide yourself with any aspect of normal existence (Mrs. W. may be able to make a new life for herself and her healthy boys but she can move in *no* direction with Annie at home), then you must question just how resentful you may eventually become about the self-sacrifice which caring for this relative will involve.

Unfortunately, the seriousness of emotional disturbance is as often dependent on the circumstances of the people around the patients as on the actual objective condition of the patient. Thus Annie's illness (now catalogued, given an APA label and a prognosis) might have gone on for years without being called anything, with Annie merely functioning at a less organized level in the community where she lived.

In case this aside prompts the reader to redouble efforts to keep the patient at home regardless of the difficulties involved, it must be said that since there is no sure guide to which kind of handling is better in certain major illnesses, you may find to your surprise that the place that was considered last choice is oddly less traumatic than choice number one, which was beyond your means, or choice number three, which seemed to offer more of the apparent comforts of home.

You may find that the hospital recommended because of its superb teaching staff is currently at the mercy of a rebellious nursing staff, underpaid attendants, or an administrative shakeup, which can sabotage the best treatment plan. You are just as likely to find that the patient begins some step toward integration and recovery by the presence, sometimes by sheer accident, of a warm individual within the hospital framework who takes an interest, expresses real concern and is extra kind. This can be a doctor, a nurse, an attendant, or simply another patient.

At the stage when it is necessary to accept hospitalization, you will find yourself hard put to accept the illogical and unending red tape involved in finding the right place for the patient. It is impossible to exaggerate the difficulties as you ask agencies and information sources for help. Painfully you see that the average doctor has only the sketchiest idea of facilities that may be suitable, and that information given even by social service agencies will often be outdated and inaccurate.

It is hard to accept the unbelievable delays in sending medical records and the confusion that exists as to what records are pertinent. Placement is often delayed as long as four months because of these details alone. It is hard to accept some of the medieval hospital attitudes that surround admission, especially in cases where the kind of illness is a heightened sensitivity to such treatment. Here is an example of one admission:

> Mr. and Mrs. Henry G. have found it necessary to bring their daughter to a state hospital for treatment. Julie has attempted suicide twice before; this time her wrists are a mass of razor slashes and her parents are rightly afraid to care for her at home during this stage of her disturbance.
>
> Mrs. G. phones the hospital to ask procedure and is told to bring her right in to the adolescent unit. They arrive, but on arrival are told that Julie will have to remain in the general admissions building several weeks for screening. The girl starts to cry, pleading that she will go voluntarily if she "can go in with the teenagers, I only want to go with the teenagers."
>
> The G.'s request an interview with the doctor in the adolescent unit and, by a miracle of timing, this is granted. After seeing Julie and discussing her history, the doctor feels she will be acceptable for their unit, but he cannot admit her until her previous records have been received.
>
> "They were sent out three weeks ago," Mrs. G. says in dismay.
>
> "Yes, well, they haven't been received. It may be harm-

ful to your daughter's state of mind to process her through general admission now. Why don't you take her home and the hospital will notify you when the records are received. Then she can come directly into the unit."

Nine days later, having received word that the records are there, the G.'s and an even more disturbed Julie arrive at the adolescent building, only to be directed back to general admission.

"But we were told she could go directly into the building for teenagers," Mr. G. says bitterly.

"That doctor had no authority to make such a statement. All patients must be screened here for several weeks," says the new voice of authority, a clerical worker with an officious ring to her voice.

Once inside, a nurse looks at Julie's suitcase carefully packed with her favorite clothes, and removes one skirt and blouse and one set of underwear. "The rest of the suitcase goes home," she says. "All she'll need here is one change; she can rinse it out every few days."

"But over the phone they told us to bring a full suitcase and a handbag," says Mrs. G.

"Don't care what they said over the phone. That's the rules here."

The G.'s are asked to sign a release for a minor voluntary commitment, and as they turn toward the desk Julie is led away before they realize it, without so much as a formal minute in which to say goodbye. Even a bank or the telephone company would have more courtesy, but in this crucial entrance into the hospital world, amenities are often ignored. When the G.'s ask if they can see their daughter for a moment to say goodbye, they are told this is impossible, the "system" has taken over, and they will be told by mail when they can visit.

Although such aspects of hospital admission and procedure are difficult to accept, you may be helped to do so by considering the alternatives: who else can care for the patient during this period when it is necessary? Are these annoyances major or minor as against the real help occasionally offered? Do these shoddy arrangements represent the whole tone of the treatment or are admission details relegated to less competent people as a result of inadequate staffing? If the latter is the case, you may be pleasantly surprised to find that even under such conditions dedicated doctors exist on the ward who may be able to help Julie over her most recent hurdle.

Accepting the Need for Hospitalization

Let's assume that you have finally been able to accept the fact that the patient must be hospitalized. If you have spent many years of your life caring for that person, you may find yourselves overwhelmed with feelings of guilt for no longer being able to do the job and pained by the impending separation. There may also be a surge of relief at the new personal freedom. Within hours you find yourself involved in feelings you never knew existed—separation anxiety, anger at fate that all your efforts did not produce a cure, a niggling doubt that maybe those efforts were wasted and misguided, and even physical symptoms such as nausea, dizziness, and an overwhelming fatigue.

These last are likely forms (there may be others) of so simple an emotion as grief. Our standards are still such that despite public communications to the contrary, placement in a mental hospital is still considered a stigma. If a relative goes away to college, or gets an out-of-town job, or marries in a distant state, you may be sad but you do not mourn. As that relative leaves to go to a mental hospital, you may find yourself mourning him as though he had died.

You cannot accept emotional illness in the family or help in any way if you too closely identify with the patient. As one woman put it, "Though I understand John's trouble I seem doomed to experience everything now through his eyes. What he couldn't enjoy, I can't enjoy. It's all wrong and I'm going to have to stop it. Especially since the rest of the family needs fun, games, and horsing around, just to keep the toothache of his new breakdown from spreading at the moment."

Try to take such a step while the patient is in the hospital. He needs you to make the most of the time in which he is not in your care, to recharge flagging spirits and build up some new reserve. You will be able to accept his need for hospitalization when you can accept your own need for relief and relaxation. As one woman describes such a period:

Now the wet sloppy sky is full of ocean smells (gulls and grass). The children miss their father but they are still looking for joy. So they are being very wild cranberryish and beach shrubbery and jogging along beside me like proper little brown barefoot duners.

Am getting slim and beautiful as will befit my new life if I ever have the courage to be happy. It always seemed disloyal to John to be happy because he couldn't. I can solve all the problems with the back of my hand and go stomping back into life because I love it so, if I can just work out this one small thought.

Married to a man in the grips of a cyclical depression, this woman found her own kind of acceptance. It lay squarely—as it does with all of us—in what she termed "my secret smile."

Accepting the Idea That Your Efforts Are Worthwhile

Dr. Walter Barton, medical director of the American Psychiatric Association, feels that some individuals have a kind of awareness that can be communicated to families as a guide in accepting the view that a relative may have an illness that will be with him all his life.

"There are families," says Dr. Barton, "who are sensitive and have seen an illness go through episodes, who are alert to the changes in behavior and can intervene or refer their relative back for treatment when necessary. There are other families whose problems are so intertwined with the patient that it becomes difficult for them to be objective." It is the first kind of family that is likely to have a measure of respect for the right of an emotionally disturbed person to some of the good things of life.

An honest acknowledgment of the patient's illness will do more toward calming him than any number of sincere lectures. There is a story by J. D. Salinger that describes what happens when a sick person is surrounded with adult falseness. Seymour Glass, a gifted young man, has come back from the war slightly paranoid and goes to Florida with his conventional wealthy young wife. We meet him for just a short time, playing on the beach with a four-year-old girl. Both are looking for "bananafish" in the water, an invention of the man's which delights his young companion. The climax of their relationship is reached when the little girl says that she has seen a bananafish with six bananas in its mouth. At this moment there is a sense of complete understanding between the child and the adult which redeems the man's pain and briefly but poetically restores happiness to life. But several minutes later, when the young man is returning to his hotel room, he turns on a woman in the elevator and asks her why she is looking at his feet. "If you want to look at my feet, say so . . . But don't be a god damned sneak about it!" Of course the woman isn't looking at his feet.

For Seymour, contemplating a life in which he has got himself married to a woman who is a combination of "hair nets, deodorant bottles, and flip psychiatric platitudes," it becomes impossible to seek help for his problem, treatment for his illness. The real people in his life, wife and mother-in-law, *deny* illness. Then where, asks Seymour, does the pain come from, because unmistakably it is there.

To recognize that you are not omnipotent, that even the gift of love can sometimes fail to pull your friend or relation from the mystery of a psychotic episode, is not to deny the value of that love, or the care which you gave him as long as you could. You hold his hand, talk over problems, help make new plans for the ninth time, and sometimes see with a sadness that cannot be recorded that people you love are gravely caught for what seems like forever in their plan. At such moments you can only help by continuing to say "yes" to their right to life, *with* the illness, yes to their right to what is left.

The nature of emotional disturbance has changed little if at all since the days when families rode determinedly into homesteading territory, descended from their covered wagons, and fed their horses and their babies. When you strip modern treatment methods to the bone, you still find an area in which some illnesses remain intractable and others flare up and subside with no pattern that you can recognize and control. Faced with this existing ignorance you must make a choice. You can either accept the patient as possessing a right to the best life he can live, even with his handicap, or penalize him for his problem by depriving him of everything else.

Chapter 3

Picking Your Way Through the Jungle: Different Forms of Treatment

After a member of your family has been diagnosed as having some form of emotional disturbance you face the question: What is the best type of treatment? If the choice is up to you, it's important to know the alternatives.

Let's first look at the range of treatments available. These include *psychotherapy* (treatment of emotional illness through psychological communication); *electro-convulsive therapy* (shock) which attempts to change the current emotional state by chemical or mechanical means; *drugs,* especially those of a tranquilizing or anti-depressant nature; and *psycho-social therapy,* which includes social goals, milieu therapy, and foster homes (treatment through changing a person's environment).

Psychotherapy

Psychotherapy, or the treatment of a person's emotional disorder through his own mind, is the most usual method of treatment today. This form of therapy may be considered a many-branched tree, with each branch representing a distinct "school" of thought. These include psychoanalysis (with all of its sub-branches); client-centered therapy, founded in recent years to enable the patient to "do it himself"; behavioral therapy, based on the assumption that humans, like other animals, can relearn new forms of behavior; group therapy, family or marriage therapy, and tangential types of psychotherapy such as Moreno's psychodrama, and hypnosis.

Psychotherapy may be compared to "fatherly" talks with a minister or teacher. Religious people or "gurus" also sometimes provide "faith cures" for emotional disturbance. Today religious and psychiatric psychotherapy exist side by side. Psychiatrists, understanding both the effectiveness and the pitfalls of religious or mystical treatment, prefer to use a less other-worldly approach. However, many realize the traditional appeal of religious faith cures, and they recognize that, as Dr. Jerome D. Frank of Harvard puts it, "religious healing in primitive societies, as in the Western world, tends to exist side-by-side with naturalistic treatment by medicines, manipulations, and surgical operations."

"The first principle of psychotherapy is that it is done by some *one* for someone *else*," according to Dr. Karl A. Menninger. Dr. Robert White lists five elements of the psychotherapeutic process: A therapeutic, doctor-patient relationship; expression by the patient of his feeling; the pointing out of a patient's feelings by the therapist, either by paraphrasing them (as in client-centered therapy), or by interpreting them (as in psychoanalytic therapy); transference by the patient (where he begins to think of the doctor or therapist as a "substitute parent"); and the formation of new behavior as a result of the entire treatment.

Let us see what a first therapy session might be like. Dr. Vernon W. Grant, a psychologist, describes a session with a twenty-nine-year-old patient named Marcella who has a great deal of trouble in getting along with other people.

Psychologist: What sort of trouble do you have with your neighbors?

Marcella: Well, they did a lot of things to bother me.

Psychologist: What kind of things?

Marcella: Some little things, and some pretty serious things.

Psychologist: Can you give me some examples?

Marcella: Well, what bothered me a lot was their getting into the house when we were away.

Psychologist: Could you be sure of this?

Marcella: I certainly could. Things were damaged. Sometimes they took things.

Psychologist: How much damage was done?

Marcella: Well, not a lot, but they had no right to enter the house.

* * * * *

Psychologist: Why was this [damage] done?

Marcella: Just to bother me. To show that they had been in the house.

Psychologist: You mean, that was the only reason it was done?

Marcella: The reason was to annoy me so much that we'd move out of the neighborhood. It was to get rid of us.

Psychologist: What do they have against you?

Marcella: I don't know.

Psychologist: Is your whole family unpopular?

Marcella: Well, my husband gets along all right.

Psychologist: Is it the children?

Marcella: I don't think so.

Psychologist: Then it's you they want to get rid of?

Marcella: Yes, it's me.

Psychologist: And you have no idea why?

Marcella: No.

Psychoanalysis

Psychoanalysis, initially a treatment for neurotic disorders, was formulated by Sigmund Freud and propagated and modified by his followers. Freud's great contribution was his theory of the unconscious as a basic part of a person's personality. The unconscious, according to Freud, universally consists of three parts: id, ego, and superego. The id is the source of various drives and instincts such as hunger and sex. The ego is the individual's conception of himself, functioning as a "check" of the more primitive and "untamed" id. The superego acts as a "conscience" and a transmitter of family and cultural background.

The basic principles or characteristics of psychoanalysis include: *free association, interpretation, transference,* and *dream analysis.*

Freud described the method and purpose of *free association* to his patients at their first therapy session:

> Before I can say anything to you, I must know a great deal about you; please tell me about yourself. . . . Your talk with me must differ in one respect from an ordinary conversation. Whereas usually you rightly try to keep the threads of your story together and exclude all intruding associations and side-issues, here you must proceed differently. You will notice that as you relate things various ideas will occur to you. You will be tempted to say to yourself this or that has no connection here . . . or it is nonsensical so it cannot be necessary to mention even if you feel a disinclination against it, or indeed just because of this. Later on you will perceive and learn to understand the reason for this injunction. So say whatever goes through your mind. Act as if you were sitting at the window of a railway train describing to someone behind you the changing views you see outside. Finally, never forget that you have promised absolute honesty, and never leave anything unsaid because for any reason it is unpleasant to say it.

Free association is a way that psychoanalysts can "get at" some of the underlying problems, since it strips away layers upon layers of defenses or "masks" which people use to cover troubling thoughts and feelings, many stemming from early childhood.

An important characteristic of psychoanalysis is that the therapist will usually offer some sort of *interpretation* of a patient's behavior—past or present.

The analyst's skill in interpreting his patient's thoughts and feelings brought out in free association may be the difference between a successful and an unsuccessful treatment. For example, the same type of interpretation may enhance the self-esteem of one type of patient and weaken that of another. Thus a patient who is overwhelmed with feelings of guilt may gain considerable support from interpretations that imply that these feelings were inevitable reactions to the actions of others and he is not to blame. Such a formulation might aggravate the condition of patients who are already too prone to transfer responsibility for their difficulties to the shoulders of others.

A patient's "feeling toward . . . the therapist" usually results in a third characteristic or process of psychoanalysis, the *transference.* The analyst becomes a substitute parent in the mind of the patient, although a more understanding one. Transference takes many different forms. During the process the patient may have one or more of the following feelings: obedience and submission, anger (because the analyst has not provided a "miracle cure"), childishness, fear, worthlessness, and a desire to control and dominate the analyst, usually out of anger at the reopening of buried memories and hidden feelings.

When the Biblical Joseph interpreted the Pharoah's dreams he was practicing an ancient form of *dream analysis.* Sigmund Freud made this an important part of psychoanalysis. To Freud, dreams represent repressed desires, mainly sexual in nature; and they contain a myriad of childhood phantasies.

Dreams, according to Freud, have two levels of meaning: a manifest, or plot-line meaning; and also a latent, or hidden meaning that contains many unfulfilled wishes as well as inner conflicts and fears. Dreams are seen by Freudians as loaded with sexual symbols that reinforce Freud's idea that everyone passes through a number of stages of sexual development. His method of treatment is based on the theory that people are driven primarily by sexual impulses.

Freudian psychoanalysis is a long and expensive treatment. The patient usually visits the analyst from three to five times a week. He lies on a couch with his back to the therapist and is usually instructed to say whatever comes into his mind. The cost per session in private practice is usually $25.00 and up. Length of treatment is often three or four years.

Because the process of psychoanalysis is so time-consuming and expensive, certain followers of Freud, Drs. T. M. French and Franz Alexander, devised a more flexible variation of

Freudian analysis called *psychoanalytically oriented psychotherapy.* Alexander and French differed from Freud in their conception of transference and the patient-analyst relationship. Alexander explained that a patient's transference may be matched by an analyst's own form of transference ("countertransference"), which sometimes produces harmful and unexpected results.

Alexander's approach stressed flexibility, "seldom using one and the same method of approach from the first to the last day of treatment." Because this flexibility means that the treatment proceeds according to the demands of the individual situation, there might be several sessions or several hundred sessions; the interview between patient and analyst might be through the traditional "couch" approach, or face to face; the analyst might be a "blank screen" shadowy figure, or become a more dynamic personality who uses such devices as psychological tests, play therapy, and hypnosis—as well as advising his patients to use activities outside of the therapy session, like recreation, family life, and work.

Although Alexander and French offered a number of important modifications of Freudian psychoanalysis, their ideas remained within the general framework of Freud's theory. Other psychoanalysts broke more sharply with Freud. One of these was Alfred Adler, who, around 1910, developed his own form of psychoanalysis called *individual psychology.*

Adler felt that the most important drive and the one which a neurotic person has the most trouble handling is power or superiority. In the words of Dr. Valer Barbu, "In order to overcome his feeling of inferiority and to hide it from himself and others, [the neurotic] develops a drive toward superiority. The only healthy solution that is possible for him is to develop social feelings."

Adler's ideas have always had a strong appeal to the "man in the street" who could see evidences of inferiority complexes and drives for power in people around him. In this country, where material goals represent the "top of the ladder" for many people, it is quite natural that a person be driven by an urge to dominate.

Another divergent branch of psychoanalysis is Otto Rank's *will therapy.* Rank contended that neuroses stem from the impact and shock of birth, called "birth trauma," claiming that the main problem of patients was to learn to assert their own will, or individuality. Rank further believed that during treatment a patient should have a "new experiencing," rather than a reliving of past experiences.

Still another form of psychoanalytic treatment is that of Carl Jung, who founded a school of psychoanalytic thought called *analytical psychology.* Jung used a highly complex and deeply mystical approach described in his book the *Psychology of the Unconscious.* He singled out as singularly important the early parent-child relationship, including such factors as the "concealed discord between the parents, the secret worry, the repressed hidden wishes."

In recent years a number of analysts called "neo-Freudians" have made important contributions to the treatment of mental illness through psychoanalysis.

Karen Horney, like so many others, began her career as a traditional Freudian analyst, breaking with him principally because of Freud's biological or sexual approach. Horney was interested in the interpersonal (people-to-people) relationship of childhood and its effect on a person's present behavior. Her ideas, which may be grouped under the heading of *character analysis,* emphasized cultural pressures as being one of the main causes of neurotic disorders. She wrote of a neurotic's pursuit of "neurotic goals" that lead him to grasp at false values; and how these goals can lead to an idealized or faulty picture of himself.

Both Sullivan and Fromm advanced a type of psychoanalysis which may be called *interpersonal.* Sullivan, a clinical psychiatrist who believed that all his work should be carefully "proved" from clinical observations and records, thought that sex, although important, is not necessarily the key force that motivates a person toward neurotic or "adjusted" behavior. He felt that we have two main goals: satisfaction and security; and the *way* in which we pursue these goals from childhood determines whether we shall become sick or well as adults. He emphasized significant relations with important people (such as parents).

Fromm, on the other hand, has been mainly concerned with "the impact of moral and ethical values on the behavior of man." He is a leading non-medical psychoanalyst and advocate of the cultural school of psychoanalysis, and his work covers a number of fields. Fromm felt that "the goal of therapy is not primarily to make the person adjusted to his culture but to develop a sense of integrity and a respect for his true self."

Today, psychiatrists still use psychoanalysis as a major form of treatment as well as a research tool, but, as we've already indicated, there are many conflicts within the field. A psychoanalyst may lean heavily on this or that "school" of psychoanalytic thought, and his orientation, as well as his innate ability to understand and work with a patient, may determine the extent of success he will have in helping resolve a particular person's emotional disturbance.

Some forms of analysis take a greater length of time than others, thereby resulting in a higher cost to the patient. For these and other reasons you should be aware of the "brand" of therapy practiced by the physician you select to treat a member of your family.

Let's look at four imaginary psychiatrists practicing different brands of psychoanalysis and compare their backgrounds and methods of treatment.

Dr. A is a psychoanalyst who uses a traditional Freudian technique. A medical doctor who specialized in psychiatry and studied under a few followers of Dr. Freud, Dr. A's basic procedure varies little from patient to patient, many of whom undergo as much as three years of treatment. For his work (about four sessions per week with each patient), Dr. A is usually paid $30 to $40 per visit. The session begins with the patient entering the doctor's office and lying down on a comfortable couch. Dr. A uses four basic techniques during a typical course of treatment: encouraging his patient to freely associate or relate feelings and impressions of childhood experiences which seem significant; encouraging a process of transference whereby the patient comes to feel that Dr. A is a parent figure who appears to be stern and understanding, depending upon the particular childhood situation; interpreting the patient's feelings and relating them to a "model," or a universal pattern of sexual feelings and personality development, and analyzing his patient's dreams, paying close attention to symbols and themes that touch on the realm of the sexual.

As a Freudian analyst, Dr. A likes to think of himself as a "blank screen" or blackboard upon which his patients can "write out their neuroses and then erase them by themselves." He explains that "if a wound in a healthy person is kept clean, and protected from interference, it will heal. In much the same way I assume that if the childhood tangle of feelings and prohibitions can be brought to the light of consciousness and understanding, it will straighten itself out without active interference."

Before becoming a psychoanalyst, Dr. A underwent a thorough personal analysis. He usually only treats patients with neurotic problems, refusing to use psychoanalysis to treat the elderly; adults with sharp hallucinations and delusions or other forms of breaks from reality; adult or adolescent psychopaths; or persons whose intelligence is too low for an easy exchange of thoughts and feelings.

Dr. B, although objecting to the use of "labels" to divide off the different schools of psychoanalysis, uneasily accepts a description of him in medical journals and other listings as a "neo-Freudian" or even "eclectic." Dr. B holds a medical degree and is an avid reader with a special interest in anthropology, the study of other cultures and ways of life. Professionally, he is most interested in the writings and works of Erich Fromm and Karen Horney, who, like himself, emigrated from Germany to the United States in the early 1930's. He is an advocate of a "cultural approach" to psychoanalysis, placing great weight on the area (environment) in which a person lives his life and rejecting many of the teachings of Freud, which he says are "too one-sided in that they essentially represent a biological, sexual, and pessimistic approach." Dr. B believes that psychoanalysis should be "direct and to the point," thereby saving a patient time and money. He feels also that psychoanalysis may be used for other types of mental disorders—rather than just for the treatment of neurotics.

During a typical therapy session with Dr. B there is much give and take between patient and analyst. He asserts his own point of view whenever he feels it would be helpful to the patient. As a follower of Dr. Karen Horney, Dr. B would heartily approve of her comment that "the analyst does not merely follow the patient."

There are a few other areas which differentiate Dr. B's brand of psychoanalysis from many others. During a session, which (like other types of psychoanalysis) lasts about fifty minutes, Dr. B is mainly concerned with his patient's current behavior and present feelings and thoughts. He is not very much concerned with early childhood experiences filled with sexual overtones. The patient usually discusses his feelings and behavior toward other people. He rarely uses free association as a technique of eliciting feelings; instead, it's mainly a question and answer session with a more liberal use of interpretation and less emphasis upon sexual implications, other than those which are on a cultural level of morals, values and taboos.

Dr. C, a psychoanalyst who always admired the work of Dr. Sigmund Freud, has incorporated some of Alexander's and French's ideas and attempts to condense his therapy sessions into a six-month period (on an average).

Many patients who have undergone treatment by Dr. C have found themselves sitting in a chair face to face with the doctor. In fact, one patient who came to Dr. C with the popular misconception that all psychoanalysts used the famous "Freudian couch" and just sat and listened to their patient's story of childhood demons was visibly shocked by Dr. C's methods. At the outset she was given a battery of psychological tests, including an inkblot test, an intelligence test, and a written personality test. Dr. C, after a preliminary interview during which he inquired only about her current problems, recommended that she only see him once a week. During the next four and a half months she visited Dr. C once a week, discussing her relations with her husband, children, parents, friends, and neighbors during the interview sessions. Dr. C, like French and Alexander, believes that transference should not be allowed, or should be allowed only in a limited and controlled manner—since the process whereby a patient comes to feel that the analyst is a father substitute is time-consuming, unnecessary, and in some cases potentially harmful to the patient. Dr. C believes he has successfully retained at least the "flavor of Freudian analysis," while taking advantage of recent time-saving modifications and improvements.

Dr. D has had no medical training. Rather, he holds bachelor's, master's, and doctor's degrees in psychology, and he has been certified as an analyst by a psychoanalytic institute after a number of years of intensive study. Because he has no medical training Dr. D may not prescribe drugs or administer other forms of psychotherapy such as shock treatment. However, he is recognized in the professional community as one of the leading analysts and is a member of an association of "lay" (non-medical) psychoanalysts and also a Society of Individual Psychologists—a group which has been strongly influenced by the teachings of Alfred Adler.

Dr. D is well read in the works of Erich Fromm, Karen Horney, and Harry Stack Sullivan. However, he has combined his own ideas with the teachings of others to provide an individualistic form of analysis. Instead of modifying or streamlining the theories of Sigmund Freud, he has broken with Freud completely, for his mentor Adler was something of a rebel.

Although Dr. D has his own method of analytic treatment, he agrees with many aspects of the Adlerian point of view and is fond of quoting Adler's remark that "the uncovering of the neurotic life-plan takes place by friendly and free conversation, for it is always better tactics to let the patient take the initiative."

The course of treatment with Dr. D will probably be a fairly short one, lasting from six months to a year. He always schedules two appointments per week for each patient, and each session lasts for 50 minutes. Dr. C charges $20 to $35 per session, depending upon the patient's means. Unlike his Freudian cousins, he makes extensive use of the technique of interpretation, attempting to "reeducate" his patients as to the best way to come back into a community, to adjust to their environment. He agrees with Adler that "to cure a neurosis and a psychosis it is necessary to change completely the whole upbringing of the patient and turn him definitely and unconditionally back upon society."

Because psychoanalysis does not suit the needs of all persons with emotional problems, your doctor may suggest other forms of treatment, less expensive, time-consuming and wearing.

A form of treatment which differs sharply from analysis is *client centered therapy.* Founded by Carl Rogers, it assumes that the patient, or *client,* has within himself the capacity to change his personality and "grow" in a psychological sense. Client-centered therapy is non-directive and involves a number of talk sessions between client and counselor. Rogers tries to create a close relationship between client and counselor so that the client can "talk as freely as possible about all aspects of his difficulties." This kind of therapy stresses the importance of the relationship.

If a member of your family is participating in client-centered therapy, you should be aware of the following points. This is not a medical treatment. The counselor is not a medical doctor, as a psychiatrist is, but is usually a man who combines some sensitivity to human feelings with objectivity and self-understanding. He has probably acquired this skill through psychological and sociological lectures plus supervised experience of actual counseling.

If your referring doctor recommends drugs, shock therapy, or other medical procedures for your relative, you should realize that a client-centered therapist would be very unlikely to use these treatments. For these measures a psychiatrist is necessary.

Group Therapy

Group therapy uses the participation of people in common efforts to develop interpersonal rapport, sympathetic understanding and mutual helpfulness. Forms of group therapy include encounter, marathon, Synanon, Esalon, and offshoots of all the standard forms of individual therapy. In one city, according to Dr. Donald Shaskan, there are vocational groups; groups for art, for acting out; for psychotics, epileptics, homophiles, addicts; for families, men, women, married couples.

Joseph Pratt, a Boston physician, started the first group in 1905. In treating TB patients he found it useful to hold weekly meetings at which patients would discuss their common problem. The therapeutic group is, as Kenneth Lamott has said, simply a particular instance of the general tendency of human beings to cluster together, whether in blood groups such as family and tribe; in occupational, social or religious groups; or in prisons and armies.

Jules Masserman describes some conventional forms and techniques of group therapy:

> *Discussion groups* are composed usually of six to ten patients, led by one or two therapists or selected participants who meet regularly to explore the relevance to their lives of current events, individual experiences, or the general human significance of past or present events.
>
> In *family therapy* the group is limited to related members whose interactions are observed and presumably improved by one or more therapists. . . .
>
> *Psychodrama* is a variant in which patients act out scenes from their past or anticipated future, using therapists or other persons in these episodes. Roles are then changed, mimicked (mirror technique) or reversed in order to broaden the subject's understanding of how his behavior appears to others. When skillfully conducted the method may be illuminating, but care must be taken to avoid excessive histrionics and to keep clear for both patient and therapist the distinctions between the fantasies of wishful play-acting and the realities of present and future existence.

The involvement of family members had been discouraged by Freud. Yet Drs. Boszormenyi-Nagy and Framo point out that treatment failures led them to believe that it was the exceptional patient who could make lasting progress if his family didn't change.

Family therapy is the end result of a chain of reasoning from "seeing the illness in the patient, to seeing it in the relationship between the patient and mother, to realizing that father and 'well' siblings were involved in the shared psychopathology (problems), and that the patient was not so much a victim but an agent who helped maintain the family pathology, to finally wondering whether the family, aside from being considered the noxious agent, contained the potential for possible change which could be capitalized upon." You will most likely find the family therapy approach at a community mental health center.

The difference between the typical two-hour session during which half a dozen patients, all with similar symptoms, get together, and encounters such as the "300-year weekends" of Los Angeles' Dr. George Bach, is enormous. Therapists like Bach keep the group session going for 30 to 40 hours during which no one is allowed to leave the room except to get food and coffee or take care of bathroom needs.

Esalon has been perhaps the most influential of the group therapy movements. Before Esalon and other group therapists, all of which make up the whole Human Potentialities movement, psychoanalysis and behavior were the two major forces in forms of treatment for emotional disturbance. Recently there has been no attention paid to this third one which stresses growth and self-actualization rather than seeking cures for existing neuroses.

You may also consider the expansion and open quality of one of the therapies described by Rasa Gustatis in her book *Turning On.*

If you or a therapist choose group therapy for your disturbed family member, be wary of some of the "fashionable" groups pushed by "true believers." Such cultists heralded torture to exorcise evil spirits in the middle ages, and they tend to accept as the final answer any new treatment publicized by the media.

Here are pointers for checking out a new form of group therapy:

Check to see that the group leader is truly qualified. Some individuals who run groups have practically no professional credentials, and sometimes their only real qualification comes from having been in enough groups themselves to have learned the jargon. Bruce Maliver warns that "in contrast the recognized postdoctoral training programs in psychoanalysis and psychotherapy take very seriously their responsibility to weed out people whose own disturbances could make them destructive to patients. Postdoctoral institute programs require at least four years of intensely supervised training before a therapist is considered competent.

"When screening a new patient, one of the critical decisions the trained therapist makes is whether the patient will provoke in him emotions that may work to the detriment of the therapy. No similar protections exist through the encounter group training programs."

Beware of the profit-hungry organizations that have hopped on the bandwagon of group therapy. More than six million people are currently in such therapy in the United States, according to psychologist Warren Bennis. Therefore organizing and leading encounter groups has become immensely profitable. It is usually a good idea to check a therapy situation with the American Group Psychotherapy Association.

You should take into account the nature and degree of disturbance in your family member. If he is suffering from a transient situational problem that has made him depressed or withdrawn, or has a simple personality disorder, he may well profit from one of the kinds of group therapy. If, however, his problems are more severe, causing disorientation, breaks with "reality," and intense anxiety, he can be badly harmed by the hit or miss quality of a group.

Behavioral Therapy

Behavioral therapy is based upon the ideas of Ivan Pavlov, who believed that the highest nervous activity, as shown in the conditioned reflex, consists of a continual change of three main processes—excitation, inhibition, and disinhibition.

One interpreter of Pavlov's methods is the controversial Andrew Salter, who practices a form of therapy called habit-training. Salter's conditioned-reflex therapy is direct and forceful. He explains to the patient that his symptoms are, for instance, due to his inability to liberate emotion. The patient learns new behavior patterns, in this case to be more open and free with his feelings, and the disturbing symptoms often disappear.

Forms of behavioral treatment can often be called *directive therapy.* This approach, usually during brief psychotherapy of about one to twenty sessions, may be suitable when a relative shows clearly defined symptoms.

One type of directive therapy has its roots in hypnotism, though an actual trance may not take place. You will find that the therapist attempts to induce change from the moment of his first contact with a patient. With this method the patient is asked to follow specific directions which involve him in a cooperative endeavor to change his symptomatic behavior. Many directive therapists are willing to take charge and intervene in a patient's life, while non-directive therapists will say that telling the patient what to do will increase his dependent attitude.

Most directive therapy proceeds by placing the patient in a situation which he cannot resolve as long as he continues with his symptoms. The therapist provides an ordeal, thereby placing the patient in an "impossible" situation. If the therapist were only treating the patient badly, the patient could deal with this. However, when the therapist is hard on the patient within a framework of benevolent help as long as the symptoms continue, the patient can only abandon his symptoms.

While the goal of psychoanalytical treatment is self-awareness or insight, the goal of directive therapy is to bring about a change. Treatment may end when one part of the patient's life is changed in such a way that change will occur in other aspects after therapy has ended. When this works you may find your relative behaving more "normally" in the sense that he has as little concern with insight as most people and is dealing with his difficulties in ways that help him feel more satisfied.

Brief Therapy

An interesting and promising new kind of therapy has been described by Doctors Fisch, Watzlawich, Weakland, Bodin and Frykman of the Mental Research Institute, Palo Alto, California. Patients or family members come with specific complaints, and treatment involves a certain responsibility for relieving these complaints. Therapy is expected to be accomplished in ten sessions with an occasional return after some time. Brief therapy looks at emotional disturbances as situational difficulties or problems of interaction. They feel these to be the simple outcome of everyday difficulties which often involve an anticipated life change or one which has already been badly mishandled by patient and family. "Brief therapists" see normal transitional steps in family living as the most common and important everyday difficulties which lead to problems when badly handled. Some of these are: change from the voluntary relationship of courtship to the commitment of marriage, the more permanent commitment when a first child is born, the whole turbulence of the adolescent period, retirement, return to single life after the death of a spouse. All these transitions need enormous adjustments, which is why so much common mishandling behavior leads to "problems."

Brief therapy makes a sharp distinction between an ordinary difficulty and what is called "a problem," or emotional disturbance. When people treat an ordinary difficulty as "a problem" or treat the difficulty as absolutely no difficulty at all, trouble can occur. Viewing a difficulty as no difficulty at all makes it more likely that normally difficult transitions will be viewed by the people passing through them as "problems." On the other hand, once a difficulty begins to be seen as a "problem," it is met with a "solution" which intensifies the original difficulty and turns inappropriate behavior into actual symptom behavior, causing intense inappropriate reactions in turn.

Even long-standing emotional disturbances or "problems" are viewed not in the usual sense of a basic defect in the individual, but simply as the persistence of a repeatedly poorly handled difficulty.

By focusing on symptoms and working in a limited way toward their relief, brief therapists offer the achievement and encouragement of small goals. Change can come most easily if the goal referred to is clearly stated and refers only to limited areas of the patient's life. Not only is it possible to effect small realistic changes in the patient's life, but once the patient experiences a "small" change in the overwhelming nature of the problem most real to him, this experience can then generate further self-induced changes.

Somatotherapy

Your relative's doctor may recommend treatment quite different from psychotherapy of *any* kind. This treatment, which may consist of various forms of drugs, shock therapy, and surgical approaches, is called *somatotherapy* and attempts to get at the disturbance in a more physical way.

Only a psychiatrist who is a physician is trained to administer electroconvulsive therapy, administer drugs, or advise on any of the forms of physical treatment.

Drug therapy makes it possible for many patients who would need prolonged hospitalization to be able to continue in daily routines and sometimes earn a living. If a relative has been diagnosed as psychotic, and he presents a severe problem getting along with other people or is often withdrawn and depressed so that he cannot pursue any daily goals, drug treatment of one kind or another may help his adjustment and make life easier for him and you.

If you take your severely disturbed relative to a physician or clinic where drug therapy is suggested, you will probably find that one or a combination of "major tranquilizers" is prescribed. It is not necessary for you as a layman to make distinctions between the various forms of drugs that may be prescribed, but you may want to have a general idea of their actions so that you can understand what to expect.

You may find your relative is being treated with one or both of two major kinds of drugs. The tranquilizers are intended to calm him, the stimulants or psychic energizers to increase his activity and help him overcome lack of drive.

Stronger tranquilizers are usually given to those who have been diagnosed as suffering from a psychosis while the milder tranquilizers are used for temporary stress situations, anxiety that is neither too severe nor prolonged, and in some neuroses. Mood-elevator drugs are sometimes used to fight sleepiness, but their main use is for treating depression.

One of the common drugs in this fight against symptomatic behavior is chlorpromazine (Thorazine). Mild tranquilizers such as chlordiazepoxide (Librium) have helped reduce anxiety when a less potent drug than chlorpromazine will do the job. Antidepressants such as imipramine or amitripytline have their uses also. All of the hundreds of such drugs currently being prescribed have advantages that only an experienced physician can know; to attempt to self-prescribe in this area is an invitation to disaster.

According to Dr. Mortimer Ostrow, "the development of the newer drugs has profound implications for the practice of psychotherapy and psychoanalysis. Perhaps the most serious intrinsic limitation of psychotherapy has been its inapplicability to the major psychoses and several other categories of illness. By combining drug treatment with psychotherapy, it is possible to establish and to guarantee the minimal psychic stability required for the effective conduct of psychotherapy."

Other forms of treatment which may be suggested include the *shock therapies.* A Viennese doctor, Manfred Sakel, was using insulin to relieve the withdrawal symptoms that morphine addicts undergo when he noticed an occasional beneficial effect of the insulin upon some symptoms which addicts exhibit in common with schizophrenics. Insulin therapy is still in use in some hospitals though in greatly curtailed fashion. The patient goes into deep coma as a result of insulin and, after a long series of treatment, improves. No one knows actually how or why this treatment works.

Convulsive shock therapy was given first by means of the drug camphor, and then metrazol to treat depressions and other affective disorders. In 1938 Cerletti and Bini inaugurated the use of the electroshock machine for the inducement of convulsions by alternating current. Although many of the patients are helped and their symptoms disappear, no one really knows how this treatment works or why the patients improve.

Shock treatments are usually given three times a week for periods that depend on the patient's response and the nature of his disorder. Unlike insulin shock, the treatment can be administered in outpatient departments of hospitals and in the offices of psychiatrists in private practice. The social implications of this are obvious, for the patients may remain in the community rather than have to be admitted to psychiatric hospitals. By the same token, however, the ease of administration of convulsive therapy also exposes it to abuses, and this must be guarded against with extreme care.

It is common belief at present that psychotherapy of a supportive type is of great value when used along with convulsive therapy. As is true throughout medical practice, each individual case must be weighed carefully and all risks properly evaluated.

Recently much has been claimed for the "niacin treatment" of schizophrenia, promulgated by Drs. Hoffer and Osmond of

Canada. A combination of nicotinic acid and ascorbic acid, the niacin treatment in huge doses, will, it is claimed, produce remissions in some previously untreatable patients. Another treatment you will want to inquire about is the orthomolecular or "megavitamin" treatment.

Results have not yet proven this to be so, but because it is harmless and also inexpensive, the treatment is still being tested in various combinations, with word here and there of good results. You may want to ask the doctor about it or write to the American Schizophrenia Foundation for further information.

Other Therapies

One important form of treatment, often overlooked because it seems to have no direct bearing on the actual illness, is occupational therapy. Supplemented by recreational and physical therapy, occupational therapy assumes that emotionally disturbed patients can benefit from a regular program of interesting daily activity, and that the closer such activity comes to meeting real desires toward a return to productive work of some kind, the more satisfying the experience.

Dr. Walter Barton points out that "when a patient develops a mental illness he usually loses his ability to live and work happily as part of a group of people. One of the principal goals of therapy therefore is directed toward resocialization."

According to the American Occupational Therapy Association, "occupational therapy is the art and science of directing man's response to selected activity to promote and maintain health, to prevent disability, to evaluate behavior and to treat or train patients with physical or psychosocial dysfunction. In the treatment of the geriatric patient, for example, the registered occupational therapist's objectives are to provide treatment and an atmosphere which will stimulate the patient to develop or maintain his highest potential in physical, social, psychological and avocational activity. The occupational therapist evaluates the elderly patient to determine the extent of his disability (motor, sensory, psychological and functional), to determine the psychological and social implications to the patient and his family, and to determine treatment goals. The occupational therapist also selects specific activities and techniques to reduce disability, maintain self-concept and capacities, promote independent function, prevent further deterioration and aid in psychological adjustment to a progressive disease process."

Sometimes it is found that, however well motivated, a particular family interacts with the patient in such a way that old unhealthy or threatening patterns continue to plague the relationship. In such a situation the psychiatrist may recommend *placement in another setting:* hospital, treatment center, halfway house, foster home, or even a room alone if the patient is able to handle a certain amount of solitude. The decisions you must make if this is necessary are discussed in Chapter 7.

Which Is the Best?

Beyond the initial one of deciding where to turn for help, the choice of treatment may or may not be up to you. If there is a community mental health center in the area, you are in luck. Probably the suggestions made there will put your relative in touch with a doctor or type of treatment from which he will benefit. If there is no such facility available and you do not have the funds for private care, a call to your state Mental Health Association will give you names of facilities and resources in the area.

Assuming that you can afford a psychiatrist but do not know which to choose because of uncertainty about the relative merits of the various "schools," you should take into account your relative's general personality apart from his illness. If he enjoys self-scrutiny, personal probing, going back over the past, the methods of an orthodox Freudian will be congenial to him. If he is rooted in the here and now, a Karen Horney therapist may appeal to him. If he resists insight, becomes silent and uncommunicative when old troubles are discussed, he may be a candidate for direct therapy or one of the conditioning modes of treatment.

You should remember, when trying to decide between different forms of treatment for a family member or friend, that no decision is final. Treatment involves a constant shift and effort; it is a continuous process, and even from a poor response in one direction, much can be learned that will benefit the person next time round.

Chapter 4
Problems of Grownups

All of you are not doomed to play Abel to a violent fearsome Cain! Some of you want only to know how to deal pleasantly and calmly with the minor emotional showers that interrupt the sunny days of normal human relationships. Others are plagued by a vague sense of worry when a friend, relative, or lover "has been feeling low for some time," is frequently cranky, especially demanding, nipping on the sly, or whatever.

The neurotic interactions in marriages or between parent and child are *one* kind of problem. Some live with emotionally disturbed people when the needs of both mesh. There is another kind of situation in which one person really is more troubled (or at least less adjusted to his environment) than the other. It is to this situation that this chapter is mainly addressed.

The first step in coping with the emotional disturbance of a family member is recognizing its presence. This is not easy to do and involves much more than just seeing a parent or child behaving strangely. You can play an invaluable role in early diagnosis and treatment by carefully observing the variant behavior of a family member. At the same time you should be aware of the following warnings in order not to jump to hasty conclusions:

Don't play doctor. Just obtaining *information* doesn't qualify you as a doctor, and obviously you should not attempt to treat the developing difficulty yourself. As soon as you suspect that some form of emotional disorder is present, medical advice should be sought.

Don't try to verify the suspected problem yourself. Because you have concluded from observation of symptoms that an emotional disturbance is present, there is no guarantee that this conclusion is correct. Verification should be left to medical sources; it's the doctor's job.

Don't label the patient prematurely. Much harm may be done by placing a family member in a fancy mental cubbyhole. Identifying him as psychotic at this stage can cause trouble, and if your hunch proves later to have been incorrect, the damage may be serious.

Don't read your own thoughts and feelings into the suspected illness. Individual items of behavior can be caused by so many passing events or moods that reading emotional disturbance into what may be simply a temper tantrum, a "feeling low" week, or a mischievous or rebellious spell may be due more to your own problems than to the person whose behavior causes you concern. It is no single symptom but the accumulation and continuation of them that gives cause for worry, so always search first for the least complicated explanation.

Remember that background may account for certain symptoms. In Boston-Irish families, for example, there is a general acceptance of a certain amount of drinking. This same drinking in an average Jewish family would be considered unusual if not abnormal.

Remember that illness is not always associated with unhappiness. For some, illness in childhood was a time of parental attention, and disabling ailments may become a way to re-create that atmosphere of parental warmth and solicitude, of hot soup and cool washcloths, of soothing and demonstrated love. You understand the child who clings to you during illness, but it is usually difficult to understand (or even like) the *adult* who uses illness to get attention. One problem you face is sometimes setting too high expectations for the patient.

In the interests of communication between you and your relative's doctor, the labels given to mental illnesses, as used by the American Psychiatric Association, are described in a glossary at the end of the book. The labels are used in this chapter simply because one of them will have been used by a doctor to describe your relative's emotional disturbance.

You will face different problems depending on the severity of the emotional disturbance in your family. Let us now look at these particular problems, ranging from temporary disturbances to long-lasting illnesses.

Transient situational neurosis is the technical name for emotional disturbances caused by an outside situation so hurting to the individual that only the greatest internal strength or understanding by the person in charge can prevent the outside pain going inwards and becoming a part of the personality.

Such temporary situations may be death of a parent or love object, rejection by a love object (as in cases where divorce is wanted by one person and not the other), overwhelming illness or accident, forced retirement, impossible financial obligations, or major natural catastrophes.

You can live with the person who has been so hurt in a strengthening or weakening way, depending on your own unconscious attitudes toward both the stress and what has always been considered a "suitable" reaction.

If the neurosis is rooted in memories of terror and loss, you can help by encouraging your relative to express those memories when he is ready, by gentle understanding of what he has been through, and reassurance when it is not possible for him to wipe out those memories sufficiently to face the day.

Dr. Louis Rose calls despair of an excessive degree for an excessive period related to a traumatic situation or event prolonged grief reaction. For example, the widow who feels hopeless and lost at the death of her husband is reacting normally to the traumatic situation. If after a year or two she still refuses to dispose of her husband's clothes or deal with his estate, and loses general interest in all activities outside of those focused on her previous loss, this is a prolonged grief reaction and help is usually necessary.

In addition to grief, anxiety may provoke a transient neurosis. Anxiety is, according to Dr. H. J. Walton, "a mood of fear which puts out of action a whole range of normal skills and functions. Anxiety can increase in intensity to produce a state of terror. If a person is appropriately predisposed, there is a wide range of life events which can precipitate a state of anxiety."

In these cases all your patience is needed to understand that this person can be frightened into a long-term neurotic reaction if he has not sufficient inner strength or does not get immediate ego-bolstering support from others in his environment. This can occur even though the cause may appear trivial.

You may also find yourself developing a matching set of neurotic symptoms. Accepting your relative's neurotic symptoms is a delicate matter, for you are liable to find yourself more likely to accept his symptoms than the underlying material that his symptoms are a defense against. If it is your spouse, chances are that you *chose* him because of his attitudes, and it is very unlikely that you will be able to accept change in him without changing yourself.

It is possible to ease the situation of living with a person who is severely neurotic and whose symptoms do not match your own needs by asking yourself just how really bothersome his symptoms are. Knowing that most neurotic symptoms are amenable to therapeutic treatment or counseling should cheer you up, for if his condition makes him really unbearable to you you can insist, *as a condition for your continued presence,* that he go for help.

Be careful, however, before suggesting that he embark on what may prove to be drastic changes, that the symptoms are sufficiently severe to warrant this "opening up." Not all people are suitable candidates for analysis or even investigative psychotherapy, and it is a dangerous thing to meddle with defenses of long standing. This is an area in which it is especially important to react sensitively to just how truly incapacitating the symptom is. Perhaps it should *not* be changed.

A person who reacts to stress by an unusually severe or long-lasting body response is said to be suffering from *psycho-*

physiologic, autonomic, and visceral disorders, which are often more difficult to accept than other forms of neurotic behavior. Most such psychosomatic disturbances have a relationship to repressed anger or defense against unacceptable sex drives. If you find it difficult to accept the fact that your relative is constantly complaining about a physical ailment which a doctor has described as emotionally based, you may become more cheerful by realizing that it is quite possible for him to be helped if he follows a plan like that suggested by Drs. Ewalt and Farnsworth:

> Conferences with the doctor to check plans, progress, or changes in management. Group therapy or classes with other patients with the same problems for the obese patient and for patients suffering from ulcerative colitis, coronary disease, or arthritis. Patients with impotence or frigidity do not always do well in groups.
>
> Provision for prolonged dynamic psychotherapy. In those cases where the person has the ego resources and the opportunity, psychoanalysis can often be helpful.
>
> Living conditions that are supportive and can supply the patient with a normal social life appropriate to his age and recreational interests.
>
> Family counseling by a social worker if one who is a nonjudgmental human being is available. Family members with pathologies that mesh and interact with the patient's physical symptoms should be treated, although not by the patient's psychiatrist.
>
> Relief of stress from work, family, or social responsibilities if possible. Some patients with these disorders want to be cared for like infants and continuously loved and fed. Neither family nor employer should be expected to comply with infantile needs for an indefinite period, but it is helpful to treat the patient as an adult who needs extra amounts of love, understanding, and confidence.

The person suffering from a *personality disorder* shows a disturbance of behavior rather than of thought and emotion. You will sometimes be repelled and discouraged by his infuriating behavior and the small likelihood of his ever changing for the better. Although the current tendency to identify these difficulties as medical helps keep your relative out of jail, that doesn't make it any easier for you. You may find that you will live with such a person for years, only to give up in despair. Your decision should be based upon the type of personality disturbance and its severity without regard for any notions of rehabilitating him by example, by education, or by therapy.

Acute brain syndrome is the name for emotional disorders with an external cause. The cause may be drugs or alcohol, an infectious disease, or a tumor. In acute brain syndrome associated with systemic (body) infections, you may find that many of the symptoms disappear after the infection is gone. In some cases depressive or neurotic behavior lasts, often for just a short time afterwards, occasionally for longer.

Problems of mental disorder related to drugs or alcohol are dealt with in later chapters. Acute brain syndrome associated with convulsive disorders such as epilepsy is often successfully treated. However, you should guard against letting the patient "deny" his illness in the sense of forgetting to take drugs regularly or running out of them.

If a growing tumor is the cause of acute brain syndrome, it will be almost impossible to accept the situation of gradually increasing impairment. Just as the patient will benefit from supportive psychotherapy before and after surgery, so the rest of the family may have the same need. Symptoms may occur before his tumor has been diagnosed and can be confused with hardening of the arteries of the brain or with depression. When you know what the condition is, there may be some comfort in seeing that the supportive care, nursing, and "being there" which you provide will communicate his last positive look at the world. Nobody can be expected to accept the illogical agony of an incurable illness, but here there is no decision and no choice. A book by John Gunther about his young son, *Death Be Not Proud,* can point you toward that small positive area that comes of knowing this painful truth.

Living with Chronic Brain Syndrome

Grandma is senile, or suffering from *chronic brain syndrome.* There is no suitable nursing home and not enough money to send her; she *has* to live at home. How do you manage in this situation?

Get an up-to-date checkup to make sure her diagnosis is correct. If her doctor, or the facility suggested by your local Mental Health Society if you can't afford private examination, feels outpatient treatment or medication can help, arrange for it immediately and *keep it up.* Inquire of the local hospital about possible help, including funds (such as through Medicare, Medicaid, or organizations named for specific illnesses). An aging relative's mental disturbance may exist concurrently with a medical problem such as heart disease, cancer, or multiple sclerosis, and help and services may be available through the Department of Welfare or community mental health centers.

Recognize that the prognosis (prediction for the future) is poor as far as improvement in the actual condition is concerned. If the patient has mostly depressive or paranoid symptoms, treatment for these symptoms may be helpful and allow another few years of more useful life before it becomes necessary to give in to the illness as a whole.

If the patient thinks something is being done for him, he may feel better regardless of the symptoms he is still expressing. It will do him good to feel useful in some way, and if the process of finding something useful seems at times harder to figure out than just plain letting him vegetate, you can request the services of an occupational therapist to evaluate the direction and extent of the senility.

Herman Schwartz points out that "one way of awakening the interest of the aged is to leave a minor task half done. He may be challenged to finish the job . . . you can depend upon it that as long as he has some energy and inclination and receives encouragement, he will seek new outlets for his remaining energies. You can toss him a suggestion in a friendly way and then leave the room quickly. You thus give him plenty of time to think the matter over and avoid the quick decision that is likely to be no. . . .

"One of the pleasures of the aged is recalling experiences that have perhaps been covered up by the dust of living. Digging up the old hurts is to be discouraged, but you should laugh with him over pleasant and amusing memories. Stimulating his sense of humor helps, for humor chases away irritations and even lessens pain. . . .

"Being human, you will sometimes fail to give the patient the warmth and sympathy that conscience dictates. Don't hound yourself into remorse, but do your best and let it go at that. When tensions arise, remember that the old person cannot alter his behavior, and make up your mind to tolerate it so long as it is not excessively harmful to the rest of the family."

Emotional states of depression or elation are part of a group which has been called *affective disorders*. In actual fact these symptoms vary tremendously; your relative may have lighter or deeper depressions; some have periods of elation, and some alternate between these in long or short cycles.

Accepting life with a person who is subject to these enormous "mood swings" is nearly impossible if you identify with the patient. You must maintain a certain emotional distance to avoid being sucked into the cyclical currents of fear, anger, guilt and depression and hurried downstream with the very person you tried to help.

People with these disorders tend to have recurrent attacks and to recover between attacks. The attacks are usually self-limited, lasting from two to three weeks to two to three years in different people, but an individual patient tends to have attacks that are similar except for the tendency to increase in length as they recur.

You may find it especially hard to accept the fact that the patient is *sick* when his symptoms are euphoria and overactivity during which he may accomplish a great deal. His difficulty may not be apparent to anyone else, and plans and precautions may falter because of lack of general understanding as to what you are up against. Sometimes creative people can only function in this way, with great compulsive spurts of overactivity followed by emotional exhaustion and letdown.

In the depressive stage of manic-depressive illness, it may be next to impossible to accept your relative's symptoms as he vents his anger in small but persistent doses. The best way to accept living with a depressed personality is by frequent intermissions. More than any other, this illness drags down those around it. Moreover, scrupulously avoid considering yourself the cause of the depression. Although this seems obvious, you may, out of love and pity, reach deeply into your behavior to find an explanation for the anguished sighs of your relative. In this direction lie chaos and further pain, for as you leap in one direction to please, then leap in exactly the other, you find that there is literally no way to "cheer up" a person caught in this pit. Nor should you try. Rather than attempting to reasonably explain the future or "reality" positives in his existence, just recognize his present need to feel down and express his pain.

The enormous group of disorders diagnosed as *schizophrenia* are characterized by "disturbances in the thought process, severe problems in emotional interaction with other persons, difficulty in group relationships, and, frequently, peculiar beliefs, delusions, and hallucinations."

It may help you to live through the pain and difficulty of caring for a relative labeled as schizophrenic to know that it is likely that some constitutional predisposition made him "susceptible."

Dr. Humphrey Osmond, a leading proponent of the theory that schizophrenia is a chemical or metabolic illness, says, "There is little evidence to support the claim that schizophrenic patients become ill because their parents loved them too little or fussed over them too much." Nevertheless, it is hard to accept the sporadic symptoms of the illness and the fact that at times a relative may appear so well that you may feel he has recovered, only to be thrown by the next episode of difficult behavior.

You can help reduce his most painful episodes by creating a special environment that is as undemanding as possible. The doctor may prescribe one or more of the tranquilizing drugs. They have different effects on different people, so respect the patient's *subjective* opinion, and change or eliminate the drug if he is unhappy with it. If he reacts well to it, it can help the patient control some of the more difficult aspects of his behavior and relieve him of a certain amount of anxiety so that other people will find it easier to accept his presence.

You will find it easier to live with schizophrenia in your family if you understand the symptoms and do not hold its manifestations against the patient. Toward this end it can be helpful to read books by Dr. Ronald Laing, who serves almost as an interpreter in clarifying the schizophrenic position to people who have never been touched by it. As you learn, you will find yourself better able to help a relative first express, then learn to control, those parts of his behavior that are motivated by primitive impulses.

Paranoid reactions make a person almost impossible to live with. Yet many who suffer from this illness are able to maintain some form of functioning in the world. This person will have a well-organized system of delusions of persecution which sound logical enough if we assume his original premise to be right. Because of this it may be hard to even consider him as ill. If you find him rigid and unable to change his beliefs in spite of a tremendous mass of evidence, you will have to make an adjustment to his special and often infuriating needs.

In true paranoia the person is not necessarily limited in his contact with the world and other people. In many ways he can be a success, but he will usually be lacking in real emotional involvement. Your relative may have no symptoms at all outside of ideas of persecution, or his delusional system may be partly supported by paranoid hallucinations relating to smell, hearing, or body ailments. Such people are often able to maintain themselves, for their illness is not incapacitating except in maintaining close human relations. The prognosis is poor, and treatment may only provide adjustment, rather than cure.

Someone who has made a normal adjustment to early life may start to come apart during old age. This shrinking in ability to cope with the environment in a positive meaningful way is called involutional psychosis. Some symptoms appear in nearly everyone who reaches sixty-five years of age; it is the severity and the crippling nature of some of them that causes them to be considered psychoses. These usually appear at the time of the climacteric (menopause and male equivalent) and are not clearly proven to be caused entirely by the shift in endocrine system function or psychological reasons alone. Our culture often provokes the disturbing emotions experienced by many at this age because it considers second rate the situation many people find themselves in at this age, being alone. Being alone can be positive if it is a time for relaxing with memories and solitary pleasures, books, music, an old motor to fix, cookies to bake for the neighbors, and other such joys.

When you find that people you know begin to show exaggerated signs of earlier personality traits such as depression, repressed hostility, or neurosis, some degree of this problem may have begun and should be watched for. Although illness typical of age may be present, don't assume that his symptoms are necessarily due to such illness, for the psychosis will not go away just by treatment of his high blood pressure, diabetes, hemorrhoids. Hospitalization may often be necessary, for the danger of suicide is great. Involutional reaction responds favorably to electroshock, with reported recoveries ranging from 80 to 90 percent in the depressed type to 50 percent in the paranoid type.

Problems of emotional disturbance begin to be solved as people understand their nature, discard fear and prejudice, and provide a more accepting environment for those who have broken down.

To stand helplessly by as a loved and once loving relative slips into a grey world between night and day where the static of anxiety drowns out joy and meaning, where he can only "hear" you while temporarily soothed by major and repeated efforts, where he spends his time nursing evidence of slights and watching for signs of injury, is painful in a way that doesn't need to be described. Living with the emotionally ill starts with the premise that you want to reduce the suffering of the patient and yourself. The North Pole of complete explanations of emotional disorder remains to be discovered; until it does every person who lives, warmly, firmly, and pragmatically, with the emotionally disturbed supports the holding action which does not reject them from society but tries to help until new discoveries come.

Those of you faced with long years of living with emotional disturbance in a relative can make it by stripping away nonessentials, embarrassment, what the neighbors think, how anything at all *looks,* and remain open toward anything alive the next day has to offer.

Chapter 5
Problems of Children

As the parents of an emotionally disturbed child, you are probably confused, badgered by guilt, and simply tired. The first thing you must do is take a rest. After a rest you mustn't be afraid to ask Grandma to take over your chores briefly, for fear she will find out; she knows already and it is time to sit down and talk things over.

First, find out how disturbed the child really is. If he has not yet been diagnosed you may be happy to find that many seemingly bizarre and disturbing symptoms of childhood are "passing," may be "outgrown," as a previous generation used to put it, or may be pseudo-psychotic. A recently expressed and constructive way of looking at differences in children's behavior is to consider that some kids are docile, some difficult and some slow learners. Make sure your child is not simply rebellious or slow and stubborn by nature before concluding that his symptoms need "professional" advice.

Children develop as a result of the endowment or constitution with which they were born, their interaction with their parents, the rest of their family and the society in which they live, and the things that happen to them.

Often the seriousness of a behavior problem cannot be properly evaluated until one has obtained an accurate formulation of the child's normal learning pattern before the problem began to alter that pattern. For example, the same degree of withdrawal will have a quite different significance in an originally gregarious, responsive and active child, than in a child who was quite placid and undemanding in infancy. How can you identify the child, recently estimated as one in ten, who shows some form of mental disturbance? When do his difficulties warrant his being seen by a doctor?

A man and a woman have a child. Five days after birth the mother wraps that child in a fleecy white blanket with blue fringe and takes him home. Once home, blankets and garments are peeled carefully off the tiny splendid thing. How pitiful it looks at some moments just before being fed perhaps, or when a passing cramp brings forth a sharp cry of pain. To the baby pain means panic: there is no way for an inexperienced baby to know that "someone is looking out for him"; that hunger will be met by food, uncomfortable wetness by a soft dry cloth; tummy-ache by gentile patting or being turned over or held in a soothing way.

Some babies are easier to satisfy than others. Some babies lose their panic sooner, maybe never even experiencing it to the extent that others do. They are the ones who are simpler to raise, who respond to love if love is there without suspicion and confusion. These babies turn into children who "know who they are" and feel that the world does exist apart from them. They are not afraid they will not get their share.

To have such a child does not guarantee that no problems will exist, for you cannot bring a child into the complicated jungle of human existence without problems developing on the way. But the chances are good that barring accident or other tragedy, the man and woman will find it pleasurable to nurture such a child, one who responds to food by seeming filled, sleep by seeming rested, kisses by smiles.

Having raised that first child with effort rewarded by the kinds of pleasure a child can give, the man and woman have another child. Suppose this time the mother leaves the hospital with more understanding of what she can expect. Accustomed to a friendly secure first child, she wraps the second baby in his blanket with that special joy that comes of going home with what has been described by the doctor as a "healthy newborn."

Considering that she now understands her job a little better, has experience to fall back on and a fairly sound relationship with her husband, won't she be likely to have another child as well adjusted as the first? Not necessarily, for as the National Association for Mental Health points out, "each story is different, as every child is different." Children differ for many reasons—they are molded by the physical background of their actual birth, their genetic heritage, their involvement with mother, father, other people, the cultural and economic accidents of their birth. Troubled children are especially aware of and sensitive to all these influences, for in terms of rearing there is no way to avoid some mistakes.

This second baby, however, is not only far more difficult to take care of than the first, but soon develops traits that are clearly "odd." The father and mother, tired now, a bit on edge and somehow finding themselves sharply critical of each other because nothing seems to help, begin to doubt their own ability as parents. Perhaps this has happened to you.

How Difficult Is Difficult?

If you think your child has an emotional problem, here is a simple procedure to follow. Write down a brief "history" of the child's habits and ways of development, his place in the family, the ages at which he was weaned from bottle or breast, how he "took" to weaning, the ages at which he began to walk, talk, play with others, was trained, the way in which he reacted to these steps. The history will list any special circumstances, severe physical illness, high fever, parent separation or divorce, deaths in family, particular strain on a parent during his infancy. This page of information will help the doctor if he thinks it necessary to see the child, and it will help you. Finding out just how real or unreal your worries are can only help, whatever conclusion you reach.

Next, make a list of your child's disturbing behavior, perhaps in the form of a weekly diary. Here are some things to look out for.

Inability to enjoy cuddling, hugging, or normal childhood play. Walling himself off from people, terribly short attention span, clinging out of panic but without real warmth.

Oddly objective absorption in parts of himself, overconcern with body motions. Inability to understand the meaning of "I." Confusion about his personal limits (what is his body, what is the outside world?). Excessive fright about simple routines such as haircuts which seem to tear away pieces of himself.

Assembling huge collections of often unchildlike objects which must be within his control. Arranging and sorting these collections.

Intense dislike of change. Often needs to have everything in his life remain the same.

His senses may be used to help him understand his world in ways that seem odd. He may need to sniff at some objects and not be able to stand certain smells. He may avoid looking at people or objects. His hearing is selectively keen, certain sounds actually seeming to cause him pain. His attention may be bombarded by all the color, movement, sound, objects, people in a room. He responds to his confusion by overactivity, withdrawal, or an activity in which he can lose himself, such as his collection.

Ever-present anxiety unrelated to any specific events, even in routine day-to-day living situations. Anxiety often increased or provoked by the most commonplace objects or occurrences.

While a new harmless toy may seem to be terrifying to him, he may often appear to be quite comfortable in a really dangerous situation. He may climb agilely to unsafe heights or cross a busy street entirely free of any sense of danger.

He may never have developed speech although his responses make it clear that he can hear and understand what is said to him. Often when he talks he may use some words in a strange way so that only members of his family can understand his "code." He may talk in an artificial voice, high-pitched, or a flat monotonous tone. Speech is not a bridge of communication but another part of the wall that separates him from the world.

He may take odd postures, assume bizarre and awkward positions and make strange motions with his body, hands, and head. Sometimes these mannerisms are organized into rituals and appear to be his efforts to bring some order and control into his environment.

In a tantrum or rage or panic, he may tear at himself, hit or scratch himself or beat his head against the wall. Although he may do real damage, cause himself to bleed, he does not seem to feel the pain or to know that he is hurting himself.

Rocking his body, banging his head and spinning around and around are sometimes apparent very early, or may become part of a pattern that he develops later.

He may have isolated islands of knowledge yet be backward in other areas.

Now here is the confusing yet vitally important fact for you to know. Your child may at various stages show one, two, or even *all* of the symptoms described. Before you run for help, consider what you can do before getting him a "diagnosis" which sometimes sets up a different set of problems. Consider first if there are present painful circumstances in your own life which the "responsibility of a difficult child" prevents you from facing up to. Your marriage may have unexpressed difficulties. First try expressing them openly and honestly, leaving the child out of it. Second, see if your child is being confused or put into a double bind by conflicting verbal or nonverbal directions from mother and father or mother and grandmother, etc. If you disagree on some aspects of child raising, that is fine as long as your disagreement is expressed clearly. Your child may otherwise be forced to mindread you to hold your love, and if he gets signals from you that indicate the opposite of what comes from your mouth, remember that children who are especially sensitive have an expanded sense perception so that their "crazy" acting is actually an accurate response to your mystification in communicating.

If your child is acting generally in a way that is unacceptable to everyone, if this has continued for some time, and if patiently waiting for him to express his feelings to the point that the painful ones are diminished has not changed anything, then at this point you will probably have to get help. Take the child to a doctor in the area who is experienced with children (a pediatrician or a general practitioner). He may suggest that it is necessary to consult a psychiatrist. If you cannot afford it, inquire about special services. You should also consult the Directory of Resources for Mentally Ill Children in the United States published by the National Association for Mental Health for a list of special services in your city or state. If any of the services in the area include mental health clinics or social service agencies, you are in luck. A phone call will usually give information about what income levels the organization serves, so that you can find a resource to fit your means.

Dr. Milton Aisenson says the pediatrician or family doctor is the one most often asked to evaluate this supposedly disturbed or abnormal child. Many parents will ask if a particular behavior is normal for that child. The doctor tries to evaluate this from a fifteen-minute examination, from behavior in the waiting room with other children, with siblings, etc.

"In this connection we have many behavior and developmental inventories that we seldom use formally; instead we rely on knowledge and experience. We are aware of the great variation in easily measured items: height and weight, age of first step, talking, red blood count . . . in normal children. So we must also consider differences in the child's personality as well as differences in his parents' standards and expectations. If we worked strictly by the charts we would needlessly refer thousands of children for psychiatric diagnosis."

How early can one suspect that a particular child is disturbed? Neurological disease may be apparent at birth; if mild, it may not show up for years: "Bizarre" symptoms should be seen in relation to age and milieu, with allowances for differences in rate of maturation and for transient regression, for example at birth of a sibling.

The child who gets into trouble with authorities—school, police—is often referred immediately. The child who has problems with fewer social or outward implications usually goes for a much longer time before he is identified as having difficulties.

Let's now assume your worry had a basis in fact. The doctor tells you that your child *is* suffering from an emotional disturbance. At this point you will find it calming to have the doctor discuss a general plan for care and treatment. Whether he suggests that treatment take place in a residential center or hospital, or that the child be cared for at home, ask for a clear explanation of the scope of the disturbance, the kind of difficulties that may be expected along with it, and possible hopes for the future.

However frightening the diagnosis, remember that it is just a label used as an aid to communication between doctors, and that there are all degrees of the same problem. Realize that just as a child can be slightly handicapped physically, even some children with a label of "psychotic" can be helped to "live" with their disability to the point of leading full and well-adjusted lives.

If you cannot afford professional treatment and there are no agencies or services in your home area, don't panic. Your child may have one of the kinds of disturbances that can be helped by awareness of the problem and supervision by his family doctor. Not all emotional illness needs professional therapy.

Suppose the doctor advises that your child's illness is probably a major one. You cannot afford further consultation and there is no sliding-scale child guidance clinic in your area. What can you do? You can take your child to a state hospital service which is available in every state for every citizen. There you can explain that if it is at all possible you want to be able to care for the child at home. Further consultation and diagnosis at the state hospital will be provided according to your ability to pay. Then a recommendation will be made. Unless a child has previously "acted out" his illness by committing anti-social acts which have involved the police, there will be nothing you "have to" do; you will simply be given advice.

Even in cases of serious disturbance, few psychiatrists will want to take a child away from home if you will cooperate in his home care by doing what is indicated (bringing him for possible outpatient or short-term hospital treatment, giving medicine that is prescribed, etc.). Michael Freeland of the National Association for Mental Health has said, "If you go to any one of the state hospitals where they have special children's units with good programs and talk to the director or the staff . . .

you will find as many as half the children are there not because it is best for them but because there's nothing else for them and nothing in the community."

Now that you have faced the situation, there is one difficulty: you don't feel a bit better. If anything, you feel worse. You now "know" what before you may have only thought, and the knowledge is not what you had hoped for, but a sharp reminder that although you are exhausted and hurt, what is ahead is not a rest, not a quick solution, but a time of continued difficulty . . . and perhaps a lifelong problem.

Everything in you wants to run from the thought. You may find yourself especially short-tempered, full of self-pity, wanting to escape into some mind-lulling activity or crawl into bed and pull the covers over your head. You may spend time berating yourself for actions which you think may have contributed to your child's illness, especially if you are the kind of person who is afraid to show anger directly. Depending upon the kind of diagnosis given, you may feel hopeless and depressed, hopeful and angry, or just plain bewildered by what has happened.

All of this is understandable; none of it is useful. What can begin to help is positive action, for even the slightest relief in a child's symptoms as a result of having "gone for help" will provide the first bit of encouragement that will be needed. Above all, don't blame yourself.

This point is important. As you begin to face caring realistically for such a child, you will recognize the wastefulness of squandering sorely needed energy on guilt. Some of this guilt arises naturally, for every parent has made some mistakes or has problems of his own, and the unhappiness of a child can be a constant reminder to both mother and father that somehow they have failed. Dr. Ralph Rabinovitch, director of the Hawthorne Center in Michigan and an eminent child psychiatrist, believes that parents must realize that "the best protection against emotional disorders in children is their own integrity and self-respect, their own cheerfulness and serenity, their honestly giving love and sustaining strength. But even those who have never changed a diaper or warmed a bottle can hardly fail to see that children are not mere lumps of clay upon which parents superimpose their own features." Guard then against a hopeless, guilty attitude that suggests that you were responsible for a child's illness or that you can hardly be the person to help him get well. Don't, however, jump to the opposite conclusion, that he was somehow "born that way," so that again, for quite another reason, there just won't be much that can be done to help.

This is your child. If he were crippled by polio you would help him retrain damaged muscles; neighbors and family would be sympathetic, the community supportive. All this would happen because frankly it seems more rewarding to help the physically handicapped child. He seems "grateful," whereas the very nature of your child's emotional illness may make it harder to get along with him, to even, let's face it, *like* him.

Now that you know the kind of disturbance the child has, just how useful can that information be? Cutting across illness labels one can divide emotionally disturbed children into the following groups. One group can continue to go to regular classes in public schools, provided there are pupil personnel services in the school and community treatment facilities are available. Another group may need to be in a special class in a public school with special teachers and intensive individual care. A third group will need special schools, combining education and therapy. Finally there are children whose symptoms have become so disruptive to themselves and others that hospitalization is needed to be able to change habits and patterns so the child can eventually return in a different way. You may then have to turn to hospital or residential center.

Of the estimated four million children with emotional disturbances, 85 percent will be in the first two groups, according to Dr. Sol Nichtern, including a surprising number of the seriously disturbed. It can be a tremendous relief to find that although serious emotional difficulties exist in large numbers so that major help is needed, most of the complaints brought to child guidance clinics and doctors by worried parents involve minor problems that can often be dealt with successfully.

Detailed descriptions of the disorders of children are given at the back of the book, but here is a brief mention of the various types. Some emotional disorders of children are called reaction behavior disorders. These are simply reactions to real events and will probably pass. Neurotic behavior and personality disorders occur when a reactive behavior disorder goes unnoticed or doesn't get helpful understanding. Less common in children is an actual neurosis. Phobias, anxiety, compulsions often appear from time to time in the normal child, and you will find the doctor considering such symptoms neurotic only if they are inappropriate for the child's age or if they are substituted for normal involvements in his life.

Organic brain disturbance and psychosis are the more serious problems.

In caring for your child, you will find real benefits in facing what must be faced and helping with what must be helped. Relieved of the "mystery," you may come to value a moment's warm communication or a new gain in a child's life as the remarkable achievement it is. Instead of constantly worrying about what others may think, you will find a private satisfaction in seeing a small improvement before it becomes obvious to anyone. As far as embarrassment, *that* will soon become the most minor of emotions! Even on the rough days, when it will seem as though what you have been trying to teach has just not penetrated, it may help to know that the child is not totally different from the rest of mankind, for whom, as Josh Billings said, "Experience inkreases our wizdum but don't reduce our phollys."

For yourself, have as much fun as you can, with or without the child. Don't make the whole week a mental health discussion. Don't "worry" the problem all the time like a dog with a bone. Be kind to yourself. Don't forget books-for-fun or delicious meals or everyone trooping down for a hamburger on impulse. Don't forget ball games or bike rides or walks. Don't forget prettying up the house. And don't forget hoping.

If your child is under the care of an accredited psychiatrist, the advice in this book can only be supplemental. The doctor's information will provide for the individual characteristics of your child's disturbance.

However, the doctor may not have time to give you detailed instructions about home care, any more than the average pediatrician will recite those useful paragraphs in Dr. Spock's famous book on raising babies. His hours are limited and you will want him to spend them on the child. The few general questions in this book are designed to help you direct your questions toward the "special" aspects of the child.

Helen Moak writes that "most parents will find, perhaps to their surprise, that life in the family is a happier one and that their relationships with all their children are strengthened when once they accept the challenge of caring for a troubled child. It could hardly be otherwise when the one who needs help so badly unwittingly gives his parents a special sensitivity to the needs of all children; indeed he demands the kind of family life which is most likely to give us men and women of responsibility in the next generation."

Sometimes it seems as though a day is impossible to get through and worries have a way of creeping up on you. Will the child have to be hospitalized? Suppose he cannot take care of himself when he is grown. How will he manage? What will become of him? These are real worries, not to be banished by a few words of reassurance. Still there are things you can do to guard his future, and you must not get so submerged in caring for him that your days become leaden and heavy. Under such circumstances marriage sags, creaks, and finally bursts its springs like an old couch. The child loses, the parents lose, everybody loses.

Try to pace yourself. If you feel yourself sinking, find some kind of relief, coffee break, evening out, a day in bed, *something.* If the child is so seriously disturbed that an extra burden of physical care past the usual age is added, then you must have a weekly change of pace or you will find yourself bitterly resenting him instead of helping. Take one day at a time, sometimes feeling reassured and seeing improvement, other times feeling that caring for a child is like trying to patch a sieve with scotch tape. You keep asking about the future; you ask the psychiatrist, the teacher, the social worker. What is the child's potential? Where will it all end?

Except in cases of simple behavioral disorders, literature from the National Association for Mental Health suggests that it is likely that there will always be a "difference," a gap that doesn't fully close. Expectations for him will have to be determined, not by what you wanted him to be, but by what he can do when reassured.

Don't neglect the possibility of family therapy. Guilt is a

waste of time, but there are situations in which the child's disturbance lessens or even disappears when the family dynamics are changed. Ronald Laing's *The Politics of the Family* can be helpful. Even if your child has already been labeled, continue to try to evaluate the prevalence or lack of honesty existing in your family, and what can be done about it. If it has been determined that your child's problem originates not in family pathology but in an external cause, it will still be helpful to clarify family roles and opinions.

You can take pride in the job begun, realizing that as you help one sick child you begin to understand yourself as well. You have done more than wait and hope; you have taken action.

Just before going to bed, let's take a look out of the window. The child is asleep and your head aches. Wind blows a branch against the window and the sound is a little scary even to us adults, for winter is about to begin and we feel we have missed summer; summer passed us by.

Learn to be satisfied with a paper flower. It is yours, and maybe next year will be better. Meantime remember what Robert Frost said as he battled every day of his life with feelings of frustration, impatience, and uncertainty:

Count our strength
Two and a child
those of us not asleep subdued to mark
how the cold creeps as the fire dies
at length—
How drifts are piled
Dooryard and road ungraded,
Till even the comforting barn grows
far away and my heart owns a doubt
Whether 'tis in us to arise with day
And save ourselves unaided.

Special Instructions

Reaction Behavior Disorders. According to Drs. Lieberman and Bower, in these beginning difficulties it is always good to educate children about their illness and to permit them to express their feeling about it. Many relatively superficial disorders such as these will seem to have no "real" reason behind them. Neurotic symptoms, whether "reactions" to a particular situation or deeper, will also seem to have no real reason, but whether they express themselves psychosomatically (through body symptoms) or not, they will have a better chance of relief if their underlying cause is understood.

Of course the cure is often harder than the illness, especially if it involves feelings or actions which the family cannot handle.

Dr. David Chasin points out that "children worry parents for such diverse symptoms as nightmares, tics, headaches, bedwetting, stealing, fire setting, beating other children, and poor school performance despite good intelligence." Often these symptoms are not signs of serious illness at all, but represent character, behavior, and personality disorders that are so responsive to proper handling and treatment at an early age that complete relief can be obtained, from not only the symptoms but the causes behind the symptoms. Here is the more cheerful side of the picture, for although some children, because of factors still medically undetermined, can never be completely cured, such disorders in others, if caught early enough, will clear up.

If a child has a reactive behavior disorder, you will be relieved to know that it is not caused by organic conditions but is simply a reaction to "what happens to him." It can include behavior that is inappropriate in our society, patterns that he uses to defend himself against unfortunate circumstances, painful events. The word "reactive" suggests that as the circumstances improve, so his problem may lift. Knowledge of his real situation is vital; you can distinguish, for example (as pointed out in a letter from Dr. Martin Myers), between grief and depression by knowing if there is a basis in reality for grief. The loss or death of a parent or beloved person is an appropriate basis; *continued* depression for no apparent cause must be looked into.

These disorders may show themselves only at school or only at home, only at camp, etc., and you can occasionally get an idea of the cause from the place in which the problem appears.

If a child seems disturbed only at home, there may be a real situation that is unbearable for him. Examine family relationships to see if his needs are met. Is there another child in the family who is chronically ill, and has this child been encouraged to express his feelings about the problem? Are there pressures brought by the neighbors or community which are too much to bear? If his behavior is disturbed only at school, investigate his learning responses or his relationships with other students or teachers.

If his behavior has begun after recovery from a physical illness or during an illness that needs special care, educating him in understanding the treatment is necessary. Let him express his hurt.

You can help the child to complete recovery from a reactive disorder by helping the situation or seeing that he gets brief direct treatment. Since here we are caring for an essentially normal child who is reacting to something real, removing the irritant or supporting him in going through, then gradually getting over, the trauma will leave you delighted with the results.

Neurotic Behavior and Personality Disorders. Sometimes a child's reaction to a specific trauma situation continues and becomes fixed—then it is called neurotic behavior and personality disorder.

Removing the unacceptable ways a child has recently found to defend himself against this previous hurt may not yet be a very complicated matter. Nevertheless it will take patience, for it is one step further than the simple reactive disorder. He should be cared for just as you would treat a normal child who has been traumatized.

A neurotic personality disorder is simply a continuation and "hardening" of reactive and neurotic behavior disorders. You will have to trace back the problem which was originally interpreted by your child as hurting. Because you will probably not have sufficient distance from your own possible role in causing him pain, or be involved in an intention that is adding to the difficulty, some professional therapy will probably be helpful. You should not be distracted by his presenting "symptoms" to the point of forgetting that these can eventually ease if he first expresses them, then begins to understand what made him unhappy to begin with. At this point there may be a stubborn quality in his behavior, so that finding the trouble may be as hard as removing chewing gum from hair. Drs. Lieberman and Bower believe that "sometimes the cure involves feelings or actions which the family cannot handle." Trying to "make up" to him for what deprivation he may have felt or was real in the past is, as Dr. Lieberman points out, "often unrewarding." Nevertheless it is worth an honest try.

Childhood Neurosis. According to Dr. Stella Chess, childhood neurosis is relatively rare, perhaps because of the immaturity of the child's personality, or, to put it another way, because the child is still in the process of maturation and his neurotic elements have not had time yet to become organized. If a child has psychosomatic symptoms such as morning vomiting, asthma, hives, etc., the important thing to do is find out the underlying cause rather than focusing all your energies on the illness itself. It is very unlikely that this will be discovered without professional help; often what appears to be the cause is only a disguise for the real problem.

You should remember that while he is undergoing psychotherapy, you can help best at home by caring for the physical symptom matter-of-factly, without anxiety. You may find that as the uncovering treatment continues, the "cure" will be harder for you than the illness, for often anger directed at a parent has been converted into an organ disability. If you can stay reasonably cool through this time, allowing him to express his previously pent-up emotions directly, you will be given a rare reward in the area of emotional illness, for you may eventually see an illness actually go away.

Organic Brain Disturbance. Dr. Chess reminds us that the outlook is more hopeful for brain-damaged children today than several decades ago when the child was treated only for the organic or physical part of his ailment, and no attempt was made to help his behavior. The new optimism isn't only because of the increased knowledge as to diseases of the brain, but because of the development cf new treatment and educational techniques. Kurt Goldstein's studies on rehabilitation show that "the child who has been unable to function in normal society because of his impulsiveness can make a better adjustment if both he and those around him learn to recognize signs of restlessness and a constructive or at least bearable outlet for his impulses is provided." Recent advances in drugs may make it possible for a child to "seem" less handicapped. Although brain tissue cannot be regenerated, you will want to ask the doctor if suitable drug therapy can help the child to better handle some of his difficulties.

If his brain damage is minimal, careful management can help him grow into a fully successful functioning member of society. If it is *extensive,* you can ease his adjustment by:

Understanding his failure to conform to conduct expected for his age. He will probably be hyperactive, lack certain inhibitions, have tantrums for trivial reasons. As he grows he may seem to have much trouble with other children.

If brain damage is suspected, his condition *must* be evaluated professionally. After diagnosis has been made and the extent of damage assessed, a psychologist can give you an idea of the child's potential. Find out if he meets the minimum requirements for education and rehabilitation by present methods before making a decision as to whether you can care for him at home.

If it is possible to live in a suburb or the country, it will be easier to raise a brain-injured child than in a densely populated city.

Since the community is likely to regard the child's behavior as a result of parental failing, it will help to belong to an organization which can enlist community support for your educative efforts.

Don't attempt to understand or explain his behavior by recalling your own at that age, or by measuring him against the other children. Don't try to compare him with a group, since his difficulties in perceiving and thought will often interfere with his understanding group behavior.

He needs a place of his own where he can be by himself in times of stress. You cannot worry about things like furniture;

his should be sturdy, for he is often unintentionally destructive.

A fenced-in yard is ideal, for he may not recognize danger at the same age as other children, and the number of his playmates needs to be carefully supervised.

This is one illness where parents must learn to recognize situations that will cause an outburst. "The outburst itself is a sign of the child's internal disorganization. It is more a cry of distress than a cry of anger." Brain-injured children cannot tolerate uncertainty. In such cases we will not wait for misbehavior to occur to "correct" it, but anticipate it on the basis of what his organic disability will not let him understand.

Keep the child's life simple: few associates; carefully purchased clothes which do not result in frustration because of his physical clumsiness—nothing too small or tight with tiny buttons. His clothes should be chosen and laid out the night before. Extreme food habits are likely to develop. Most of them are comparatively harmless and may have to be accepted; overeating may need to be dealt with when it happens just because he cannot stop eating. Frequently he will eat exactly what he is given to eat, no more and no less. A utensil called a "pusher" (a small plastic device shaped like a hoe) will help him get food by his own fork, a process in which he is again held back by his motor clumsiness and difficulties in perception.

Remove all extraneous objects from the dining table and indeed from this child's life. The more severe the tissue damage, the simpler and less confusing his environment will have to be for him to remain in control of it. This does not mean grim surroundings (if anything these youngsters are more affected by pleasant color and cheerful decor than the average child). But he will not be able to function unless his possessions are few and arranged in an orderly, predictable way.

"Punishment" won't help him if it is used to correct behavior that is an aspect of his handicap. He can be helped to make changes that are hard for him by getting him into a quiet situation before attempting to explain.

Taking away a thrown toy is better than scolding, since it eliminates the disturbance the object created and shows him that when he throws things they are lost to him.

Do not try to explain anything to him while he is doing something else. Learning will require his full attention and you will be wasting your words. Give instructions in a sequence and do not leave anything out.

Some of his grimacing and walking problems may be noticed in public. You will have to strengthen yourself against embarrassment and at the same time strengthen the child by explaining that some people are rude. Simple expedients like facing him to a wall in a restaurant will reduce his distractibility at the same time it minimizes prying curiosity.

Explain to the people in the child's immediate environment that he has a handicap that needs their understanding and support. His life is a constant struggle to perform through repetitive training what to most people "comes naturally." Recognition and praise for his achievements, however short of his age level, will help him use what function he has been spared in the best way possible.

The Psychotic Child. If the child has been diagnosed as suffering from a functional psychosis, you will be confused as to its cause (still unclear), and *what* it is (there is a strong tendency to consider it to be many diseases rather than one). Leo Kanner, for example, refers to "the schizophrenias of childhood." Drs. Lauretta Bender, Leo Kanner, David Levy, Leitch and Escalona are only a few of those who have investigated early differences only to emerge with some feeling that an infant probably brought a "constitutional sensitivity," "maturational lag," or "biochemical disturbance" to the beginnings of his relationships. Getz explains that rejected children are found to have serious problems, but schizophrenia is not noticeably or statistically prominent among them.

Dr. Lewis Robbins, director of New York's Hillside Hospital, says, "Some people are unsuccessful for one reason or another in completing this maturation of steps, and continue to be dependent and need some kind of assistance in completing it."

Base your approach on the principles of rehabilitation, for whatever the diagnosis is, this is no excuse for a hopeless attitude.

Many of the suggestions directed at living constructively with brain-damaged children will apply here. Just as alternative methods of achieving the same function are worked out for the physically handicapped, so your aim must be educative, and this education directed at substituting what the child can learn to "work for" in an area in which he cannot and must not be expected to function normally.

Ask the doctor about prescribing an appropriate medication for the child. He will have to be watched carefully during the period of dosage adjustment, for some of the most helpful major tranquilizers which "screen out" much of the ever present anxiety may have side effects such as drowsiness, feelings of helplessness, feelings of physical restraint, skin rash, etc. For a psychotic youngster drugs may spell the difference between being able to care for him at home and sending him off to an institution where only custodial care may be available. It is your continuing responsibility to see that he takes the dosage that was prescribed, and to get in touch with the doctor when it has adverse effects or doesn't seem to be doing the job. This is a delicate matter; from time to time medication will have to be adjusted as much as if you were asking the doctor about a formula change for a brand-new premature baby.

Don't fall into the trap of hoping for a therapeutic result similar to that which might be attained with a neurotic child. It will be more helpful to proceed in the same way that we would with a physically handicapped youngster. You may have to retrain some functions, train others not usually involved to assume part of the loss, and clearly define situations that the child will not be able to handle without help.

If a child is getting professional help, see that he benefits from some retraining in patterning his thoughts, behavior, and awareness of his own reactions. You can help in such retraining by looking at his present performance as objectively as possible. Where are the weak spots? How does he "ruin" friendships? What baffles him most? His schooling will have to be adjusted with the utmost delicacy. It is a constantly shifting matter, and you cannot take a firm stand without losing ground; the nature of a child's illness involves as much variability in mood and ability to take tension as the weather. One month he will be able to achieve good grades in a regular classroom situation, the next he will be floundering, feeling that "everyone is staring at me, nobody likes me." This will signal an intruding screen of anxiety and you will just have to lower your expectations and help the storm cloud pass. He should not be told that you are disappointed in him after combating a bout of anxiety and losing ground meanwhile. It is a wonder he can integrate himself at all, and he needs praise.

Direct a young child's social life as does a traffic dispatcher for a railroad. He cannot coordinate the social needs of more than one person at a time and is apt to unwittingly confuse and hurt. If allowed to proceed on his own, as your normal children, he will only succeed in being rejected in fact rather than just imagination. Help him plan his activities, insist on enough rest, suggest activities rather than contact with people on what you will come to recognize as his "off" days.

Investigate all types of schooling available. There can be no generalities as far as school placement; one child will do well in the relaxed atmosphere of an ungraded class for the emotionally disturbed, another will mimic every deviation of each child and can proceed at his own rate in a regular class if there is no pressure to continually do well. There are innumerable variations to the kind of schooling that will help a child's illness, from excellent day schools such as the League School for Severely Disturbed Children in Brooklyn, New York, to experimental public school programs like those in Livonia, Michigan. Included in the list of services at the end of this chapter are outstanding day schools, both public and private, and such superior residential treatment centers as the Hawthorne Center in Northville, Michigan. Sometimes parents of very severely ill youngsters will have to accept the fact that a residential treatment center will be helpful. Such schooling is usually accompanied by active treatment and the child returned to his home when conditions are favorable. If this procedure is not possible, either because of finances or because the child is not able to endure a sudden or prolonged separation, alternate plans will be given in later chapters.

Accept a child as he is, even while trying to progress. He is looking for signs of rejection, and this may often make him seem unlovable. Face into the wind and show him, by a kiss, a handclasp, a cuddle if he is small, that you are there. Even if he doesn't seem to accept it, stiffening, lying inert, not responding, let him see that your acceptance is real, to be offered again and again. Keep disciplinary measures short and clear so that he will not confuse your anger over an unacceptable action with permanent feelings about him.

Provide him with a daily respite from all pressures, a "rest period from having to worry about growing up." This psychological rest may be exactly what he needs to gather strength for later progress. For example, a psychotic child who is managing in a special class in the public junior high school has a seemingly regressed hour every day as he arrives home from school. This time of babyishness marks the intermission between his intense efforts in school and his late afternoon efforts at homework and control of anxiety. Such needs are not uncommon among healthy children; among the disturbed they are universal.

Caring for More Seriously Disturbed Children at Home (General Advice)

Arrange family life to suit the needs of the whole family. Attempt realistically to meet the extra needs placed on you by a child's emotional illness in the same way that you would recognize the extra needs of a child with a chronic physical ailment. You should have household help if it can be afforded; it will be worth some sacrifices of extras to save your strength. If this is not financially possible, take a relative into your confidence or arrange through the nearest mental health center for a rotating pool for some care or recreation so that each mother of a disturbed youngster will have regular time off.

Respond only to reasonable demands from the child. It will take much energy to listen to continued pressure of excessive ones and you ought to respond with firm willingness only to those that are appropriate. Resist the temptation to secure peace through granting such demands when tired.

Take advantage of good moments. Offer warmth and extra attention when there are *not* excessive demands. There are few illnesses so overwhelming that the eventual connection of affection given freely rather than on anxious demand will not eventually get through to the child.

Try to steer a middle course between keeping a child's illness an uneasy secret from friends and neighbors and using his "diagnostic label" to explain all failures of behavior, or to draw pity for yourself as his parent. This is a delicate matter, for depending on the extent and possible permanence of his disability you will have to pick your way over some hot coals. People come to visit and a schizophrenic child acts especially trying, talking too loud or too fast, asking unsuitable questions. Should you always try to hide the illness, passing it off as ordinary misbehavior, or identify it to your guests, thus exposing your child to a possible community stigma?

Neither reaction is helpful. You cannot completely disguise or "talk away" a child's disturbance, and the community may not be ready yet to know its "name." The average person becomes terrified by words like brain injury or childhood schizophrenia, feeling some connection with danger. The helpful way is to explain that the child may have some odd symptoms which will require patience, since he has an emotional problem. It is pointless for you to identify it further except to use the words "mild" or "temporary" if they are true. There is no need to say "severe" if it is, for that will be obvious.

Set up a household schedule that will "work" to provide some relief to each member of the family. For example, fathers need a period of rest from tension at the end of each workday. If a child has developed defenses against anxiety that make mealtimes a test of will, feed him earlier. Keep him company by having fruit or salad or one course with him, so that he is helped to consider mealtime a socializing experience. If the other children are distressed by his behavior at mealtime, set up a schedule where certain days they can enjoy a relaxed meal with one parent while the other eats ahead with the child who makes mealtime difficult.

Since insatiability or greediness is a frequent defense against the kind of fear felt by many disturbed children, it may help to have food served to the family in precut portions. Extra amounts can be left on the stove for second requests; this can do away with some of the anxiety over "not getting enough" of what is on the family platter, often a source of mealtime despair.

Establish a schedule. A schedule even for weekends is a tremendous help to the child with emotional problems. The kind of unstructured existence that is possible with the other children makes him frightened. Lewis and Lehtener point out that he is relieved of having to continue his compulsive and unsuccessful efforts to control the whole world. He sees that he can have confidence in his parents; they are in the driver's seat and they know how to steer. . . . Usually one change at a time is all either the child or his parents can manage.

Let relatives help. Many parents of emotionally disturbed children make superhuman efforts to hide their child's disabilities from grandparents or other relatives. Parents often feel somehow "ashamed," or think that they have failed because the grandchild they present does not bring praise as did their previous efforts to please. Far more important than praise is any help that can be offered out of sincere family concern. It is a sign of maturity to accept it unless those relatives, because of their own problems, have an adverse effect on the child.

Try not to identify with all of a child's problems of behavior. If they are serious you may need trained help to sort out which are "his" and which are "yours," which are primary and caused by his inner differences and which are "secondary" and aggravated by your handling.

Do not ask back guests who, for reasons of their own, are unable to "stand" the child. If it becomes clear that a visitor has a strong feeling of fear or prejudice, you have to face dropping him as a friend, or seeing him in other surroundings.

Do not be overconcerned about violence. It may be reassuring to know that violence in mental illness occurs "in only about the same proportion as airplane crashes to general airplane travel." If you are sensitive to a sick child's emotional climate over a period of time, you will know his weak spots and can take only normal safety precautions.

Chapter 6

Survival Tactics I: Office Treatment

Psychotherapy and psychoanalysis have been so thoroughly discussed in popular media that mere mention of "my analyst" is apt to bring a series of comic responses. Unfortunately, it isn't always funny. If someone in your family is in therapy, other members of the family may find themselves in a trying situation.

If the patient is in individual therapy with any but a "family" therapist, there will be little or no consultation with the doctor, little or no explanation of the patient's conduct, and little or no guidance for other members of the family as to how to act toward the patient's new and surprising attitudes. Implicit in the Freudian or related schools of psychotherapy is the idea that the confidentiality of patient to doctor is literally sacred, for if the patient felt that there was going to be some feedback of his expressed free associations, he would be tremendously inhibited.

On the other hand, the family can go through a bewildered few years faced with unfamiliar behavior and tremendous mood swings on the part of the patient, until it seems to them that instead of "getting better" as they expected, he has "gotten worse."

You will have to take it on faith that the patient's trust in his doctor's exclusive concern with his own problems rather than that of other members of his family makes it rather more certain that he will unburden himself of whatever load he has been dragging around.

Let's see what kinds of problems can lead people to therapy.

Jules M. is a married man in his early forties who has been "playing around" for some time. In the last five years he has had numerous affairs, most of them situations where he did not find himself seriously involved emotionally. Recently, he has entered an affair which seemed to matter more to him, causing him to suggest to his wife the possibility of divorce. The tentative way in which he phrases this leads his wife to conclude that he doesn't know his own mind. He makes the sketchiest attempts to conceal his unfaithfulness, forcing his wife to conclude that there is something in the situation of having two women know about each other that he finds exciting. Faced with actual evidence of his continuing adultery she confronts him by saying that if he does not want a divorce, he will have to go into therapy and find out what is making all this happen. Thinking of how unsure he is about his own desires, he *does* go into therapy, complaining all the time that it is *her* neurosis and *her* problem that he is going to get help for.

Robbie L. is a twelve-year-old child who is afraid to go to school. Each morning he procrastinates, hangs back, and then finally vomits, ending up so physically sick as to preclude the possibility of school attendance. Various attempts made on the part of his family to find out just what the trouble is have failed; at this point it may be helpful to take Robbie to a psychiatrist who will keep his reasons confidential, and let the doctor probe his unconscious desire to rebel against his parents which leads to this school phobia.

Catherine P. is a forty-two-year-old woman whose husband is extremely successful financially. She lives in a large suburban house, drives a new convertible, has servants so that only time she desires need be spent with her children. Yet she is wretchedly unhappy, possessed of a gnawing feeling of dissatisfaction with herself and those around her. She constantly feels she is unacceptable and looks for rejections on the part of her friends as evidence that this is so. Some years before, she gave birth to a retarded child who is still hospitalized. Her need to work out irrational guilt about the sick child, and her unexplored feelings of anger at her husband and parents, bring her to a Freudian analyst for treatment.

Eric L. is an outwardly thriving commercial artist who has started a firm of his own that is going remarkably well. Still tied in desire to fine arts, he works at his real love in a desultory fashion on Sundays, half afraid to step toward it for fear it will jeopardize his precarious grasp on "finally making a good living" for his family. He buries most of his really creative impulses, allowing them to emerge only slightly in the area of his daily work. He sublimates these desires most evenings by making wine, a relaxing and creative hobby but one with which he is not content since he is really a "born artist."

Billy F. is a painfully obese young man who has had overt sexual experiences with other men but who really wants to be heterosexual. Afraid of being rejected by women, he leads a timid life working as a clerk during the daytime, writing poetry weekends and at night. He crash-diets three and four times a year, taking off anywhere between thirty to forty pounds, but he puts it back again and then repeats the cycle of rejection by women because of his overweight.

Lauren T. is a charming young lady who is attending a school of social work for her master's degree. She appears on the surface to have no problems, but throughout her life we see that she is oddly drawn only to men who, for reasons of their own, cannot reciprocate or are already married, and that the eligible ones forever seem unattractive to her. This effectively bars any possibility of her getting married. Marriage is surely not the goal of every woman, but Lauren does well to go into psychotherapy to determine why she seems to so *want* to get married, while unconsciously undermining any possibility of that really happening.

All these people share in common a need for further probing to find out why their outward activities do not match their expressed desires. To live with them during treatment (from six months for brief psychotherapy to four or five years for a full Freudian analysis) is extremely difficult and requires a lot of patience. It may be helpful to trace some of the ups and downs of each of the patients described and see how their treatments can prove disturbing to other members of their family.

Jules M. has been facing for some time the increasing knowledge that his sights are shrinking. At twenty he wanted to be a writer, and the fact that he is successful in the related occupation of editing doesn't change his view of himself as having been left behind by his writer friends who have "made it" in their original direction. The fact that he has a family, has outwardly the fullest and most rewarding life of all his early friends, is not enough to pull him off the hook. About ten months before, he had finally gotten himself to write a novel in his spare time and on weekends, and this had not been accepted by any of the major publishers.

Along with the realization that his earlier ambitions would not be fulfilled went complicated lifetime feelings about his wife, his mother, and his still unresolved difficulty with his parents who had separated when he was twelve, plaguing and haunting his present marriage. Jules has always required the excitement of two women at a time, and for a while this occurred through confrontations between his wife and mother. Later in the marriage when his wife, after receiving psychiatric help herself, refused to allow this to happen, it became a series of affairs that were never really secret, always communicated to the wife in one way or another.

In therapy, Jules explores with his doctor those reasons provoked by the past which led him to this kind of behavior. His wife, if she wishes to preserve the marriage, must stand patiently by while he rids himself of years of accumulated anger. Through his analysis this anger will emerge from time to time without regard to the actual immediate cause which provoked it.

Trying to her patience also may be a depression Jules undergoes while in the course of treatment, for analytic treatment not only does not protect against outward difficulties during it, but may even *cause* them as material from the past is brought up, examined, interpreted or not interpreted, and allowed to go back into the past again.

Only when you clearly realize you are not the cause of the patient's heightened emotions during therapy can you find peace with a person who is going for office treatment. If you take all the blame, or, just as destructively, reject *any* blame and get incensed by the patient's irrationally heightened reactions toward people in his present life, you will find it rough going.

Robbie R. may be going for supportive or investigative therapy. Either way he will be more emotional, more inclined to storms and upsets, and unlikely to weather the treatment with the kind of smoothness that a parent may expect upon sending his child to "get help." His parents find to their dismay that instead of the situation getting better, the therapy, which is often costly and secured at great financial sacrifice to the family, seems to be making the problem temporarily worse. They request a consultation and the therapist explains the difficulty. Because confidentiality of patient to doctor must be respected, even more so if the patient is a child who expects that his criticisms not be repeated to his family, a child psychiatrist is not like a pediatrician with a responsibility to report back to the parent all of his findings as he comes upon them. It is hard for the family to accept this, particularly when therapy is entered into as a quick panacea for the presenting problem, and the family has a tendency to grow irritated with what seems like a slow, frustrating approach to what was seen by the parents as the actual problem involved.

Robbie's reluctance to go to school stems from his sense that his parents are using him as a vehicle for their own ambitions that were frustrated. Forced to leave school for economic reasons at a young age, Robbie's father has always looked forward to having a son who will stand out academically. Although he and his wife have never voiced this special ambition, it has come through to the boy that he is in some way expected to perform perfectly. Frightened of this expectation, he becomes so physically sick that he is unable to travel. An hour or two after the time of going to school has passed, the boy slowly recovers and shows no neurotic traits for the rest of the day.

The stages in Robbie's psychotherapy will probably be such that his parents have to bear the brunt of his anger as he slowly develops insight into his phobia and how his parents have unconsciously used him to further their own ambitions. Robbie's family may well have to swallow impatience and alarm as his rebellion in this one area turns into a less pointed rebellion in many areas, gradually weakening and diluting the boy's violent response to school alone.

Catherine P. may prove still more of a challenge to her relatives. Whatever happens to her in therapy is seized as an excuse for one of her long monologues about herself, her new insights, the thing she has "just learned." This proves monotonous as well as confusing to those around her, who dimly perceive that the ennui which first brought her to the psychiatrist still motivates her every action. It will be a long time before her doctor gets to the root of that almost total preoccupation with self which makes her life so formless and without value even to her family. Living with her, therefore, becomes a matter of patience to withstand her constant new "insights" and to realize that she is still defending herself by these too easy realizations from getting to bedrock where her actual problems are concerned.

Eric L. has been in therapy before and it is a tribute to his wife's ability to deal with the situation that he is once again going for office treatment. Eric had stopped the first time when he was on the brink of discovering how to resolve his parallel drives and ambitions and accepting that one of these goals must be given up. His wife is reassuring yet firm in her understanding of the stages he must pass to work through this difficult material. She doesn't fuss when he temporarily loses his temper, realizing that his therapy involves much reliving of old or childhood experiences, and that anger will be spun off on whoever is around at the moment.

Billy F. will have a hard time conquering his deep homosexual urges, based on early childhood experiences. His numerous attempts to diet, to help himself out of the bind of being rejected because of physical ugliness, then feeling so rejected that he eats more to overcome the feeling, is an old pattern. A few months ago, Billy lost a much loved younger sister who died of Hodgkin's disease. Despite discouragement on the part of his psychiatrist, Billy has temporarily taken refuge in a kind of formalized spiritualism, a sect that believes in the return of the spirits of absent dead ones, and which promises him some comfort regarding the aching void which right now constitutes his life.

For Billy's family, much gentleness with regard to his odd forms of assuaging grief must be shown, for Billy is balanced precariously on the edge of not being able to continue therapy without his "comforts" at the moment. If he can just be encouraged to continue, there is a strong possibility that after his grief for the young sister has diminished, he will be able to really take advantage of his Freudian therapy to find out and be able to act on what has been causing so many of his previous troubles. Billy's family may find it easier than some of the others, for Billy's anger is so deeply buried that he presents an almost uniform picture of sweetness and light, rather than the kind of belligerence shown by the other patients going for office treatment. It will be a long time before any of Billy's anger surfaces; his family can expect to take it as a sign of progress when this happens.

Laura T. is not so much a burden to her family during her therapy as an enigma to them. She grew up with an older retarded brother who was kept at home until she was eighteen, and it is hard for her to approach anything in therapy without the most violent feelings of rage for this injustice that she feels was "perpetrated on her" by her parents. Throughout her childhood she was always afraid to bring home friends for fear they would see and mock her older brother. Moreover, she fancied that each time her parents looked at her they were saying to themselves, "Why couldn't it be Lauren instead of him?" for people of their ethnic background tend to value a son more than a daughter. That this may have been her own idea projected onto them has occasionally occurred to Lauren, but she was never really sure.

She continues her inability to form lasting relationships based on choosing as love objects only those people who are inaccessible and is a cranky, irritable family member, putting her parents through daily torments of guilt and self-investigation as she proceeds in her analytic treatment. No matter what goes on during her sessions, she is violently annoyed at her family for true or imagined misdeeds directed specifically at her. Living with her during her therapy is therefore immensely difficult and takes great strength of mind.

How can living with all these different kinds of people as they undergo office treatment be eased, in fact made possible? For from time to time the families of all the above patients have despaired of simply "getting through."

It may help, if your relative has a neurotic disturbance which the doctors have said is curable by psychotherapy, to remember how much luckier you are than a parent or spouse of a patient whose illness offers no such hopes for relief at the present.

Apart from the emotional difficulties, the financial strain of having a member of your family going for office treatment can be discouraging. If the family income is very low and psychiatric help is needed, you should go to the local or state mental health association and ask if there is a social service agency or community mental health center in your area. These mostly are run on a sliding income scale, so that there is a possibility of getting the help your family needs without draining resources. Community mental health centers which service "neighborhoods" provide facilities of the clinic, including outpatient care and treatment with psychiatrists, at a cost that runs from fifty cents a session up to twenty dollars. Private agencies such as Jewish Family Service in New York are run the same way, thus bringing in for treatment a whole group of people to whom ordinarily the world of psychiatry would be denied because of income difficulty.

Jules Masserman points out that a patient is encouraged to regard his therapist in these three ways:

First, as a kindly and protective parental figure who provides a source of security and comfort.

Second, as a learned and experienced teacher whose counsels for more restrained and balanced, and therefore healthier and happier, modes of life can be followed on rational and practical grounds.

Third, as a personal mentor uniquely interested in the supplicant's complaints and difficulties ("present illness") and willing to explore their relationship to his past experiences, their meanings and values and acquired patterns of goal-directed action in order that the verbal understandings so derived would lead to more satisfying, lasting and useful adaptations.

It may be helpful to you to know exactly what a therapist is and how he can help your family member. The psychiatrist, first and foremost, is a physician who is equipped to recognize and evaluate mental and physical illnesses. He helps people to realize their potential through the removal of internal handicaps and conflicts. At one time or another he encounters the psychiatric components of nearly every body illness, and proceeds with full recognition of the body as important in his work. Just as the GP views his job as a multifaceted one of soothing aches, patching broken bones, relieving rashes, giving preventative shots, excising unwelcome growths, lowering fevers, aiding in the reduction of annoying symptoms, so too the psychiatrist is faced with not one job but many, for there is no single solution to all the problems of emotional disturbance.

A psychiatrist helps the healthy as well as the sick. The role of psychiatry is not limited to treating the seriously disturbed or dangerously ill. Salk vaccine administered to normal people lowers the threat of polio; similarly, almost everyone can benefit from psychiatric attention. Ideally the skills and insights of psychiatry, if available to the general public, could help all. Imagine men, women, and children of all classes guided to be more balanced in personality, capable of richer, more fully developed lives, better able to withstand stress and adversity, less inclined to manipulate and be manipulated out of fear and inadequacy. Think of us all subtly assisted to have a little more "give," a little more "fun," better able to "roll with it."

Since a therapist is in the position of being able to help not only people with obvious symptoms but also those whose difficulties are less clear, he must be wise enough to decide the question of urgency himself. Roughly speaking, potential patients fall into three groups: people who seek help because their problems cannot be concealed and are causing trouble to the patient and others, those whose problems are not apparent to anyone but the patient himself, and those whose problems become apparent to the patient during interview.

To many people in the community, a psychiatrist or therapist becomes symbolic of magical help in emotional difficulties. Often he can't spend a social evening without facing the problem of an acquaintance or friend expressing his "patient" needs. No matter how skillful or experienced the therapist may be, his therapeutic effect in this setting falls short, for this is not a situation in which he can properly work.

There is no exact point when the therapist ceases to be a patient himself, and suddenly becomes a professional. As part of his full training, he must first be a patient (called analysand), for he cannot hope to help others until he has first worked through his personal qualities which might interfere. Whatever the needs that made him decide to become a psychiatrist or psychologist, the process of his training carries him beyond them. Often he perceives that here is a profession in which he can consistently and constructively push the "growing edge" of his own maturity. By these standards, the therapist has "a certain earnestness and dedication to getting on with a difficult job. . . . He feels a deep humility in the face of the vast and varied ignorance that confronts him, but he has arrived at a point where, as Santayana put it, we can begin to define the limits of our ignorance." Though psychiatrists seem to be divided into schools with differing theories, the most enlightened are tolerant of other points of view.

The image of the therapist is not a static thing. Just as the expectant mother in the course of the stages of childbirth finds her feelings toward the obstetrician in flux, so a patient's image of the therapist will vary during office treatment, depending on what is going on. Yet there is a quality, hard to describe, of needful respect. It pervades the relationship when the doctor, as is often the case in these more hopeful days, is really able to help.

A psychiatrist who is a dull moralist is a contradiction in terms, for his access to the deepest feelings of others implies a tolerance that can only be achieved by a wide-angle lens. His aim is to be right but never righteous, firm but not punitive, and a firm ally, accepting of the patient though never willing to abandon him to his illness.

The psychiatrist would appreciate the lines, "What after all is a halo? It is only one more thing to keep clean." Trained to run his beat through the devil and the deep blue sea, he knows that the healthy person is one who can adjust thoughtfully to his own nature and that, like nations, no virtue can exist for long half-slave and half-free.

This world begins with what Dr. Lauretta Bender has called a birth crisis and goes on to an awesome awareness of mother and of milk. Around these simple matters exists the dark possibilities of birth injury, chemical or metabolic imbalance, maternal deprivation, psychological trauma, anything everywhere. To grow is to court injury and insult of all kinds, yet through this dangerous situation we call life, the possibility of joy and freedom exists. The psychiatrist is a person who understands the pitfalls yet helps people to face whatever metabolic accident has determined their general limits with stoicism and occasional enthusiasm.

All psychiatrists need a certain amount of specific training to be accredited, but the difference between an adequate practitioner, technically acquainted with therapeutic methods, and the inspired healer is enormous. Infinite skill is required to chisel away at the most malignant parts of the personality while not destroying, out of sheer ignorance and clumsiness, those parts which pulsate with vitality and a special quality of their own. To free a talented writer from the corrosive effects of some of his early experiences, while helping him maintain his unique creative vision, is as challenging as any surgical procedure. Genius is not dependent on neurosis.

Dr. John Romano, in writing of his own experiences, said, "As a psychiatrist I never fail to be astonished by daily opportunities to grow in knowledge and wisdom. Psychiatry affords many occasions to acquire and pursue specialistic skills and interests . . . however in it, if one chooses one may also retain that which is indeed rare in one day . . . namely a generalistic approach to the nature of human behavior. It is the most personal, the most human of the medical sciences. Terence's maxim will be as appropriate tomorrow as it is today and as it was to Charcot a century ago. 'I am a man and nothing that concerns a man do I deem a matter of indifference to me.' "

The good psychiatrist does sometimes get results without

exactly knowing why. Yet he very definitely knows *how* and this particular how is not due to the simply persuasive powers of the therapist. His method, while less technical than the surgeon's, is quite different from the hit or miss advice of friends.

The image of the psychiatrist is inextricably interwoven with the image of emotional disturbance. As long as prejudice against emotional illness exists, it will be likely that the physician directly responsible for administering to that kind of illness through office treatment will remain associated with the fear. Just as a criminal lawyer does not draw the same interest and sympathy as the stalwart D.A., so much of the popular disparagement of psychiatrists by means of humor and ridicule has at its core feelings toward the emotionally disturbed which still carry faint overtones of a more barbaric time.

Happily, most psychiatrists view anti-psychiatric humor with little ruffling, often adding to the humor themselves. Dr. Carl Binger cheerfully states, "I have always felt that jokes about psychiatry are a *healthy* sign. They give evidence to interest and understanding and are far better than the other attitudes so frequently encountered, especially in our medical and surgical colleagues—one being a total unawareness of our existence or of any feeling that we could be the slightest help; and the other a conviction that it is downright improper to suggest to a patient that he see a psychiatrist because he will be further confused by our so-called 'probing methods.' "

Of course there have always been psychiatrists like the Menninger brothers who were neither frightened nor repelled by the overwhelming problems of mental illness and attempted, with whatever means were at their disposal, to help those patients in their care. Regarding the image of the psychiatrist, Dr. Karl Menninger had this to say, "No, you don't lose touch with medical science and you don't become a second-class citizen in the medical world. Or at least you don't need to. Some psychiatrists have let themselves feel a little bit outside the medical world partly because they are dissatisfied with the lack of interest on the part of some medical scientists with the intangible. To many people science means measuring tangible things. To them things that can't be measured are not scientific data."

What your relative's psychiatrist is may to a large extent

determine what he does. Dr. Robert Coles, familar with problems of child psychiatry under the crisis of desegregation in the South, says that "psychiatrists have to know a lot about what patients are thinking and about what they themselves are thinking. In the United States they are called in consultation on so many problems that one would suppose they know a good deal more than they sometimes do. The demands on them are enormous and some of them inappropriate. Unlike the work of their friends in many other fields, their work is still to be satisfactorily defined, and information badly needed by others from them is sometimes simply not to be had at all."

Even under ideal conditions the therapist does not necessarily make people happy. That goal is questionable, even if it were capable of achievement. What he can do is simpler and perhaps more important; he can help reduce unnecessary and unrealistic pain.

If you are unreassured as to the value of the office treatment a relative is getting, there are ways to check the qualifications of the psychiatrist he will be seeing. You can call the local branch of the National Association for Mental Health to get information about the doctor's qualifications, and if they do not know they will direct you to an organization that will look up his schooling, his degrees, and his experience so as to set your mind at rest. If his qualifications seem inadequate and progress seems to come to a standstill or is non-existent, you can talk the problem over with an interested person from the National Association. Perhaps a consultation or even a change of doctors is indicated, for not everyone does well with every doctor. Trust your instinct. If you feel that the psychiatrist is too busy, unimaginative, trying to impose his personal values rather than finding out and validating the patient's natural urges, consult a different one.

Psychiatrists are not the only kinds of mental health personnel who help through office treatment. Significant also are psychologists, social workers, occupational therapists, and occasional volunteers.

The clinical psychologist is the person usually thought of in the popular use of the word psychologist, for he is the psychologist who is specifically involved with treatment of emotional disorders. Although the clinical psychologist does not have a medical degree, he is usually highly trained, having gotten a doctoral degree from a university graduate school where his training emphasizes research as well as therapy.

The psychologist often sees patients in his office, much as a medical psychiatrist does. He is interested in behavior and how behavior patterns can be changed if necessary. His training and practical experience can qualify him to identify deviant behavior when it is potentially self-destructive.

The psychologist's training encourages him to measure personality aspects such as motor skills, aptitudes, speech, etc. He is usually primarily concerned with emotional attitudes that go beyond his "testing." Your relative may have received some of the following tests from a psychologist: I.Q., manual dexterity, Rorschach, T.A.T. and other methods of attempting to evaluate his state of mind.

The clinical psychologist has training in such techniques as individual or group therapy. He may practice alone or with other therapists or members of a psychiatric team, one which conventionally includes a psychiatrist, psychologist, and social worker but which is expanding to include many radical arrangements today.

Your relative may come in contact with a psychologist as a consultant in an office setting. He works with all ages and in numerous settings in an attempt to determine what sort of treatment is needed. Psychologists are important in school systems, in welfare agencies, and in military services. They are often found in industry where advice on proper job placement is only one of their many duties.

Another person who may be seeing your relative in an office setting is the social worker. He is often a member of the professional team that provides services and counseling. The social worker sometimes serves a kind of community facility coordinator because of his knowledge of agencies, programs and professional personnel. In places where there are few resources the social worker often revives community interest and encourages leaders to work toward getting some of the resources that are necessary.

A social worker will often be the first member of the "psychiatric team" to have contact with your relative if he is consulting a family agency or organization where office care is being arranged on an outpatient basis. You may find yourself questioning him in detail about your relative when the psychiatrist or psychologist seems too rushed and busy to answer the dozen questions you have about this unfamiliar situation. Sometimes you will be lucky enough to encounter a really human social worker who can be a key person in the patient's life during office treatment or after a traumatic event like hospitalization. Such workers can give emotional support and guidance, provide regular counseling, and bring your relative in touch with any one of a dozen community resources such as halfway houses, job placement centers, vocational rehabilitation courses, and free therapy groups.

A well-trained psychiatric social worker develops a keen sense of the attitudes and prejudices of the community in which he and you live and he can be enormously helpful in a practical way as a kind of liaison person. A small residence in London maintained by R.D. Laing was staffed with visiting psychiatrists plus a radical, totally nonconformist social worker who lived on the premises and acted as general custodian of the emotional attitudes of the residents, communicating their special problems to the visiting personnel. He also saw, on an informal basis which resembled office treatment, those residents who needed special help of one kind or another.

If you are a parent of an emotionally disturbed child you may find the school scheduling appointments with a psychiatric social worker who is often in charge of what is called "guidance." You may regard this correctly as a kind of office therapy.

Social workers vary in education. Usually a college degree is required to be admitted to a professional school of social work for the two-year program which leads to an M.S.W. degree. Occasionally applicants with college grounding in the social and biological sciences are given jobs as social workers in organizations which have enormous needs and few qualified applicants to choose from. The New York Department of Social Services employs applicants with only a B.A. degree, and some of them prove to be as helpful in counseling as those with more specific training. In selecting a social worker as a counselor, follow your instinct about his qualities of warmth, humanity, and directness. These traits can go a long way toward replacing academic credits.

Other helpful mental health personnel are occupational therapists and psychiatric aides. It is unlikely that your relative will see either of these kinds of workers in an office setting since they mostly work in a hospital.

Patience is the most valuable trait in living with a relative who is going for office treatment with either psychiatrist, psychologist, social worker or counselor. You will find yourself disagreeing with the methods as well as the actual objectives in many cases, and you may be alarmed to discover that your quiet if troubled relative has suddenly become an angry aggressive personality with the most incredible criticisms of persons in his daily life. If you can live through the total expression of feelings, some old and repressed until therapy helped bring them out in all kinds of "unsuitable" ways, you will have made an excellent start toward emotionally supporting the person who needed help.

Chapter 7

Survival Tactics II: Hospitalization

When you say goodbye to a relative or friend who is hospitalized, you feel a rush of guilt and helplessness which seems to say, "If only I could have handled it better, this wouldn't have been necessary."

To take upon yourself the blame for a loved (or feared) relative having to go to hospital is like playing God. Just as your power was not sufficient to help to the point of avoiding hospitalization, so you cannot be considered responsible for the worsening of the situation.

There are many ways to hospitalize a relative. One is voluntary, where the patient himself declares that he wants to go. If he is under eighteen years old it will be necessary for a parent or guardian to accompany and sign for him; if over eighteen he can sign himself in or out on a voluntary basis. You should be aware though that even in so-called voluntary hospitals, if three or more doctors agree that the patient is self-destructive or possibly dangerous to others, he can be detained indefinitely against his will.

A patient can also be admitted involuntarily. The requirements for such commitment vary from state to state, but usually two or more doctors are required to sign commitment papers for a person who does not want to go into a mental hospital of his own accord. If possible, it is better to have the written opinion of at least three doctors, and allow at least one or two of them to interview the patient in depth. Often the presenting symptoms, no matter how bizarre, are cover-ups for feelings that become accessible to the psychiatrist quickly, and are treatable outside of hospital.

The decision to send your relative for hospital treatment is as often or more often motivated by a family's inability to cope any longer with the patient's behavior, as an actual worsened condition of the patient. This is not something to be guilty about. If for example there is a chronic schizophrenic or elderly depressive person in the family, the other members may just simply need some relief from the unending extra support and responsibility.

To help deal with your feelings of guilt and pain it may be a good idea to examine some of the different ways in which emotional disturbances are viewed. Dr. Humphrey Osmond and Miriam Ziegler, in their study of schizophrenia, outlined six "models of madness," each of which provides a definition of what is being treated, the function of the hospital or treatment, and rights and duties of the patient and his family. These models are called the medical model, the moral model, the psychoanalytical, the family interaction, the conspiritorial, and the societal. The purpose of these "models" is to help you find a treatment situation that is congenial to you and to your relative. Most hospitals do not clearly follow one model rather than another, but knowing the alternatives may help you choose from what is available.

According to the *medical model,* the function of this hospital is to care for patients and treat disease. Mental hospitals resemble other hospitals for long-term illnesses such as tuberculosis sanatoria, etc., and as soon as medical science provides a short-term treatment for emotional disturbance it is understood that mental hospitals will quickly revert to the appearance of general hospitals. There are two versions of the rights and duties of the patient in the medical model. In the "factory" version, in which experts work on different parts of the patient, your relative has only the right to demand that the experts be really expert. He has no right to inquire about the kind of illness he has, the reason for his treatment or the hopes for his future. The other version is that of the "responsible" patient. Here he has the right to know anything about his illness that he can understand.

In the medical model families are expected to bring their emotionally disturbed patients to the hospital where the experts will care for him. They have the job of learning about their relative's problems and being cooperative with the staff in regard to treatment. They have the right to be told about the difficulties and their relative's progress. They also have the right to expect that they will be treated with courtesy, for they are not to blame for the patient's disturbance.

The main concern of the *moral model* is with the unacceptable *behavior* of the patient. Whatever unacceptable behavior exists is called sin or irresponsibility, and is the target for change. There is no "illness" and the patient is not allowed to hide behind his label.

The hospital is a correctional institution, different from a prison in that, although the patient-inmate has broken social rules, this is not a place to punish. Keeping the patient-inmate in the hospital is to remove him from acting out; he understands that he can leave when his behavior is better.

Therapists need to be responsible moral people. Experimental psychologists and ministers of religion might qualify; psychiatrists *wouldn't,* since nothing in their medical training would give them such skills.

Your relative has the right to be released from the hospital when his behavior has improved. He has the right to have his behavior taken seriously and literally, not treated as delusional or wishful. He does not have the right to regard himself as "sick." It is his duty to cooperate with the sanctioning system as best he can.

Families have the job of bringing relatives for therapy because their own sanctioning system has somehow failed. Deviant families are unlikely to bring in deviant relatives. These patients would only be seen if the community itself was sufficiently offended by their behavior. The *phychoanalytic model* sees the emotional problems of psychotic people as more serious than those of most people and of a different kind.

The function of the hospital is to bring your relative into the most extensive contact with psychotherapy and a psychotherapeutic environment. At the same time hospitalization removes the patient from his home environment where, according to this theory, the problem originated.

Your relative has the right to expect that his words and actions will be regarded as symptoms and not judged morally. It is his duty to cooperate fully with his analyst who gives him sympathetic understanding for the difficulties he has had living in an emotionally unhealthy environment.

By this view, the family should cooperate fully with the therapist who may ask you to limit contact with the patient since even your presence may interfere with therapy.

According to the *family interaction model,* it is your whole family that is sick, not just the so-called "patient." The designated patient has been selected by his family to act out the family problems. The family is ill because the parents themselves came from families who were similarly ill.

Hospitals play along with the desire of the family to maintain this situation by extruding one member.

If the designated patient were hospitalized, he would be released when the therapist had successfully transferred the definition of the illness to the whole family. Therapy would then take place in the doctor's consulting room or the home itself. If the whole family were hospitalized (so far only for research purposes), the family would leave when all members could show insight into their ways of interacting.

The designated patient has the right to expect that all other family members will agree to being defined as patients. Each family member has the right to expect that the therapist will treat him as his patient. All family members have the duty of cooperating in their group therapy. Families do not have the right to scapegoat one of their members by declaring him "mentally ill."

The *conspiratorial model* focuses on the civil liberties of patients. In its milder form the conspiratorial model calls attention to the fact that patients are often not treated like human beings. Dr. Thomas Szasz, who is its chief proponent, says that there is no such thing as mental illness at all and there should be no mental hospitals. He points out that it is up to the individual to decide whether or not he ought to change his personality or behavior, and that if he thinks this is wise he ought to contract freely with his therapist for treatment. Szasz believes that such a free contract is vital to therapy and that involuntary therapy can be only a form of brainwashing.

The presence of emotional illness is sometimes held to be related to the poor functioning of *society.* This theory is not directly connected with any practical measures for identifying or rehabilitating the emotionally disturbed but sees a high divorce rate, drug addiction, juvenile delinquency, etc., as an indication of an increase in mental llness. A "folk" version of this model vaguely equates the emotionally ill with the poor, and sees the hospital as a kind of shelter for people who are too battered by life to live outside. This philosophy in a hospital program can subtly undermine and confuse programs for getting patients well and out again.

Underlying all these ways of looking at emotional disturbance is the fundamental definition of the hospital's function to rehabilitate, treat, or provide therapy for patients. The hospital protects the community from the criminally insane. It may also protect patients from the community, offering them asylum or respite from pressures of daily living with which they just can't cope. In addition the hospital is a teaching, training and research institution.

All hospitals are medically directed. Their staff is headed by a doctor and includes nurses, possibly other therapists, and aides who are formally responsible to the doctor in charge in addition to other supervisors in the hierarchy.

You may have a tremendous amount of feeling about the difference between private and public hospitalization in terms of how you react to where a relative *is.* This may be justified, for some states have pitiful facilities, but in many cases you may be surprised to find that state facilities, which are either free or based on a low sliding scale according to income, can give the same basic services as private hospitals, in some cases better. If you are looking for anything beyond emergency short-term hospitalization, a trip in advance is well worth the time. Individual differences are subtle and not reflected in pamphlets about the hospital or even telephone conversations.

In bringing a relative to hospital, private or public, here are some practical points you should not overlook.

If you plan to visit your relative (and visits may spell the difference between success and failure of the hospital experience), how close to your home is the facility? A hospital so far as to make the trip an exhausting day is bound to spoil visits since you will feel too put upon and end up taking it out on the patient. Visiting hours will probably be more flexible in a private hospital.

What is the ratio of psychiatric personnel to patients? How often will your relative come in contact with therapy in some form—individual, group, occupational or vocational? If the facility is enormous and there is a serious shortage of personnel, you may see a ward in which everyone is walking around like zombies. This usually indicates overmedication, a remedy which keeps the ward quiet and prevents incidents of violence, but doesn't really do patients any good. Chemotherapy designed specifically for the amelioration of particular symptoms or to reduce anxiety in a particular patient is quite different from the mass prescribing of major tranquilizers which goes on in understaffed hospitals simply as a means of keeping patients quiet.

The selection of what is called paramedical personnel is very important. Psychiatric nurses and orderlies play an enormous role in making a hospital stay a terrifyingly traumatic or helpful and therapeutic one. Some hospitals draw their paramedical help from a transient and constantly shifting work population, people who are the opposite of trained and dedicated, but turn to this work because there is always an extreme shortage of personnel. Other hospitals are in a luckier situation, with a reasonably stable group of people who go into psychiatric nursing and become orderlies and attendants with all intentions of staying in the field and are often at the same job for a long enough period of time so that they form attachments among the hospital population.

All the expert therapy and forward ideas will fail to be of help if your relative has to spend the balance of his time among rude, impatient, totally overworked, and often sadistic attendants or aides.

If the time period for your relative's hospitalization is likely to be brief you might consider the psychiatric unit of a general hospital.

The psychiatric ward of a general hospital could be compared to psychological services near the front line during war. In both the place of treatment is near to the scene of stress, in one case the battle zone, in the other the home and community; quick restorative measures attempt to forestall the development of chronicity; and the person is returned to the original situation with a minimum of separation from those close to him and the best opportunity for a complete return to normality.

Let's see some of the problems of coping in as helpful and guilt-free a fashion as possible with the painful situation of a loved one undergoing psychiatric hospitalization.

Anna R. is the mother of two children, one ten, the other three. She has always had some minor psychiatric symptoms but managed to live a full and essentially normal life until the sudden death of her three-year-old daughter of asthma complicated by pneumonia. She and her husband went through a period of normal grief which seemed to be receding slightly as the other child moved into the foreground of their thoughts.

One night, as the husband put it, "Anna just suddenly went berserk. She had been acting strangely all day, and was crying and carrying on. I was terrified and sent for our G.P. who didn't even attempt to make a diagnosis but gave her a shot of tranquilizer that sent her to sleep for twelve hours. In the morning he gave her another shot and suggested that I bring her, while still sedated, to a large receiving hospital where she would be diagnosed, treated and then eventually referred to another hospital.

"At the hospital we waited in line after line. I observed other patients and the facility and got more and more upset. We finally managed to see a young intern who told me that if I had any private means at all I should think of taking my wife to another facility since that particular receiving hospital was a snakepit of overcrowding and hideously unsanitary conditions.

"So, I took her to a general hospital which has a psychiatric ward. While she was there I was allowed to visit her every day and I soon grew hopeful as I saw that she was receiving extensive psychotherapy and gentle nursing care. Her obvious irrationality soon left, to be replaced by a more subtle but still serious set of symptoms, and although she only had to stay in the hospital three weeks, she needed to continue in therapy with the doctor in his office for another three and a half years before she was really over her breakdown."

Getting along with a patient who is experiencing brief hospitalization involves patience in waiting for normal conditions to return and not panicking about the whole idea of having *had* to go to hospital. You should keep the channels of communication open, even though it is not likely that the patient will be grateful (at least while disturbed) for your signs of warmth and affection. He or she will be frightened and embarrassed about the breakdown and will need tremendous reassurance.

Elizabeth R. is a widow with one son of army age and a recently married daughter. Her husband had been a high school principal and she'd been crushed seven years before when he succumbed to a heart attack. However, she managed to hold together and got a job which she continued with some success despite frequent bouts of depression. After several years she began to see a man regularly. His work was that of spotter in a dry cleaning establishment and she considered him beneath her both socially and educationally, so that she had no thought of marriage. However, the relationship brought many satisfactions that were very important to her. When the man said he was moving to California and she could either marry and come with him or stay east where her children were, she was torn with indecision. After he left she found herself in the grip of an enormous depression which so overwhelmed her that she had to be hospitalized for a period of five months. During this time she received psychotherapy, drugs, and twelve electroshock treatments and was discharged eventually in the care of her married daughter.

Hospitalization of more than a few weeks requires greater adjustment. You must look carefully at the state of the family finances, trying to judge whether it is better to spend all on an extended private hospitalization or reserve funds for the psychotherapy that may be needed in office treatment later.

Elizabeth's daughter and son-in-law found it difficult to visit her as the private hospital that was chosen was over two hours from their home. The visits proved supportive to Elizabeth, despite the fact that she seemed barely to respond to them, and more frequent ones would have been even more helpful.

In visiting a depressed person in the hospital, words like "Cheer up, you have everything to live for, don't feel sorry for yourself," are of no help. "Why don't you pull out of this, Mother?" elicited no response at all, but when Elizabeth's daughter told her mother of a letter the former boyfriend had sent from California telling how sorry he was that she was ill and offering to come back if that would be of any help to her, the woman raised her head from the fretful apathy into which she had lapsed and answered, "Maybe . . . Maybe. . . ."

Toward the end of a hospitalization, the way arrangements are discussed in reference to coming home can mean a great deal in the success or failure of the patient's struggle to readjust. It must be taken for granted that the return home will be a positive one, that the patient is still desired and desirable as a family member, and that hospitalization has in no way been a disgrace but simply a way of dealing with the difficulty in much the same way that an appendectomy would have been handled had it been necessary.

Living with the idea of a family member being hospitalized for a really long time, permanently or intermittently, is even more difficult and requires tremendous understanding. It is painful to see a beloved person in the grip of a chronic emotional disturbance that often seems stubbornly unresponsive to treatment of any kind. Often anguishing is the knowledge that sometimes hospitalization is no help and may make things worse, but there may simply be no other alternative.

Jonah L. is a twenty-three-year-old boy brought up in a wealthy suburb. The first of four children, his family gave him a great deal of affection, but even as a child his responses were suspicious and angry. Jonah was given to brooding rages, later supplanted by the idea that people were after him, banding together in conspiracies, poisoning his food. Diagnosed as a chronic paranoid, Jonah was hospitalized first before he was eighteen, on a voluntary commitment requiring his parent's signature. After age eighteen he was released for eights months and led a marginal existence, first in his parents' house, until his paranoid symptoms made it impossible for him to get along with them or his younger brothers, then in a shabby rooming house where he made no attempt to occupy or rehabilitate himself except when he would sporadically visit the aftercare clinic of the local hospital. He soon stopped taking the medication they prescribed for him and gradually became sicker and sicker. One day he got into a fist fight with a storekeeper over the price of a can of beer, was picked up by policemen and taken to Bellevue, and then committed to a state hospital.

Life for his parents, who still love him, becomes reduced to finding a way to remain his family and protectors both in and out of hospital. He will probably spend a major portion of his life in a hospital, for they find his disturbance too hard to handle at home. All they can do to help is keep the family communication lines open and assure Jonah that even though he cannot live with them they still want to help in any way they can. They should at least allow him to freely express some of the pain he must feel at his virtual imprisonment. Perhaps from time to time they should also explore alternatives such as halfway houses, etc.

In order to be truly helpful to a relative who will be spending most of his life in a mental hospital, you must give up certain illusions with which you may have lived for years. Chronic emotional illness is a chilling, draining experience to the rest of the family and is never easy to accommodate. If you decide in advance, however, that for a certain group of people life as it is set up in the world outside is literally too difficult to face, that the things ordinary people take for granted such as getting up early, earning some kind of living, carrying out tasks that involve caring for oneself and even others, are simply so taxing to the disturbed individual that he is in *more* torture and anxiety outside than inside of the hospital, then you can and have to adjust to the idea that the hospital may provide the best setting possible for him at this time.

If hospitalization is for longer than a year, you will probably have to make the often heart-breaking transition from private to public hospital or the cost of private hospitalization (usually $80 to $100 per day) will send you into total debt. This transition may be extremely difficult to make if your relative has begun in a private hospital where the appointments are luxurious, the nursing gentle, and the dignity of the patient carefully maintained, but a steady search may yield a public facility which offers just as good or better medical staff and therapy of all kinds. Before you make a final choice of a hospital where a long stay is expected, inquire of the local mental health association about facilities and residence requirements. Every state will have a branch of the National Association for Mental Health which provides, among other information services, a directory of such resources.

State hospitals serve usually a particular area, but if, on inquiry, one hospital seems better suited to your relative's special needs than another, you can request special placement. For example, some have special schools conducted either by the hospital itself or by the Division of Vocational Rehabilitation, some have special kinds of therapy for your relative, some maintain halfway houses to which patients can go when they are in a less acute stage of the illness.

When your relative is admitted to a state hospital, admission may be for as brief a period as several days in a facility that has put extra attention toward this problem or up to approximately six weeks in a hospital that considers general admission a time of observation as to which ward or unit the patient actually belongs.

The period during which the patient is in the general admissions unit can be traumatic. It is usually a large unit and even today sometimes resembles the "snakepit" of popular interpretation. The purpose of the general admissions ward is to give the diagnostic personnel a chance to observe the actions and problems of patients just admitted to hospital.

In actual fact state hospitals are so badly understaffed that you may find your relative literally neglected in the general admissions ward for a much longer period than is necessary, under heavy medication which reduces ward problems but veils and masks the actual symptoms and makes observation a very hit or miss affair.

It cannot be stressed too strongly that often your role in helping long-term hospitalized relatives is to act as some sort of battering ram between the patient and the administration. After your relative has been admitted, you should try to maintain close contact with a particular doctor on the psychiatric staff so that he gets to know the patient's name. You can share with him your anxiety and hope that the patient stay only as briefly as possible in the admissions or "unclassified" ward.

One adolescent girl, admitted to the general unit of a state hospital, found herself exposed to the scuffling of two lesbians on the bed next to hers, fist fights in which she was beaten up, and the most painfully depressing scenes which would be heartbreaking to a person without psychiatric problems. The girl's mother kept coming back, even on non-visiting days, urgently reminding the staff that while her daughter did have a chronic emotional illness and might need long-term care, the girl had been gently raised and had never been exposed to the kind of acting out she met in this ward. Simply your presence and persistence pointing out over and over the uselessness of your relative idly sitting in an unclassified ward can often be sufficient to bring pressure on the slow-moving administration, clogged by red tape, and bring about improvement.

Vigilance about the kind of care that is being given to your relative is one way you can help. The kind of absolute reliance on the judgment of the doctor as an authoritarian figure that you must maintain during a surgical procedure, for example, is out of place in long-term psychiatric hospitalization. In many cases the shortage of personnel means that there are errors of judgment made on the basis of staff having small knowledge of the individual patients. You have to keep a sharp lookout for your own, unless the facility is one which has proper staffing. If the tone of this chapter is warning rather than reassuring, it is because the United States has unfortunately not yet reached anywhere near an ideal standard of public mental hospitals. Here and there you may find a hospital where constant vigilance on your part may not be necessary, but all in all it is advisable to keep watching during visits for signs that little or no psychotherapy is being given, or that the attendants and orderlies are not negligent or sadistic.

Be careful, however, not to mistake the natural course of discipline in a psychiatric ward for sadism. Your relative may be a chronic complainer or have paranoid symptoms. If his complaints go beyond the normal indignity of being in a hospital, you should investigate discreetly and carefully, using all the evidence possible, to disentangle what may be the patient's resentment against rules necessary to maintain peace and harmony in a ward from rules which are unfair or discriminatory against him. It isn't easy to know, and you should try to avoid jumping to quick conclusions.

Suppose your relative is likely to remain in hospital for most of his life, either because he is potentially dangerous to himself or others or because there is no one in the outside world prepared to take care of his exacting and time-consuming difficulties. You should not pamper him to the point where he is permanently deeply dependent on one person in the family for emotional support. If he continues what is to him a supportive but too close dependency on your visits, letters, phone calls and general reassurances, your illness or unavailability—and, let's face it, your eventual death if you are a parent or person older than he—will remove all his props and probably subject him to a total breakdown. Do not make the mistake of provoking guilt in other family members to replace this overprotection. Brothers and sisters of long-term hospitalized patients bear a burden of irrational guilt simply because they are freer than the handicapped relative. To add to this guilt by an admonition that, "When I am gone Jim will have only you to depend on," is unfair. It would be more helpful to spend as much time and energy adjusting the patient to the idea that there is often someone among the hospital personnel to whom he can relate, and to guide him toward putting increasing effort *toward* that kind of relating. In addition, if you are careful about loosening some ties gradually, your relative can come to have a certain dependence on self, an ability to exist even without constant obvious signs of affection from other people, that can go a long way toward helping him form good mutual friendships with other people at the hospital.

In all honesty, it is hard to generalize about how to do your best for a hospitalized relative because of the enormous difference between quality of hospitalization in different institutions and even sometimes among different wards in the same institution.

If you live in a state where there is little choice and a hospital is strictly indicated, your only hope is to keep vigilant regarding abuses and complaints in much the same way that you would if a child were in nursery school where *his* word would be given little weight but the parent might be heeded. If, on the other hand, a relative is hospitalized in a forward-seeking facility where every attempt is made to support, protect and treat patients with as much optimism as possible, it is wiser to let the authorities take over. If you have misgivings (and even the most modern of community mental health centers can make mistakes or have personnel who treat a patient badly) these misgivings should be discussed—with as little rancor as possible—with the director of your relative's unit. Often a situation in which the therapist is trying to accomplish one thing, the family another, can be ironed out before it gets overwhelming.

It can be frightening and depressing to have to trust a loved and potentially loving person to treatment in an area in which, as Richard Lemon says, "It is a startling fact that nobody can say how well [various forms of psychotherapy] work." "There's almost nothing I can say that many of my colleagues won't disagree with," Dr. Laurence Kubie of Baltimore's Sheppard-Pratt Hospital has stated.

Nothing in the way of institutional care, however gentle, concerned, and sophisticated the personnel, can ever replace the patient's knowing that his family still cares, still takes an interest, still visits as much as possible, listening to complaints with a truly open mind and requesting to discuss those complaints with the person in charge if they appear to have even the faintest possibility of truth.

For the family who must cope with the possibility or probability that there is a relative who needs long-term hospitalization, there can be comfort in the knowledge that you have done everything that could be done to make a wise choice of facilities, to ease the way, to retain as much contact with the hospitalized person as is suitable for his condition and the family configuration. Biochemistry is on the edge of enormous breakthroughs in the area of chronic emotional illness, so much so that we can expect cures or partial cures in our lifetime. Certain groups in our society, like a hippie commune, are growing more tolerant of behavior differences. Toward the goal of eventual return to the community, the gentlest possible hospitalization, with locked wards only when all other resources have failed, can provide a holding action.

At such a time lines like these, by a poet and teacher of the 1920's, Eda Lou Walton, may prove prophetic.

> Haze gone and the outline clear:
> Each tree its own extension and its round,
> Hills suddenly perfected and the mound
> Hollowing the field near.
>
> Day whole and the summer over,
> Each leaf, each grass blade, every laurel spun
> Waxen and veined beneath the noon-day sun
> As lake its light, shadow its clover
>
> Hours of acquiescence cannot sever
> Nor is completion bitter yet, nor frost
> Come to inscribe the garden. Nothing is lost.
> Autumn is early and is forever.

Chapter 8
Home Again

Any person just discharged from a mental hospital has to get his sea legs. If he has been a cipher in a large state institution, at some distance from home and friends, his transition from "in" to "out" is bound to be stormy, plagued by panic and beset by self-doubts of all sorts. If his hospitalization has been brief, in the psychiatric department of a general hospital or a smaller, closer-to-home community mental health center, it is likely that the adjustment will be a little easier. You must not assume, however, even though his treatment was modern and the symptoms that sent him are less obvious, that he is now secure. Despite our modern enlightenment, the stigma still attached to emotional disturbance becomes enormous when hospitalization has occurred. Often friends, prospective employers, etc., feel that if a person was in such bad shape that he needed to be "confined," he is a bad vocational and even friendship risk. However disguised with terms like "nervous exhaustion," however luxurious the setting may have been, there is still a sense of humiliation and despair at not having been able to cope with or keep private one's psychic life.

Therefore you are going to have to handle a two-sided problem: keeping the former patient from regarding himself as a second-class citizen, and not allowing the situation to become the same as it was before treatment was necessary.

A general uneasiness or nervousness will characterize any person who has undergone psychiatric hospitalization, which will last as long as he feels present judgment of him is based on his previous "record." You can help relieve his anxiety by assuming that hospitalization has served its purpose and discharge means he is now ready to assume functions and obligations—bit by bit—with which he was unable to cope before. To coddle him and keep him relieved of all real stress and strain will frighten him further, for the former patient knows the difference between life and hospital or family shelter, and will gradually lose confidence in his own ability to return to a regular existence unless some regular demands are gradually put upon him.

You should expect a relative back from hospital to assume, over a six-month period, all former obligations except those therapeutically determined as so stressful as to have caused some of the difficulty.

Knowing that certain requirements exist helps him to overcome what can be a long drawn out post-hospital inertia. Contract psychology can be a helpful technique in the adjustment process. A family clinic or an objective third party can help work out the details of such a "living agreement." Here is a typical example of such a contract negotiated between a teenage boy and his parents. The youngster was in the process of emotionally rejoining his parents by degrees while establishing himself in his one-room apartment where he, the agency involved, and the family, all felt he would do better than living at home entirely. The contract reassured him as to scheduling, helped him see that his family was not deserting him but was ready to stand by with continued support and occasional "chicken soup" as he finished school, yet not allow him to infringe totally on the rest of the family as he had done before his hospitalization.

FAMILY CONTRACT

A. Parties

On January 4, 1972, John L., son, and Mabel L., mother, hereby enter into this contract agreement. This agreement is effective upon signing by both parties as of 5 p.m., January 4, 1972.

B. Terms

The following terms are hereby agreed upon:

1. There shall be a clearly defined schedule indicating when John L. shall stay at home (see "C. Schedule" below).
2. John L. shall have a clean, safe, definite apartment of his own as soon as it is possible to obtain same.
3. Mabel L. shall aid in obtaining such an apartment two weeks from the effective date of this agreement.
4. John L. shall be responsible for obtaining food and cleaning his apartment at all times. John L. shall also be responsible for cooking or otherwise obtaining his own meals at all times except when he is eating at home (26 Smith Street).
5. John L. shall be responsible for keeping his own hours (curfew) on the nights that he is sleeping in his own apartment or any other place.
6. Mabel L. shall aid in setting up John L.'s apartment howsoever John L. desires.
7. Mabel L. shall support John L. by payment of the sum of $200 per month.
8. Mabel L. shall backstop John L. up until 8 p.m. on those nights which John L. is not scheduled to be at home. After 8 p.m. John L. shall avail himself of other agencies and persons for aid, comfort and any other purpose whatsoever.
9. John L. shall not telephone Mabel L. or otherwise attempt to contact Mabel L. from Saturday 8 a.m. to Sun-

day 10 a.m. thereby allowing Mabel L. one totally free day.

10. John L. agrees to live at the ——— Hotel or other suitable place, mutually agreed upon, until an apartment (as stipulated in term #2) is available.

C. Schedule

The following schedule shall be rigorously enforced:

1. John L. shall be allowed home for only two and one-half nights per week. And he shall have his own room.
2. The nights are as follows:
   a. Sunday, 5 p.m. to 9:30–9:45 a.m. the following morning.
   b. Thursday night, 4:30 p.m. to 9:30–9:45 a.m. the following Friday morning.
   c. Tuesday night, 4:30 p.m. to 10:15–10:30 p.m. (only Tuesday evening).
3. The house rules at 26 Smith Street shall be as follows and shall be in force at all times that John L. is present therein:
   a. There shall be a curfew of 11:00 p.m. to 11:15 p.m.
   b. Girls, dates, or other friends shall stay only up to curfew time.
   c. Any mess made shall be cleaned up by John L. if made by him.
   d. He shall have no sexual intercourse at any time at 26 Smith Street.
   e. John L. and any friends of his shall have their clothes on at all times.
   f. All doors shall remain unlocked.
   g. No dirty laundry shall be brought by John L.
   h. John L. shall not act in an intentionally "crazy" manner.

D. Penalties

1. For each and every infraction of the above rules and/or terms, John L. shall forfeit one night at home during that week.
2. For each and every infraction of the above rules and/or terms, Mabel L. shall allow John L. another night at home during that week.

E. Trial Period

There shall be a trial period of approximately two and one-half months from October 21 to January 10. If after such a trial period there is a mutual agreement that the above contract has not or cannot become valid and enforceable, then John L. shall go or be taken to a hospital. However, there shall be the following conditions attached to such hospitalization:

1. Any attempt shall first be made by Mabel L. and any other agencies and/or persons to secure John L. a place at a private, rather than a public, hospital.
2. There shall be no mention or threat whatsoever of such hospitalization or of "insanity" or "craziness" at any time during the above trial period either by John L. or Mabel L.

Having been in the hospital can seem like a punishment. The patient feels punished by the community because he's been in a hospital, punished by his friends because of the former isolation, labeled and punished by the family who sometimes inadvertently find themselves saying: "My God, we've paid $10,000 for you to be in that place. You're no better than you were. And you've had help; why don't you do something now?"

James H. left the "best" ward of a state hospital two months ago. His depression remedied by psychotherapy, shock treatments, and a continuing medication, he has returned to the same life situation he retreated from, possessing a little more insight and physically rested. He is divorced, has a marginal job, and is living with a second wife whom he loves but who feels resentful that most of his salary goes toward supporting his first wife and children. She tries not to give in to her understandable feelings of resentment that since the marriage she has had to work steadily to support herself, absorb the shock of his illness and hospitalization, and welcome him back with a measure of emotional support and warmth, despite her own feeling of deprivation.

Family therapy can help James's wife to express those feelings directly, rather than letting them carry over into a guilt-provoking underground attack on her newly returned husband. It can let James ventilate those feelings (based partly upon a realistic problem) that formerly made him become so depressed that he could no longer function.

If family therapy is not available, you can get through by trying to reconstruct the situation that seemed to worsen the former patient's symptoms, this time allowing all bitter feelings to be expressed. Any attempt at total "tact" or picking your way around the situation is doomed to failure, for unexpressed anger will revive the kind of behavior that sent your relative to the hospital originally.

Jimmy R. has been discharged from a voluntary mental hospital for the third time. His first hospitalization lasted for two and a half years and occurred subsequent to heavy drug experimentation at college. The schizophrenic symptoms began after an acid trip which simply did not end but produced extreme anxiety culminating in the breakdown which led him to enter the psychiatric unit. Since he was of draft age and had problems at school, it is possible that the drug experience provided a ready excuse for his unconscious desire to break down and be relieved of the terrifying responsibilities that were piling up.

Jimmy enjoyed the first hospitalization, apart from his own symptoms, which were a necessary adjunct to staying there without being bothered by conscience. He liked the freedom from having to make decisions as to his future and the mildly physical pleasures of this private hospital which was organized around civilized non-punitive measures. He became acquainted with several girls with whom he carried on long philosophical conversations over coffee, interrupted only by the mild dictates of the daily routine.

Jimmy found the outside world harsh and unstimulating upon discharge. He made no attempt to find a job, stayed with his parents in his former room, and took a few haphazard college courses. A chronic anxiety made his symptoms return with overwhelming intensity, and he spent literally months in bed, physically well but sleeping enormously and masturbating perhaps twenty times a day.

On returning to hospital he was disgruntled on finding that his former groovy companions were gone and the company was bland and uninteresting, a bunch of "drab middle class lunatics" as he put it. This lack of interest in other patients led to a faster discharge and this time he managed to hold on to a kind of direction that led to his starting to write poetry and short stories and enroll in a college to take a master's degree.

He functioned reasonably well except for being unable to take competition from anyone to the point that he destroyed his best friend's relationship with a woman by telling the woman a series of supposed revelations about the friend and his continued infidelities. Recognizing his need to make trouble, the woman decided to end friendship with him, so that Jimmy lost two friends at one blow by his disloyal confidences. Jimmy's pattern of messing up his life and relationships in order to be sent back to the hospital is a familiar one to him and one followed by many people who actually prefer a hospital setting to life outside.

Your relative, just out of hospital, will be likely to sleep late and find assorted unconscious ways of fending off facing the outside world. It may prove aggravating and frustrating to have to contend with this when you want him to be able to return as quickly as possible to normal functioning, but you must exercise a great deal of patience, for too much pushing in the initial stage is very likely to result in an enlarged fear.

If Susan L. sleeps until one or two in the afternoon every day, arising long after all possibility of securing a job has passed, the question of *when* she is ready to be awakened earlier and a gentle but firm pressure exerted on her to begin to really look for work inevitably comes up.

It is well to consult the discharging doctor on your relative's individual needs as well as turning for help to whatever after-care agency your community provides. Here are some general points which will hold.

Try to maintain standards which do not put the former patient in a bind, for example expecting him to quickly return to his former job or earning capacity in the face of his need for a more gradual transition time.

Accept "odd" or bizarre behavior in private, while pointing out calmly that this behavior is not acceptable in the outside world as it was in the hospital and will make it harder for him to be accepted by former and new friends.

Try to arrange a kind of sliding scale of successful functioning, starting with his freedom from former annoying symptoms and very slowly putting new expectations upon him.

Accept the fact that improvement cannot come in all areas at the same time and learn to live with what you consider the least disturbing aspects of his behavior in favor of producing improvement in a few important ways.

Be totally sincere with him, for any deceit in your relationship comes through as enormous to the former hospitalized person. After all he is at the time especially conscious of how people seem to him and how he seems to other people. Not yet finding satisfaction in his work or creative outlets, he is shaky and likely to consider his world bounded by the nuances of shifting feeling and relationships.

Do not be too solicitous, for an excess of sympathy can paralyze him to present action. Assume with him that his hospitalization was a step in treatment which is no longer needed, that however traumatic it may have been (and probably was), other people have faced other traumas and recovered from them. You might guide yourself by thinking of him as a person who has been through a grief experience in which much pain was present. By this device you will learn to sympathize without letting the former patient sink into a hole of self-torment and guilt.

On the other hand, as Dr. Schwartz points out, "Do not dismiss the patient as silly when you know very well that he is working on your sympathy. Very often he will be, but remember that he cannot help acting the way he does." The former patient's emotions are like a child's, but his understanding is an adult's. Your most important need is patience.

The good rapport between you and the former patient will help you discover the difficulties under which he is laboring. Such information, plus the data that you collect from others of the family and episodes that you remember, may be of some help to the doctor. He may be a keen observer, but very few are Sherlock Holmes, and he must depend to some extent on what he is told by the patient and his family. At any rate, don't you attempt to dig into the former patient's subconscious and probe into his psychic wounds.

Be natural with your returned relative. Act toward him as you do toward the other members of the family, but be slightly kinder, less emotional, and less critical. Make him feel that you accept him as an equal. He will be quick to detect and resent the slightest condescension in your attitude. Tell him casually about the affairs of the neighborhood but not too much. Watch his expression. If he seems to be annoyed at what you are saying, change the subject or say nothing.

Don't be annoyed if he blames you for his troubles when his bitterness overflows. Be a good listener. If you don't permit him to talk freely he will think you are indifferent, callous or afraid. Besides, it is good medicine for him. But don't try to draw more information out of him than he wants to give. In fact, it is better for both of you if you prevent him from talking too much. It is a drain on his vitality and an equal drain on your patience.

Be careful not to set yourself up as a paragon of virtue. If you lose your temper, make a ready admission. If you were wrong, admit it. Such an attitude on your part may help him to make like concessions. When he questions you, be as honest in your answers as possible. Even if he is confused, take for granted that he does understand many of the things you say; he will respond more easily to your attitude of kindness and sincerity. Show him that you are interested in him.

Don't try to control outside events too closely. You can be helpful without being omnipotent.

It may be useful to remember, if you are trying to live with a person recently out of hospital, that the quality of your own mental health and the amount of insight courageously probed for and felt is likely to make the other person's adjustment a little easier.

Dr. Humphrey Osmond points out that in a family where there is one person with a psychological problem, there are odds of about one in ten that there may be another disturbed person in the family. Two psychotic people don't get on better together than a psychotic person and a well person. This is especially true if the disturbed person is a schizophrenic. When he leaves the hospital, the schizophrenic faces problems that can be predicted, so that you can give him a little map of the surroundings to which he's going, both physical and emotional. In addition, a person recovering from this illness must be given his own room, even if it is the merest cubicle. A schizophrenic cannot live all day in the company of other people; he must have some privacy to rest from the continuous assault upon his perceptions occasioned by the differing reactions of others. In addition he needs, as crucially as food, a simple well-regulated schedule. His life should be as structured as possible, with little leeway left for frightening initial moves and forays into what will always remain a somewhat unknown and threatening world, inhabited by people who perceive it differently from him.

If you are living with an elderly ex-patient, you face several problems. There is the problem of personal hygiene, if your parent or in-law doesn't want to bathe or keep up to the family standard of cleanliness and you have to struggle to get him to bathe or wash or change his clothes.

Your relative may be chairbound and not able to walk without assistance. The physical strength to lift him out of bed and into the chair is often more than you have. Or the former patient may not sleep at night and keep the family up, leading to twenty-four-hour anxiety over his care.

You can arrange for a trained person to accomplish those physical chores, which can leave you enough energy to handle your relative's psychological problems. If you cannot afford private help, many communities have social service agencies who can send a "home visitor" or visiting nurse into the house.

Rhoda Scherer, registered occupational therapist and consultant at the Sephardic Home for the Aged in Brooklyn, believes we have to first consider the aged as individual persons who have gone through all kinds of experiences. The aging process is no different from any other stage of life. A person grows from childhood to adolescence: it's stormy; he grows through the forties and it's stormy; he grows into the aging process and fears begin to take over the way fears have taken over in all other stages of life. Older people have to face that their jobs are over, their children are grown, they're not needed any more. Hopefully they are on pensions and have time on their hands. They are simply unable to focus on what to do with themselves and it makes them frightened, unless of course they've planned for it.

The very active human being with keen interest all through life is set for aging. The person who has been working since late adolescence to support a family and may not really be skilled in reading, now has time to read but has difficulties. The person who has never had an opportunity to use his hands in any way but to earn a dollar has difficulties. To put hands into clay is very frightening; it won't come out creative. Put the same hands into dough and fingers will automatically turn out rolls or cookies if that's been the lifetime experience. When someone is comfortable with what he's doing, his capabilities grow, he becomes pleased with himself, becomes proud to show what he's done; and one good feeling interacts on another. A result is a human being who doesn't have time to grow old, he's simply too busy. Often the reverse happens.

Unfortunately the person who has not found a satisfying life, the person who struggled to make ends meet, settles very quickly into hospital routine where someone takes care of him. He becomes institutionalized very readily, feels more comfortable in a nursing home being sheltered from the trials of cooking and shopping. A person who becomes comfortable in the hospital setting can cause you worry, for a highly motivated human being of any age will insist on caring for himself as much as possible.

Occupational therapy plays a great role in rehabilitating people who have become unmotivated in this or other ways. If a person comes into a rehabilitation setting unsure if his living situation can work out, the occupational therapist will test activities of daily living. When it's determined what the limitations are, activities are chosen to help that patient increase his skills. As treatment continues, the patient has a choice of going two ways. The person who has a family and is really needed, or has an unfinished job or strong hobbies or is involved in a Y or a Golden Age Club or a political group, has forces at work to keep him a whole active human being. When there is no input and the patient begins to feel sorry for himself, accepting outside help such as the hospital offers, he begins to lose sight of the days of the week.

In a hospital there is very little to mark season from season, there is very little involvement with commitments, and as a result days run into days, the brain is not actively used, depressions start, and as a result the patient begins to forget. There is a theory that says senility is reversible, that you can take a patient who sits day after day staring into space at the side of his bed and greet him with his name and tell him clearly what the day is, the weather is, what happened in the news today, expose him to certain daily questions and expect answers of him. The most remarkable thing begins to happen. The patient then begins to look forward to whoever it is who comes. The OT or nurse, therapist aide, can go just so far to help the patient stay aware that he is a vital member of society still. But the family must understand that when the patient goes home he can easily sink into staring into space again unless a family member continues to remind him that he is a whole and warmly accepted human being, both for the work he has done and the contribution he can still make. Demands must be made of him.

Families who find themselves facing aging parents are often influenced by traditional concepts that interpret aging and nonfunctioning synonymously. Grandma Moses, Einstein, and others are clear examples that the human mind continues to learn and develop as long as the person allows (even encourages) input of problem solving and ongoing exposure to life's daily crises.

Mrs. Scherer points out that the retirement concept that provides for increase of avocational skills will prolong human potential and provide for satisfaction and even happiness in later years.

Living with the neurotic patient after discharge from hospital is mainly a matter of patience on the part of the whole family. People are rarely hospitalized for neurotic problems. Sometimes however these coincide with some temporary situational crisis. At "rough" times the usually slightly depressed or slightly hypochondriacal or overly ambitious person becomes overwhelmed by the circumstances. His symptoms get worse and he can land in the hospital.

Circumstances can include grief over a loss in the family (especially a sudden one or that of a child), some sudden threat to occupational success or security, a decision on the part of a mate to separate or divorce, a sense of impending age and shrinking possibilities for achievement or even a natural disaster such as flood, war, or hurricane.

Such patients often benefit greatly from the psychotherapy available in *good* hospitals, and are liable to come out with a great deal more insight than when they went in. Others, mortally wounded by a traumatic hospital experience, may emerge full of roaring anger which they let out on family or caretaking persons as soon as they are released.

If you are going to live with a relative who has been hospitalized for paranoid behavior, a character disorder, or clearly antisocial behavior in which the law may or may not have been involved, you must be prepared to take stock of yourself, perhaps in the following way:

Be honest about your motives in wanting to take care of the patient. Are you sure that you love him more than you hate him? Do your pity and sympathy for him outweigh whatever grudges you have against him? Are you assuming a thankless job because you really want to help him, or merely from a sense of duty or guilt because the sick person happens to be your father, mother, husband, wife, child or some other member of your family? If you are doing it primarily because you are duty bound, the chances are that someone who is paid for taking care of him will do a better job.

Your relative understands more than you think. He observes everything, or almost everything. While it is true that he is egocentric and thinks entirely too much about himself, for this very reason he is highly observant of all that goes on around him. He will feel strongly your scorn, indifference, callousness, anxiety, fearfulness or any other emotional expression that you permit to show in your face or manner. It is worth repeating that if there has not been friendship or affection between you and the patient, then these cannot be established at this crucial time, and it is best that someone else take care of him.

Recall the relationship that existed between you and the patient before his illness. If you got along well then, you will probably have a background of sympathy and understanding of his distress.

In the same way that bringing up a child successfully implies acceptance of his person but often non-acceptance of his behavior, so you must be careful in dealing with a person formerly hospitalized for paranoia or antisocial behavior to make it clear that, although you may care greatly for him, certain aspects of behavior cannot be accepted and do not correspond to reality. Once out of hospital, the person who continues to say, "Everyone is plotting against me," is often reacting to an interior feeling which is quite the opposite of that expressed, a feeling that he is in fact being ignored by the world, that very little attention is actually accorded to his ideas and desires.

Keep an open mind and don't try to decide it all in advance.

For example, you may find that a total home situation simply does not work. Either the former patient is still difficult enough to exhaust his family, or there is a certain amount of ill will that develops over his spending *all* his time in a close interior situation like the family. In that case, you may want to think of possible part- or full-time alternatives, still hoping that the time at home will be a qualitative if not quantitative success.

These alternatives to living fully at home will be gone into in detail in the next chapter, but keeping an eye out for "how to make it all work," rather than keeping to an original plan just for its own sake, may produce better results in the long run.

You can tell if one of these alternatives may be needed if there is a heavy crushing sense of responsibility that is so pronounced that it prevents you from ever "enjoying" the former patient, even on the very simplest of terms. If he proves totally exhausting, time-consuming, depressing because of the constant rush of problems, then you cannot help any more by just being on the scene all the time. At this point a partial removal becomes not an admission of failure, but a way to save the situation. Giving yourself a series of brief vacations from the problems of the former patient may be exactly what is needed to continue to maintain your strength.

Gloria K. has been out of the hospital eight months, so that the initial phase of her adjustment at home may be considered over. Yet she is still so driven by a compulsive wish to make friends to fill an aching void that her family cannot for a minute consider her recovery complete. Gloria has no resources within herself; she cannot spend any time "alone." When she is left alone for several hours, her anxiety fills her with an enormous dread; she can neither read, watch television, listen to the radio, sew, paint, housekeep or cook, nor do any of the constructive things with which less anxious people fill up their time when not surrounded by friends or other people.

Gloria was discharged taking a major tranquilizer which she was told to use for the rest of her life, but it poses a problem. When Gloria takes it she can barely function at school (she is in her second year in college): she sleeps half the time, awakens with great difficulty in the morning, is unable to pursue her studies. On the other hand, when she does not take the medication she becomes confused; thought distortions and occasional hallucinations disturb her functioning; and her speech attracts much undesirable attention, for it is unpredictable and sounds "odd." In trying to decide whether or not she should take her medicine, her family is in a quandary, for it is almost impossible to know which set of circumstances proves more discouraging to Gloria in the long run.

What may be helpful in this instance is for her physician to prescribe a minimal daily dosage so that she receives the benefit of at least a little of the needed medication without showing so much drowsiness and dizziness as a side effect that it causes her to be unable to function in the rest of her life.

If it is decided that medication interferes too much with the kind of functioning toward a successful goal that is so deeply needed for people like Gloria, then a strict regime corresponding almost to the old-fashioned ideas of "mental hygiene" must be set up. Without her tranquilizers, Gloria needs a rigid though gentle schedule, constant calm supervision and as much rest as is humanly possible.

One of the most troubling questions to families is when to know the ex-patients are becoming or are now dangerous to others or to themselves. There is no simple answer to this, for angry or self-destructive moods come upon the most "normal" of people occasionally, and are dealt with by the family as exactly what they are. Once a patient has been labeled and identified, we are much more likely to see bogey men where there are none.

Suppose your burly brother, three months out of hospital for treatment of what was called manic-depressive illness, has a bad day looking fruitlessly for a job, and comes at you with a knife. It is important not to panic or show fear, for helping him express his disappointment and anger in words will do more toward helping him drop that knife than calling the police and running all over being chased by him.

A simple "I'm sorry, Jim, it must have been terribly hard for you today" will probably produce the desired effect. If not, you owe it to the former patient to continue explaining, with both sympathy and patience, why his urge toward violence will accomplish nothing but get him back in the hospital, and how if he will put away the foolish weapon, you can sit down and talk over how help can be gotten in the situation.

Follow the same method with threats of self-destruction or suicide. It must be made clear that you wish to talk to the upset person out of general and real caring, not because the threat has proved too intimidating. It makes sense to say something like "Jim, you can threaten to kill yourself until the cows come home and that threat isn't going to make me change my mind about what I think right for and toward you."

You should watch your relative's weight, for sudden losses sometimes indicate return to the previous depression. If you suspect a real suicidal intent, never leave him to himself, for he needs someone's presence at this time.

He should be kept at reasonably pleasant work, if not formal work then a hobby or vocationally directed therapy that will fill his brain as well as his hands and time. If he is subject to violent tirades during which he destroys nearby objects or has tantrums, you should remind him gently, without implication of threat, that if this behavior continues there is no choice but to return him to a hospital where such behavior can be dealt with more easily than in the home.

He should be kept apprised of your feelings toward his behavior, while at the same time assured that you think he can surmount it, that you still feel hopeful and optimistic about his chances for recovery despite this temporary setback. Make it clear that you do not confuse his temporary behavior (which may be due to real discouragement or obstacles placed in his path, such as the difficulty of securing work to fit his desires after he has been discharged from hospital) with *him.*

You may have to follow hospital procedure in instituting a series of penalties for violence or threats. By the same token, small rewards can be used for expression of the *feelings* on which this violent behavior is based. Expression of feelings always helps clear the air. If your relative is so constituted that he cannot express feelings except accompanied by frightening action and behavior, a strong attempt should be made to help him untangle one from the other.

If safely channeled, laughter can be your best aid in establishing warm rapport with the former patient, for nothing is as conducive to friendship and understanding as a good belly-laugh together.

Dr. Schwartz feels that "Once the dangers of the patient's

possible violence have been removed, you are in a position to go ahead with a positive program. In most cases if the means for self-destruction are withheld during the critical period of despair, the very desire fades and the basic will to live revives more or less spontaneously."

If he has been belittling himself, complaining how worthless and useless he is, and saying that he wants to die, then suddenly or gradually starts to find fault with other members of his family, this is a change for the better.

Living with a former patient after he has been discharged from hospital is something like skiing. It is impossible to avoid taking chances; you must develop the habit of taking advantage of the bumps, *using* them to go careening out on a dangerous journey that is vastly rewarding to all involved. If you approach all this pragmatically, deciding from month to month how best to handle the situations that come up, it will reflect an openness to the former patient, a sense that he is still the master of his own destiny, that will prove in the long run far more helpful than some simple authoritarian attempt to lead him only in paths you want him to follow. Without this respect for his own "direction," however lopsided or ill-advised it may seem at first glance, no lasting help can be shown, for squashing down the former patient's real desires can only lead to secret or open rebellion later on. Better to let it all out, deal with it from minute to minute, and then encourage his moving on to ways that might objectively be considered more desirable.

Chapter 9

The In-Between World: Halfway Houses, Residential Centers, Emergency Hospitalization, Night and Weekend Hospitals

Between hospitalizing your relative and having him live at home, there is the in-between world of halfway houses, residential treatment centers, emergency hospitalization, and night and weekend hospitals. Each of these institutions has unique functions, and you may want to or need to know about them.

The main function of a *halfway house* is to provide a reasonably supportive place for former patients to live without their having to fulfill pressured family goals. It provides breathing room until a firmer cure is achieved, and this cannot be underestimated. Unfortunately, there are far fewer halfway houses than people who need them. Let's look at some halfway houses to see how they work.

Woodley House, in Washington, D.C., was started in the mid-fifties by Joan Doniger and Edith Maeda, with a few colleagues from the National Institutes of Health, $3,000 of borrowed money, and later some grants.

Their chief idea was that very disturbed people could live out of the hospital and work. Even though they did not understand the true nature of mental disorder, they believed that the forms it takes are often socially determined. They expected, therefore, that people's behavior in a halfway house would be substantially different from that in a hospital.

Woodley House has room for more than twenty patients. People who have left still use the house like boarders by coming back for meals and social gatherings.

There is no age limit for the residents, who have found their way to the door through many paths. Each is sponsored by a therapist, hospital or agency who will continue to see him as long as he is in the house. One of the secrets of success at this halfway house has been a loose intake policy. They ask only one question, What are the best and worst things a sponsor guesses could happen to his client in a year? They also try to keep the group balanced and mixed.

The goal of Woodley House is to help residents find a place in the community. The director urges people to seek as full a life as possible outside of the house in jobs and social activities. Their fee system is unusual. The more a resident works outside the house, the less rent he pays. Work is defined as school, volunteer job, paid job or even day-hospital attendance. Rent includes whatever one would expect to find in a middle-class home, newspapers, phone, meals, midnight snacks.

The two women who run the house split the work. They cook the meals, help keep the house clean, run errands, meet the psychiatrists, talk with families, write papers and do research. They are available to residents for company, a limited amount of supervision and the kinds of personal services family members often give each other.

All the features of this halfway house are directed toward rewarding healthy behavior and penalizing sick behavior. In contrast to hospitals, residents are denied a "patient" identity.

The women feel that the "open kitchen" is an important difference between a halfway house and a hospital. People prepare their own breakfasts because they have to leave at various hours.

Dinner is the one meal and time of day that brings everyone together. It can be the most pleasant time, often with company. Miss Doniger considers the meal a success if they linger for hours talking.

She feels that whatever its faults, life for most residents was better in Woodley House than in a hospital. Just because someone is diagnosed as schizophrenic is no reason he should have to eat institutional food for the rest of his life, be regimented at meals or other times, or be shut out of the kitchen and grocery stores. His enjoyment of good food and freedom may not treat or cure him but it may make life better.

Miss Doniger denies that Woodley House engages in "rehabilitation" or "therapy," feeling that simply providing a friendly easy-going atmosphere in which former patients can gradually adjust to the outside world is reason enough for being.

Two people will illustrate the two kinds of claims made for Woodley House. Jean J. came to Woodley House from a hospital and spent her first few weeks sitting around, saying very little, and having little to do with the other people in the house. She warmed slowly, made friends, got a job and left town, and her letters indicate that she is doing well professionally and socially. Jean is a girl of great strength, youthful vigor, and intelligence. Joan Doniger thinks she will continue to do well. Jean said often how much Woodley House helped her, but Miss Doniger says, "Even in retrospect, I cannot claim to have done more than provide room, board, living space and company, which Jean used herself to recover from whatever ailed her."

Gloria S. illustrates another and very different kind of claim, that in Woodley House people can adjust to a non-hospitalized life of chronic schizophrenia. She was a fifty-five-year-old spinster who came from a state hospital, very passive, very thin, very depressed. Her sister, who lived near Washington, took the initiative in having her come to Woodley House, her goal to keep Gloria in Washington so that she would be eligible for the better hospitalization that the District of Columbia offered. Gloria found other advantages of the halfway house over the hospital. She put on about 20 badly needed pounds. She had not even known the names of any people who were in her ward in the hospital, but at Woodley House she became more involved with people. With some urging, she took a volunteer job which gave her additional satisfying daily contacts.

"Despite her limited intelligence and very poor prognosis," says Miss Doniger, "we were able to show other people, who thought of her as just a hopeless chronic, that Gloria was a nice person. They took more interest in her and she responded to the interest. But Gloria's chief accomplishment was to obtain her social security pension. Her sister and I urged her for months to apply for it. Finally, I just went with her to the office to fill out the forms. Though Gloria was still depressed and weepy, and though she continued to act in psychotic ways and hallucinate, the quality of her symptoms was different after she got the pension than before. She said herself quite eloquently that with the pension she lost the feeling that she would be abandoned, penniless and completely helpless."

Other halfway houses have quite different objectives, though all agree that such residences exist to provide a place where patients recently discharged from hospital can gradually acclimate themselves to the demands of the outside world.

Barrett House is a residence for disturbed adolescent girls in New York City. Youngsters here have suffered economic and physical deprivation, as well as emotional deprivation. The aim of the program is to provide total treatment, to know and understand every aspect of the girl's living situation and bring her through the trying state of adolescence to an independent self-sustaining adult life in the community.

The girls live in an old five-story building in a shabby residential area. There are six full-time housemothers and one part-time housemother. Housemothers wake the girls in the morning, get them to bed at night, give medicines, mend clothes, eat with the girls, and establish penalties for breaking the rules. Each of the four evening housemothers is also assigned three to five girls for whom she is responsible for developing a close maternal relationship, encouraging good personal hygiene and room care; supervising clothing care and purchases, budgeting of allowances or earnings and being an interested and concerned confidante. There are one casework supervisor and two full-time psychiatric caseworkers who handle supervision, intake applications, direct daily morning reports with combined staff. Caseworkers see girls once, twice or three times a week and engage in psychoanalytically oriented therapy. In addition, they maintain all community contact with friends, school, and agencies, and see parents as indicated in the treatment plan.

There are also a recreational director, an educational supervisor and a psychiatric consultant who does not engage in treatment but sees girls for diagnostic evaluation at intake and also as required under care.

A preplacement case presentation is made to the staff during which room and staff assignments are announced and potential initial adjustment problems are highlighted. The case record is made up and all staff are advised of the date, with a housemother ready to welcome the new girl, take her to her room and help her unpack.

After her first two or three weeks in residence a postplacement conference is held with all staff sharing first impressions. On the basis of the joint observation, a set of treatment goals is tentatively established. Family contacts and visits are discussed and a decision made as to how these will be followed through. Before a girl stays overnight a caseworker will make a home visit to determine the situation. Parents will be involved in casework where indicated. School visits take place throughout her stay.

Most girls remain at Barrett House until they finish school and are ready to move out on their own. Girls are not permitted to drop out of school and very special recognition to graduates is given (a watch or gold chain bracelet and a big celebration). In addition there are rewards to recognize school achievement and attendance. Housemothers become regular PTA members and attend school meetings.

Girls are counseled about finding jobs after they leave Barrett House, helped to locate living quarters (usually in Y's) and often leave with a nest-egg of earnings which they have accumulated. They are offered aftercare help and may be seen once a week for a six-month period to help them adjust to their new situations.

Elizabeth Lyon, director of Bierer House, says that "We try

to be understanding when our residents are struggling and have a problem; where perhaps they can't differentiate between different kinds of reality or certain feelings which are *really* their problem. On the other hand, we don't say 'that's all right' if a resident decides that he is going to get out and run down the street barefooted because he thinks that is funny. We say you do live in a community and you have to have some respect for other people's values.

"I think that some of the kids at the house are always going to be 'different' even when they're much healthier. Often with our residents there is a thought distortion, a great deal of magical thinking, and a lack of integration between the feeling and the ego. At a halfway house we have to learn to live with people still severely troubled by these problems, in a way that is not overwhelming to ourselves. We ask ourselves how can people living with others help not to be frightened by remaining symptoms and understand what some of these symptoms mean. And, if possible, to substitute some satisfactions that overwhelm or drown out the disturbing symptoms."

At a halfway house no one is exclusively and personally involved with the patient the way a parent might be, yet he is surrounded by a group of people, some of whom *do* care, with whom he can identify. In a halfway house a threat to jump out the window is likely to be met by this kind of answer: "I hope you don't. I hope you find other ways of handling your anger, which is so great. If you can talk about how angry you feel, or if you want to tell me something, fine."

Halfway houses have a responsibility to their residents, but it is a limited kind of responsibility. The director of such an organization usually feels that his basic responsibility is to live his own life with as much dignity as possible, to extend himself to others as best he can without losing his dignity or sanity. As a healthy human being, he must know that he must be involved, but he can't lose himself in the residents or he would not be of help in his liaison role.

You might also be interested in the kind of residence that exists in New York City. Called Friendly Homes, Inc., these small residences are set up like a large family. Limited to about ten adolescent boys out of hospital, the "home" usually consists of a married couple with some previous training in a mental health discipline, and a very large apartment from which residents can go to work or school. Their smallness helps them retain the structure of a family rather than an institution, and remarkably good results have been achieved so far within this framework.

If you are interested in gathering a group of parents, all of whom have children, adolescents or young adults who they feel cannot be properly cared for at home, you can write to the Small Grants Department of the National Institute of Mental Health. By describing the project you may very well find there are federal funds or further grants available for helping just such an undertaking get launched.

Residential schools for disturbed children are another way of coping with some of the situations that develop when home care isn't feasible but hospital is too brutal a solution, especially when only large distant state hospitals are available.

Two such schools are Cumberland House Elementary School in Nashville and the Wright School of Durham, North Carolina. The National Institute of Mental Health made a demonstration grant to Peabody College in 1961 to develop residential schools for disturbed children in which concepts of reeducation could be formulated and tried out. The states of Tennessee and North Carolina, represented by their departments of mental health, joined with Peabody to translate a general idea into an operational reality. The grant further provided for a training program to prepare a new kind of mental health worker, called a teacher-counselor, and for a research program to evaluate the effectiveness of the schools to be established.

Both schools are pleasant places, open, friendly and homelike, where children can climb trees and play dodge ball, go to school and at night have a good meal and a relaxed amiable evening.

Both schools have nearby camps that are used in the summer and on occasion throughout the year. The camps are simple, even primitive, with children erecting their own shelters, preparing their own meals, making their own schedules. For staff and children alike there is a contagious serenity about the experience. Cooking is a marvelously instructive enterprise; motivation is high, cooperation is necessary and rewards are immediate. Children for whom failure has become an established expectation at home and at school can learn to do things successfully. Nature study is a source of unthreatening instruction. And there is nothing quite like a campfire or a dark trail and a single flashlight to promote a sense of community. In this simple setting where avoidances of response are few or weakly established, the child can take the first risky steps toward being a more adequate person.

The teacher-counselors are chosen on the basis of being decent, educated, well trained adults, able to give and receive affection, to live relaxed and to be firm. They are committed to children and to the proposition that children who are emotionally disturbed can be helped by the process of reeducation. The total school staff and especially the teacher-counselors who work directly with the children are backed by a group of consultants from psychiatry, pediatrics, social work, psychology and education, an arrangement that makes available to the schools the best professional talent in the community and that has the further attractive feature of multiplying the effectiveness of scarce and expensive mental health and educational personnel.

What kind of children do the residential schools work with? Susan was eleven with a diagnosis of behavioral disturbance with some brain damage. She had attended school one day, the first day of the first grade, and had been in play therapy for four years. A pupil at Cumberland House for a year, she stayed longer than most children. She has now been in a regular classroom for three years, an odd child still but no longer a prospect for lifelong institutionalization. Ron was a cruelly aggressive child, partly as an expression of inner turmoil and partly as an expression of class values and habits; he is much less destructive now and is back in school. Danny was simply very immature, so that school was too much for him. Dick was extremely effeminate, wearing mascara and painting his nails. Both boys responded to masculine activities guided by a trusted male counselor. Billy was a gasoline sniffer and an ingenious hypochondriac; he returned to a reunion recently much more mature though still having trouble with school work. Larry, aged twelve, was quite bright yet unable to read, nor was the school able to teach him. So it failed with him.

The schools' goal is no longer "cure" but rather doing what

they can to make a small social system work in a reasonably satisfactory manner. In this they contrast sharply with the practices of many other residential treatment centers.

Parents were no longer viewed as sources of contagion but as responsible collaborators in making the system work. The children go home on weekends to avoid the estrangement that can come from prolonged separation and to give the child and his parents and brothers and sisters an opportunity to learn new and more effective ways of living together. This requires new strategies to involve home, neighborhood, school, agency and community in a contract to help the child. It has led to the development of a new kind of mental health worker: the liaison teacher who is responsible for maintaining communication with the child's regular school, to prevent alienation and to arrange conditions for the child's early return to a regular classroom.

There are many residential treatment centers throughout the United States, ranging from the Orthogenic School run by Bruno Bettelheim and Fritz Redl in Chicago, to the Montanari Clinical School in Florida. Some of them are more successful in treatment than others; all of them share the uniform disadvantage of being hideously overpriced. Unfortunately, you must consider that even as these words recommending the achievements of a particular facility are being written, the facility may have changed or deteriorated. You must yourself check out the facility suggested. If it is at a great distance from your home, try to stay for at least several weeks in the town nearby so that you can poke around and see for yourself if your relative's complaints are valid and how residents are actually treated. A couple sent their daughter to a private treatment center that was very expensive and highly recommended, only to discover that the place had deteriorated as it expanded.

You will probably want to be familiar with some of the procedures of admitting patients with psychiatric emergencies to the general or mental hospital and to know a bit about emergency programs. A pamphlet prepared by the Joint Planning Service of the American Psychiatric Association mentions that *emergency care* is a service to deal with an acute medical emergency. This care is generally provided in a hospital. In some circumstances, it may be provided in a jail. Patients may come for such care voluntarily or be brought by friends or relatives. Others, because of the acuteness of their mental or physical illness, may resist such care and may resist being brought to a hospital.

Emergency hospitalization is a temporary measure, usually for less than twenty-four hours, with limited short-term goals. It is concerned with the immediate protection of the patient, or with prevention of conduct on the part of the disturbed patient that appears to be dangerous. Emergency detention may be voluntary or involuntary. Facilities for emergency detention may be found in psychiatric services in general hospitals, psychiatric receiving hospitals, private or public hospitals, or jails.

Disturbed persons who require psychiatric emergency care fall into the following groups:

—Persons who seek help or who will accept it voluntarily.

—Non-resistive persons who may not accept care voluntarily at first but who can be persuaded to do so (such as some senile or depressive persons).

—Resistive persons who will not accept care voluntarily and whose behavior may be or may become actually or potentially dangerous to themselves or others.

An alternative to emergency hospitalization is the program that makes psychiatric personnel available, on an around-the-clock basis, to go to patients' homes and provide emergency care. Through the intervention of such professional staff, emergencies can be mitigated in a high percentage of cases. The base for such emergency service may be the psychiatric service of a general hospital, a mental health clinic, a special county psychiatric service or some other community resource.

Many general hospitals, perhaps the majority of them, have charters that forbid the admission of psychiatric patients, although physicians may use subterfuge and admit such patients under non-psychiatric diagnosis. These same hospitals, however, do receive and treat patients who have unsuccessfully attempted suicide. Many of these hospitals will discharge such patients, when they have recovered from the acute medical or surgical condition, without psychiatric evaluation. Even hospitals that require psychiatric evaluation still may not accept such a patient until after the suicide attempt, when he has become a medical or surgical emergency. For this reason you should have at hand the telephone number of the nearest Suicide Prevention Control Unit. Most large cities have at least one hospital which maintains a twenty-four-hour-a-day telephone answering service and makes the service of a professionally trained person available for telephone consultation and immediate service. Should help be required, such centers are empowered to dispatch police or medical help to the person in psychiatric need.

If your relative is doing reasonably well outside of the hospital but seems to need the sense of security that comes from a hospital situation, partial hospitalization may be the answer.

Partial hospitalization as an alternative to full-time hospital care is regarded as one of the most significant innovations in clinical care in this century. Whether in a day, night, evening or weekend service, the patient is treated in a comfortable environment even as he maintains his family ties. As he recovers or suffers a relapse, his activities and treatment are both adjusted.

Although for years it has been known that full hospital patient care is costly both in money and its often adverse effect on many patients, other methods of care have been adopted very slowly. In 1935, the first day care facility in the United States was created when Dr. J. M. Woodall admitted day patients to the Adams House Sanitorium in Boston. Dr. Helen Boyle admitted day patients at Lady Chichester Hospital in Hove in 1938. Facilities for day patients opened at the Yale Psychiatric Clinic in 1948 and at the Menninger Clinic in 1949.

A survey by the National Institute of Mental Health reported 142 psychiatric day and night units in operation in the United States. Some of these units are affiliated with a psychiatric hospital. Others are operated in clinic or general hospital facilities in the community. Of the day-night units, 139 report day service, 26 evening service, 23 weekend and 26 night programs.

The National Institutes of Health define partial hospitalization this way:

> A psychiatric day-night service is one having an organized staff whose primary purpose is to provide a planned program of milieu therapy and other therapy modalities. The

service is designed for patients with mental or emotional disorders who spend only part of the 24-hour period in the program. A psychiatrist is present on a regular scheduled basis and assumes medical responsibility for all patients. Or, the psychiatrist may act as consultant to the staff on a regular basis. Under the latter arrangement, at least one of the following then assumes professional responsibility for the program: a physician, a psychologist, a psychiatric nurse or a social worker.

Partial hospital care can be highly adaptable, both as to type of program and range of treatment opportunities afforded the therapist.

If the patient enters a *day hospital* service in the community, he can return to his home and family at night. The patient's treatment in a day care center has a high degree of flexibility. Staff and patient both participate more freely in the different kinds of programs. Often staff consultation with members of the patient's family helps in his rehabilitation and treatment. Each patient becomes actively involved in his own treatment in a day hospital program, thereby helping to counteract feelings of hopelessness.

The *evening hospital* program is designed to give sustaining help, five evenings or less a week, to the patient who can continue to work at his job and live at home. The *night hospital* is for patients who can handle their jobs during the day but aren't able to deal with their home or family situation at night. The night hospital also fills the specific need for an intermediate residence similar to a halfway house between the time when the patient leaves a twenty-four-hour hospital and when he becomes established in an independent life again. It can serve as a temporary residence for the patient with no family support; as temporary living quarters for the patient who hopes to become independent of his family; and as an overnight service for psychiatric emergency cases.

The *weekend hospital* service is another form of partial hospitalization. Patients may devote weekdays to their accustomed pursuits and obtain intensive treatment on Saturdays and Sundays. Such a program is very useful for patients who live too far away to get day care. Intensive treatment is possible in two consecutive days. For example, four group therapy sessions alternating with recreational therapy can be given over a weekend.

The part-time hospital program gives therapists the chance to diagnose the patient's symptoms early and begin treatment before the illness has accelerated to the point of needing full-time hospitalization. Often patients who resist admission to a mental hospital because it requires separation from their families, agree to treatment in a day program. Many families, reluctant to surrender a sick member to full-time hospitalization, have been found to accept this kind of care more readily. With the patient spending his nights and days at home, his family feels more involved in treatment and they learn to accept and understand his difficulty as they would other illnesses.

Often partial hospitalization lessens the patient's preoccupation with his emotional upset. Some patients learn to get along with others as well as to develop tolerance for the day's routine. They learn to assist in their own rehabilitation.

When partial hospitalization is one in a range of community mental health services, as it is in the centers program, a central system makes information about the patient available among the various services he may use. This is another dividend in his overall treatment. The integration of service helps to provide and to ensure continuity in his care.

Partial hospitalization programs are as varied as community life itself. The therapeutic community in the day hospital provides for recreational, vocational and social activities as well as treatment. The patient can be encouraged to work, to find new hobbies, to go back into the community in various ways and to return to school. Partial hospitalization services may include group and individual psychotherapy, drug therapy, electric shock therapy, occupational and recreational therapy.

According to National Institute of Mental Health statistics, one in three mental hospital beds is occupied by a patient aged sixty-five or older. As community treatment for the emotionally disturbed aged is expanded, the large number of admissions is expected to decrease. Meantime many elderly patients may benefit from the services of a day hospital while they are under care in a nursing home.

In programs giving partial hospitalization for the elderly,

inquiries show that the more active patients have fewer body complaints than totally hospitalized patients, show better adjustment patterns and assume more interest in outside and community activities. They feel better because they have things to do and people are interested in them.

The elderly may be handled in part-time hospitalization via various forms of therapy, adult education, social group work services, social and recreational activities, individual casework and public health nursing homes; transportation to a psychiatric day care center may be provided by volunteers or by bus.

Not only is the financial burden on community and you reduced by partial hospitalization, but you and your family become participants in the patient's recovery. It makes the patient a co-therapist in a setting in which disapproval is replaced by social acceptance, regression by communication.

All these forms of hospitalization and gradual return to the community by means of halfway houses have one goal in common, to return the identified patient back to his largest potential in the real world, as quickly yet as gently as possible. Ideally they form a bridge across which troubled people can surmont their troubles and rejoin society. In a community sufficiently educated to understand the needs of our emotionally disturbed, such bridges will not be necessary, for it is possible to envison a society in which the channels of tolerant communication remain open both ways throughout the new terrifying period of a person's emotional difference.

Chapter 10
Addicts

So much myth and nonsense exists about the causes and meaning of drug addiction that we must clear up some popular misconceptions before giving advice. Notice that suggestions are made for continuing family and community relations with people who are still involved in their addiction, rather than limiting counseling to attempts to cure. This is done for a strong reason: any lasting help involves real acceptance of the person *where he is at.* In the case of an addict this will fluctuate between periods when he is "cleaned up" and periods when he is enmeshed in his temporarily satisfying method of problem solving: addictive drugs. Any hope for his rehabilitation lies in your understanding of the anxieties behind the drug abuse. To put it even more strongly, the addict in your family needs your attention focused not only on the technical aspects of helping him get unhooked, but on his inside troubles, the reality problems he finds hard to deal with, and the feelings of helplessness or pressure, either emotional or social, that drive him to compulsive drug use. Usually he has no authentic relationship with *anybody,* let alone many people. He suffers from this isolation while fostering it by immature and shallow behavior, need for fast gratification of his urges, inability to truly involve himself by acts which denote caring for others.

In this country addiction is largely a problem of addiction to heroin, barbiturates, or amphetamines (speed). Although the term addict cannot be applied to abusers of marijuana, or the psychedelic drugs like LSD, DMT, or psilocybin, psychological dependence has created a new problem which will be described later. For the moment however, let's proceed for you who need help in dealing with a friend or family member who fits the most common connotation of addict, a heroin user.

Heroin is one of the opiates, derivatives of opium and classified as depressants. Opiates remove pain and anxiety, producing a blank peaceful state. Probably the second most common drug used by addicts is morphine, which is similar to heroin in its effects. Although heroin and morphine then are extremely similar in a physiological sense, they are quite different in the kind of people likely to become addicted to them. Because heroin is only purchasable illegally, the people who become addicted know from the beginning that they are involved in a dangerous situation. People who become addicted to morphine often develop their addiction through its medical use as a pain killer. Sometimes doctors become addicted to morphine since they can get it easily. Such people are known as medical addicts and are probably different in social group and direction, as well as moving in entirely different worlds.

Dan Wakefield points out that the ordinary person who becomes addicted unknowingly to morphine often becomes pushed into the world of the addict culture. If he can't continue to supply his addictive needs by getting prescriptions for morphine, he is forced to turn next to the pusher and illegal traffic in heroin. Perhaps the most powerful example in literature is the mother in Eugene O'Neill's *Long Day Journey into Night.* Hooked on morphine as a result of illness following birth of a child, her inner guilt and pain over loss of another child lead her to both a medical and a psychological dependency that plunges the whole family into tragic despair.

Social disapproval has lots to do with the overwhelming problems that face the heroin or morphine addict. The report of the AMA-ABA Joint Committee pointed out that "addiction to and intoxication with alcohol or the barbiturates may produce withdrawal symptoms which are characteristic of opiate addiction. Addiction to barbiturates may be even more dangerous and harmful than addiction to morphine or an opium derivative." Because our society has no taboo against sleeping pills or alcohol, people hooked by them are not forced into the addict culture, which creates as many problems as the addiction itself. Although cocaine and marijuana are not the main drugs of the addict, these drugs involve the addict culture. This may be because both drugs are illegal, so that the possession of either brings similar penalties as possession of heroin. The main question among medical authorities about the bad effects of marijuana is the AMA-ABA report statement that "the use of marijuana frequently precedes experimentation with more powerful drugs such as heroin." The sanest comment to date is probably that of psychologist Charles Winick: "Many persons who take heroin have previously smoked marijuana but many marijuana smokers never go on to taking heroin."

Cocaine, derived from the coca leaf, is not a physically addicting stimulant. As Dr. Winick explains, "cocaine speeds up the activities of the user while heroin slows the user down." The strange effect of both together is that of "going fast slow."

Living with an addict can be so difficult that anger and loss of temper on your part are inevitable and should not cause you guilt. Let's look first at a group that is growing bigger, youthful addicts.

Only a few years ago adolescent drug abuse was a problem that seemed limited to the ghettos, economically or emotionally deprived kids, and those who were already labeled as seriously disturbed. Today affluent white suburbs have their "drug" problem. Kids from seemingly good homes where there is no obvious trouble experiment with drugs, as they used to with tobacco and alcohol. Some of them are able to test out the mind-expanding psychedelics, marijuana and even the so-called hard drugs and make an individual decision not to pursue them at all or to pursue them in a social way that is not compulsive and addictive. Others try them and are hooked, setting up a pattern of problem-solving which becomes more and more destructive to their lives. Drug abuse is the term given to such a terrifying and often tragic continuation of the normal gropings and experiments of kids who want to identify with their peers by trying what everyone else is trying.

Dealing with this intelligently represents a fairly new problem to parents. The old shocked injunctions that take the form of, "If you smoke pot you're no child of mine," simply aren't working. No better is the all-permissive attitude of, "Try it out, I trust you to use your own judgment." What is needed by parents who hope to keep their youngsters from becoming too dependent on this method of not looking at their problems is first a genuine understanding of what the real rebellion is about and what the drug experience, in the framework of our time, represents. This comes first! Without understanding, any disciplinary method, gentle or punitive, will fail. You can't help your kid until you understand what he is trying to escape from, and what the options are that are open to him. If he is smoking pot it may reassure you to remember Winick's conclusion, borne out by a statement in the *New York Times* by James Goddard, former commissioner of the F.D.A., that many marijuana users never go on to taking heroin. (This popular fallacy has arisen by asking heroin users if they have ever taken marijuana. Almost all will have, but they have also probably tried liquor, cigarettes, and before that tea or coffee. The addict is likely to have experimented in the course of his anxieties with every possible stimulant or artificial "mood modifier" available, including pills of all types.) Many "pot-heads" and even "acid-heads" have a deep fear of heroin and stop at the psychedelics which suit their life style, rather than going on to a drug which they have heard is not only addictive but constricting rather than expanding in terms of consciousness.

Let's assume that you have an addict in the family, or that your closest friend, for whom you feel a deep responsibility, has become addicted. First off, recognize that you are not all powerful and that your absolute best efforts may never be sufficient to persuade the addict to "kick." This pain is similar to that of having a relative with permanent brain damage, senility, or other conditions that may not respond to even the most intelligent and loving care. This by no means implies that the situation is hopeless, only that you should be aware that with some deeply self-destructive individuals the addiction may be more desired than the love that should seem sufficient to substitute for the drug.

Therapeutic techniques which have too high goals or which focus on the past are not the best ones for dealing with drug abusers. Since addiction is already a technique for saying goodbye to the past, the addict needs a new means of solving his here-and-now problems. You can guide him toward changing his present life style, but this can't be done in a long-term confined prison-hospital setting since he is there protected from ever facing what could be his real or emotional problems out in the world. You should take advantage of the fact, as pointed out in the helpful book, *A New Connection,* by John Frykman that "drug abusers, especially youthful ones, show a ready willingness to experiment in finding new styles of life, new living environments, and new types of meaningful relationships." Therefore you can very well forget about the past, and deal with the individual directly at the point of immediate need which you can see and hear. From the outset draw out alternative choices to help formulate a program for change in his immediate future. Gradually work toward long-term planning for change of life style, a process of taking charge of himself.

Living with an addict involves a lot of patience and the toughest possible discipline. If he is still on his habit, unwilling to stop but simply giving lip service to "kicking" in order to stay at home, you must check his source of money to support his habit. You may find the addiction is only a small part of the trouble, since he may be in constant hassles with the law for stealing, conning, pushing or dealing to support his habit. Are you prepared to encounter and cope with the anger-punishment backlash of society or the law? If not, you cannot keep him at home until he has "cleaned up," for your annoyance at having to literally and figuratively bail him out will eventually strike him as punitive and nagging.

If your personality is strong enough to handle this side of his addiction, you can care for him at home even while he is still hooked. Lots depends on the extent and amount of his habit; some habits are so large that they simply cannot be supported except by criminal means.

Assuming that your family member can stay at home and that you want to counsel him, it is important to understand what must happen in your relationship before any valid counseling can occur. You must convince him that he really has a problem and that it's essentially his own, not someone else's. Your decision to continue to live with him will fail unless he is ready to actually look for some kind of solution. In point of fact he may still be simply "maintaining," that is neither increasing nor decreasing his dosage, but unless he has at least a glimmer of insight as to the way in which he is avoiding problems, your life with him will be a series of broken promises, lies and quarrels.

Your first step, therefore, is to help him get the kind of help that will guide him toward recognizing where he is really at, whether anything specific can yet be done about it or not.

As the Haight-Asbury counseling program points out, one of the things that you will become aware of as you live with addicts is that the "drug problem" usually drops out of the conversation very quickly. The "drug" is only incidental to the "problem," and the problem is usually similar to many of the problems you may be aware of in yourself.

Your relative must be willing to accept you as a counselor no matter what your qualifications or attitudes are, and he must do this voluntarily. Don't attempt to talk him into it if he does not trust you. He needs counseling from someone else, then, and your role must be much more limited. If he will accept your role as concerned adviser you may find helpful the training advice given to counselor-trainees at the Haight Asbury Clinic.

You must operate in an atmosphere of kindness and friendship that is absolutely real. The addict must be given positive support, which doesn't necessarily mean agreement. You need to understand the problem as he sees it. Lots of times we are able to see problems that the person does not see, or things we would like him to do, or values we would like him to hold; we push these strongly and thus effectively eliminate the possibility of real communication.

You must maintain respect at all times for him as a person. Because he happens to believe in astrology, for instance, is no reason for treating him as though he has to get over that "problem" before real progress can be made. It distracts from the real problem when counselors aren't willing to accept a young person's commitment to astrology and see this as a significant part of the problem.

In an authentic relationship each person is willing to risk something of his own personal security with the other person and allow the other person to hold that portion in trust and confidence.

You must be careful not to try to solve the person's problem but guide him to find some method of solving the problem itself. You can help him to do this in a number of ways, such as gently steering conversation toward what is obviously being left out (usually on purpose), being aware that the person is probably sensing or imagining what your responses are going to be, and being careful not to second-guess where the person is going—not finish sentences for him, for example.

Try to stick to the problems that the person himself describes even though you may be aware of far deeper ones. To decide for him what his problem is will break down trust and involvement with you. You can provide clarification of issues and problems but cannot force someone into a "right" solution.

You should attempt to project your own consciousness into his emotions so that you can almost "feel" the way he is feeling. Accept on face value the person's attitudes and feelings instead of continually questioning his motivation. Don't interrupt because of your own anxiety. Sometimes the addict is overcome by a feeling that makes it almost impossible to get anywhere with counseling. He becomes depressed, and no matter what is said doesn't seem able to snap out of it. In these situations you try to get the conversation dramatically off the area that is being expressed to spring the person loose so he can start to deal with the feeling in a better way. You can say something like, "I know you're feeling bad right now" (showing that you accept the feeling he has), "but if you really had a choice about things, what would you like to be doing; what would be your wildest dreams?"

Try to lead him into taking some specific action that he can follow through on. Listen and lead. Listen to the person and lead him to the place where he's able to hear the truth—more precisely to make some decision with respect to the truth which he himself has been able to comprehend.

If you are living with an addict who is not a family member, there are two words you need to get acquainted with: transference and countertransference. My relating to you with a feeling I normally have about somebody else is transference. If you respond like the person I have made you out to be, countertransference is happening. I relate to you as if you're my father (transference); you respond to me as if I'm your child (countertransference). Transference then is simply what happens when a person pushes on to someone in authority the feelings he has about someone else.

When the person goes out and "does up" just at the point when you feel you are making progress, remember that he is probably doing something not to you but to himself—a pattern of action that has "worked" for him many times in the past. He can't be so sure that the "help" you give him will work!

You should try never to say, do, or communicate anything that places the addict in the position of having no way out. *You* need a way out and *he* needs a way out. Ultimatums are never part of a good counseling relationship or of any good human relationship. When we make such absolute demands we are telling about *our* needs and not the needs of the person we wish to help.

You can best help the addict in your family by understanding the kind of emotion behind his compulsive habit. Dr. Charles Winick believes that most addicts are in effect telling their family and society that they believe everything possible has been done to deny their real needs. Addicts then rebel by indicating that they won't die but will show how close to death the family or society has brought them. Addicts in treatment sometimes say, "If I don't get on I'll kill myself or someone else; would you prefer that?" Many addicts rationalize by explaining that they are misunderstood.

Heroin addicts are often proud of the scars caused by their needle. Many actually allow themselves to be quickly caught by authorities, in that way calling attention to their suffering and blaming others for it. When they take drugs they seem to achieve what they can't in ordinary life, particularly if they are needful of instant gratification. They need the drug and at the same time resent it.

Fancy Freudian interpretations exist, described by people like the saxophonist who described another musical addict with disturbed Oedipal relationship, "He's carrying a horn for his mother."

There is no one psychiatric diagnosis, however, which applies to all addicts. The diagnosis certainly does not influence the progress of his addiction, for a person with a severe psychosis may recover from an addiction quickly while one with a simple neurosis may just not be able to stop taking drugs. In each case the drug fills a personality gap, but the subtleties of the need are difficult for the average psychiatrist to see, and you may also find yourself mystified as to why his need exists.

Drug slang reflects the addict's preoccupation with family relationships. His frequent use of "daddy" in referring to males, his common use of "baby" in referring to females, and his description of the supplier of drugs as a "mother" are revealing. Although addicts may be either hetero- or homosexual, opiates often take the place of sexual activity. The needle sometimes indicates a kind of sexual play, and Simmel has pointed out the strong autoerotic and masturbatory components in the addict's preoccupation with his body. Very often you will find that addicts are sexually passive, concerned with their own rather than their partner's gratification.

There are a few aggressive addicts whose use of drugs is an expression of anger toward the community, family or self, but most dependency on drugs is based on a need for passively receiving supplies from the outside, much as an infant takes milk. As in all dependent relationships, when you withdraw the drug, you as the caretaking person must be prepared to face what in your friend or relative is a period of severe bereavement. John Frykman, former director of the Haight Clinic Drug Treatment Center, now community counselor in Carmel, California, explains this: "When a drug user stops using he severs his dependent relationship with the drug. Many 'heads' in fact look at their drug in a very personal way. The bereavement he must live through is much like a problem after divorce; the estranged drug is still painfully around, as is the estranged person."

At the end of this chapter are descriptions of the various drugs, narcotics or opiates, sedative hypnotics (downers), major stimulants (uppers), minor stimulants, hallucinogens or "psychedelics," marijuana, tranquilizers, glue and other inhalants, as well as the "pattern" that a user goes through.

A wide variety of other substances will be sold by street dealers to unknowing people. These people are "burned" by thinking they are buying one thing and getting another. Some of the things that are sold for speed are Drano with magnesium removed, photo developer, sugar, powdered milk, rat poison, and epsom salts. Substances that are sold for psychedelics are barbiturates, animal tranquilizers, and sugar substitute tablets (cyclamate, saccharin). For heroin, sugar, procaine, or combinations of other things are sold.

If you are taking care of an addict at home you should know some simple first aid for emergency situations, such as those listed at the end of this chapter.

In today's culture, a large group of alert, well-adjusted youngsters experiment with psychedelic drugs. The experience can be destructive, useless and wasteful, or helpful, depending on the person's general motivation. All in all, however, despite enormous publicity given to "bad trips," it is likely that the so-called drug-induced psychoses involve breakdowns which would have occurred in those individuals anyhow. LSD, mescaline, and certainly marijuana rarely turn an emotionally healthy person into either an addict or a psychotic. Much more of a national problem is the question of opiate addiction or addiction to barbiturates or speed. If your relative is dependent on one of these substances you may have to face the painful fact that unless his inner problems and reality problems are resolved, he simply may never shake free of the addiction and you will find yourself a caretaker forever.

If this is the case, you must make a rational decision as to how much you can take without draining yourself of energy needed for other family members and for fulfillment of yourself as a person.

If seeing to the certainly excessive needs of the addict in

your family is beyond your emotional and physical ability to give, perhaps he can be persuaded to go to a rehabilitation center. Places like Odyssey House or Daytop Village in New York, and hospital units or "therapeutic communities" or residences with a methadone program, sometimes offer a chance of cure. Many people have had excellent experiences at places like the Synanon centers which combine group therapy with group reinforcement of the desire to kick the habit.

Addicts seem to display anger and aggression toward their families in the way they behave, both lying and cheating to get the immediate gratification which they need so much. Your impatience and pain at his behavior cannot be concealed nor should you attempt to conceal it. Nonacceptance of his irresponsible behavior is part of the reality he must learn to deal with. Before condemning his total character, however, because of the immature behavior, it is really helpful for you to adopt a nonpunitive attitude toward his addiction itself, thereby leaving your mind open to explore the whys and wherefores of his reliance on this method of problem solving. By looking behind the obvious problem, your only real possibility of changing his behavior may exist, for you may recognize certain needs which are unmet in him, and help him to meet them in a less self-destructive way.

A few addicts are what are called sociopaths, individuals who for unknown reasons are incapable of a caring involvement with anyone else and who remain on the fringe of society and relationships despite the most caring attempts at help. If, after exploring every therapeutic and human avenue with warmth and enthusiasm, it becomes slowly and progressively clear that your relative is truly a "hollow man," you must find a way to preserve your own strength and that of the rest of the family. Under such circumstances you must realize your own lack of power and relieve yourself of the responsibility of care, leaving only concern in its place. You can help some addicts to withdraw, and you can help some addicts to solve their underlying problems in a way that makes future addiction unlikely, but those who cannot be helped and are destructive to those around them must not be allowed to drag down everyone around them. Such a decision cannot be reached quickly but it will spell itself out in time.

Special Aids for Living with Addicts

Following is a description of the types of drugs and how they work. Further details can be found in the book *A New Connection* published by Scrimshaw Press, San Francisco, from which most of this information is derived.

Narcotics or Opiates

Heroin, morphine and codeine, the natural and semisynthetic derivatives of opium as well as a variety of synthetic products; Demerol, Percodan, laudanum are included. They relieve pain and also relieve anxiety. In addition they depress some body functions such as bowel mobility (paregoric is used to stop diarrhea) and respiratory reflexes (codeine is used in cough syrup). When heroin is injected into the blood stream there is an immediate "rush" of an overwhelming feeling of well being. The "high" is this feeling of well being and absence of pain.

Physical and psychological dependence build rapidly with continuous daily use of the opiates. Death comes quickly to those who overdose, usually in less than an hour. The cost of maintaining a heroin habit can easily run as high as $100 to $200 a day. Withdrawal symptoms include cramps, vomiting, runny nose and eyes, extreme anxiety, headaches, muscle aches and spasms, and other complaints. Detoxification usually takes from three to five days. A person is usually able to cope with these symptoms well if he is in a friendly, drug-free environment.

Sedative-Hypnotics, "Downers"

These include the barbiturates, "minor" tranquilizers such as miltown, equanil, etc., alcohol, Freon gas (the pressurizing agent used in spray cans), nitrous oxide, ether, a group of widely prescribed anxiety relievers, Serax, Librium and Valium, and the bromides.

The main effects of the sedative-hypnotics are to relieve anxiety, induce sleep, and at higher dosage levels to produce general anesthesia. The HIGH of the drug is a disinhibited feeling of well being, more commonly described as being drunk.

Physical and psychological dependence are serious dangers with the sedative hypnotics. Many deaths occur due to overdose. For example, barbiturate poisoning causes more deaths in this country than any other type of poisoning. Barbiturate detoxification or withdrawal has many complications and must usually be done in a hospital because of the high risk of convulsions. Detoxification takes from eight to eighteen days. An additional danger is that when two or more of these drugs are taken together they have an additive effect.

Major Stimulants, "Uppers"

"Speed" (methamphetamine HC1), cocaine, Benzedrine, Dexedrine, Desoxyn, and a wide variety of "pep" and "diet" pills are in this family. These drugs "speed" up almost everything about a person—his breathing, heartbeat, even his speech (speed rapping). There is an almost abnormal cheerfulness, and the person "does" much more than usual. Major stimulants are prescribed for use in depressing appetite, warding off depression and for putting off sleep in the treatment of narcolepsy.

The HIGH is euphoria, a feeling of maximum creativity and self-confidence, that the user has "the world by the tail" and can accomplish anything he wishes. To most intravenous users, the "flash" or "rush" which one feels immediately after injecting is the most important action of the drug. It has been described as "a total body orgasm." When a person first begins to use "speed," there is some enhanced performance and concentration.

There is no clear evidence of physical dependence with the amphetamines. However, psychological dependence can develop rapidly. Most people using speed compulsively do not believe that they have a problem. They are "feeding" their veins with the ultimate energy food of speed.

Minor Stimulants

Caffeine (coffee, tea), nicotine (cigarettes), and wyamine are in this family.

The HIGH is getting "up" for things through their use, e.g., the person who can't go to work in the morning without his morning coffee and/or cigarette.

There is some evidence of physical dependence to nicotine,

though most of the dependence is psychological. These drugs are listed with the other drugs of abuse because (1) in some ways they are far more dangerous forms of drug use (deaths from lung cancer and other diseases from cigarette smoking); and (2) they represent a very compulsive style of drug use—(is it more compulsive to stick a needle into your arm twice a day, or a cigarette into your mouth twenty to sixty times a day?). In withdrawal from cigarette smoking, there are some of the same conditions of irritability and depression which accompany amphetamine withdrawal.

Hallucinogens or "Psychedelics"

A wide variety of different substances make up this family. They include LSD, DET, DMT, STP (DOM), MDA, TMA, mescaline, peyote, and psilocybin. Many other naturally growing things have some of the same qualities—morning glory seeds, Hawaiian wood rose seeds, nutmeg, cinnamon, catnip, etc. Although these drugs cause an initial mild stimulation, the main changes are psychological. The way the mind perceives things is changed; e.g., colors are seen more brightly or vividly, or no color is seen; the person feels heavier or lighter, longer or shorter; or the walls may seem to breathe with him. Most of the time true hallucinations do not occur (seeing something that is not there).

The HIGH is mind expansion. The person looks to the drug as a way of getting a deeper understanding of himself, experiencing new dimensions of the mind and thinking.

Again, there is no physical dependence; the potential for psychological dependence is much lower. The real dangers of the hallucinogens are that the "trip" can sometimes precipitate a psychotic break, which can mean long-term trouble for the person. Suicides have occurred as a result of some of these "bad trips." Most such "bad trips," however, are likened to the setting in which the drug was used, or the state of mind of the person when he used the drug. The phenomenon of the "flash back" is probably more a function of memory than of drug effect—e.g., if your mother has been killed in a car you were driving, you could easily "flash back" on that experience anytime if something in your experience provided a "reminder" of it. Contrary to popular belief, there is no convincing evidence of brain damage or permanent chromosome damage with the use of hallucinogens.

Marijuana—"Grass"

Marijuana is made from the dried and crushed leaves and flowering tops of the female Indian hemp plant. They are usually smoked, but sometimes eaten. Hashish is the most potent form of *Cannabis sativa* (the botanical name for the plant), and is made from the sticky resin that forms on the flowering tops.

The effects of the drug are interesting and peculiar. It relieves anxiety and disinhibits (much as the sedative-hypnotics), tends to relax muscles, in some persons is mildly stimulative, and has at times evoked rare experiences which have been likened to "psychedelic trips." Marijuana is a relatively innocuous pharmacological substance (less dangerous than aspirin or sugar).

The HIGH is similar in some ways to alcohol, without the morning-after hangover. There is a feeling of relaxation and euphoria, and usually a sense of increased awareness and a desire to look in on oneself.

By far the greatest danger of marijuana use is the possible encounter with the law. (This danger is also present with the other drugs which have been mentioned.) There is no physical dependence built up with its use (one reason it should not be listed in the sedative-hypnotic family), though there is some indication of psychological dependence in certain individuals. There have been "bad trips" in connection with its use, but to a much lesser degree than with the hallucinogens.

Tranquilizers

This family consists primarily of the phenothiazines; brand names include Thorazine, Mellaril, Sparine, Compazine, and many others.

These drugs have some things in common with sedatives; for example, the heart and breathing rates become slower. There is an important difference, however; whereas the sedatives release inhibitions stored in the primary brain stem, the tranquilizers wall off this primary area. Where the sedatives tranquilize by letting loose some of those things in the deep center of the brain, the phenothiazines *tranquilize* by locking in those same primary impulses. That's one reason why phenothiazines have been so effective in the control of psychotics; this is their primary clinical use.

There is really no HIGH with phenothiazines; there is only a depressing DOWN. Everything seems in control, but it isn't a very pleasant experience. This is one of the most important reasons why these drugs are so far down the list of potential for abuse, especially when you consider how readily available they are.

The greatest dangers with these drugs are the many possible side effects and bad reactions. It is also true that many people attempt suicide through overdoses with phenothiazines. Some are concerned about the "legal" abuse of these drugs; they are widely prescribed by physicians to "control" or "manage" patients or inmates in institutions, especially convalescent hospitals for the aging and prisons.

Glue and Other Inhalants

Model airplane cement, automobile ignition spray, benzine, carbon tetrachloride, shoe polish, lacquer, paint and gasoline are but a few of the substances in this family which are currently in abuse.

The effect of inhaling the fumes of these various substances is much the same as for alcohol or other sedatives. Anxiety is, relieved and the person is loose and disinhibited. There is, however, more drowsiness, more lethargy, than with alcohol.

The HIGH is similar to alcohol intoxication.

There are strong indications of psychological dependence being built up by glue sniffers. Often it is a very difficult problem to deal with, because it is associated with early adolescent drug use, is a part of the same "growing up" pattern as thumb sucking, and can be very compulsive because of this. There is a good deal of evidence that the use of glue over a long period of time may cause permanent damage to the brain, may lead to liver and kidney problems as well, and alpastic anemia (the breaking down of bone marrow). For many young people, it should be made clear that it is probably safer to experiment with some of the "harder" drugs than to get involved with glue sniffing.

Miscellaneous "Drugs"

Amyl nitrate—a drug that is inhaled, is a vascular dilator and is used medically to relieve the pain of heart attacks. Through a lot of folk gossip, aphrodisiac powers have been attributed to it, and it is used in connection with sexual activities to increase the satisfaction of orgasm. The usual sum effect, however, is a rather uncomfortable headache.

Angel dust—One of a variety of forms of smokeable replacements for marijuana when marijuana is in short supply. Usually it is dried parsley flakes (kitchen cooking variety) impregnated with either a barbiturate or a hallucinogenic drug.

THC—the initials for tetrahydrocannabinol—is a synthesized variety of the active ingredients in marijuana, a very difficult chemical to produce, and very costly. Therefore, almost all of what is sold to people for THC is not. Usually it is PCP or a barbiturate. (PCP is an animal tranquilizer; trade name for one form is Sernylan.) PCP is also widely marketed as mescaline or psilocybin.

Simple First Aid for Emergency Situations

In the treatment of narcotic overdose, death is not caused by sedation leading to coma but by drowning caused by the lungs filling up with body fluids. Death from overdose comes in fifteen minutes to one hour. The treatment is very simple (an injection of nalorphine or levallorphan), but if a doctor is not available it may not be possible. Try to get a doctor fast, letting him know that the problem is opiate overdose.

If this is not possible the person should be treated in the same way as for an injection-induced barbiturate overdose. Keep him warm, in a shock position, and, since respiration is also depressed by opiates, keep him breathing. Though they have provided help at times, amphetamines should only be used as a last resort.

The danger with Nalline and Lorphan is that they put the patient into immediate withdrawal symptoms and you must therefore be ready to help him with certain problems when he regains consciousness.

For withdrawal the right clinical treatment is with the drug methadone ("dollys"), the substitution of this long-acting synthetic opiate for the short-acting heroin.

If a person has no "dollys" (there are long waiting lists to get into methadone programs at all facilities) the following drugs can be helpful in reducing some of the withdrawal symptoms:

Ask your doctor to prescribe Bentyl, Antrenyl, or Pro-Banthine with phenobarbital to reduce nausea and vomiting. Thorazine in dosages up to 150 mg. is also helpful for this symptom and capsules can be inserted rectally in emergency where vomiting makes the use of oral medication impossible. The doctor should not give Thorazine (or other phenothiazines) with Talwin, history of reaction to any phenothiazine, history of epilepsy, heart or lung condition, or present liver disease (jaundice).

In the case of overdose of barbiturates you must remember that withdrawal from barbiturate addiction is more violent and dangerous, without the proper medication, than even from heroin.

The use of barbs will often precipitate violence and irresponsible behavior. If they are mixed with alcohol there is an additive effect.

Although barbs are usually taken orally, they may be injected intravenously. They must be injected under high pressure because they are so hard to dissolve, so often large ulcers and abscesses caused by missing or blowing the vein can be found. Best treatment is in the hospital, but here are a few emergency suggestions:

If the person has overdosed by mouth, induce vomiting with syrup of ipecac or warm soapy water. Keep him awake, moving and warm. Slap him to keep him awake. He can be permitted to sleep for half an hour at a time after about four hours, if his air passages are watched.

A cure used by street people is an injection of speed (amphetamines). This is effective but must be repeated every few hours since the speed wears off. Other stimulants such as coffee, tea, coke, may be used if the patient is conscious.

In cases of overdose by injection or if the person is unconscious, forget vomiting. Use speed if available (this can be given rectally). Keep the patient breathing through mouth to mouth resuscitation. Keep the patient in shock position with mouth down so mouth and throat can drain. As soon as he is conscious, begin waking him, moving him around, etc.

If there is doubt as to whether the overdose is caused by heroin or barbs, treat for the heroin overdose first. You can help your relative withdraw from barbs by substituting long-acting phenobarbital for whatever short-acting barb the person has been using, then decreasing the phenobarbital slowly over a period of ten to eighteen days.

In cases of mixed addiction (the person may be using alcohol, heroin, or speed at the same time as barbs) he must be hospitalized and withdrawn from one drug at a time while being maintained on the others.

If your relative is strung out on speed, you may find his overdosing very hard to handle. Medication is usually necessary to offset the effects of the stimulant, and here again sedatives seem to have a better effect than tranquilizers.

Compulsive use of amphetamines is often accompanied by lack of sleep and poor diet. These lead to paranoid feelings, malnutrition and deep depression. Deep depression may follow withdrawal from the drug.

Hepatitis is not uncommon as a result of the "speed scene." In helping your relative withdraw from speed try to provide him with a very supportive drug-free environment, making it possible that he gets lots of food and sleep. Drinking several glasses of cranberry juice daily will help him get the amphetamines out of his system faster. Sleep therapy (three or four days of sleep) seems to be helpful in warding off "amphetamine psychosis." Once he is off, you should be careful about putting demands on him for some time.

The use of hallucinogens or psychedelic drugs usually does not come under the heading of addiction except possibly in a psychological sense. However, if your relative often takes such drugs, there is much that is helpful to know.

The most common problem with the mind-expanding drugs is what is called a "bad trip." This can mean anything from paranoid feelings about inner or outer events while the drug is still in his system to a violent anxiety reaction. Anxiety is the common denominator of most bad trips.

A person who is taking LSD, mescaline, etc., for the first time usually feels that his behavior is so changed during the experience that he cannot encounter the outside world without being "found out." In point of fact, it is often difficult for a non-physician to tell if someone is tripping, and many everyday activities can be done before the drug has even begun to wear off.

A bad trip usually occurs when your relative has taken a psychedelic at a moment in his life when he is beset by deep anxieties or depression or in a setting with people he does not really trust or like. The insights that are triggered by the special non-inhibiting qualities of these drugs then appear to have portentous and often painful or destructive aspects. Painful (psychic or physical) moments that occur briefly during almost every trip are held onto, hallucinations are seen as threatening and ominous, and the darkest aspect of every experience is the one that is dwelt on, to the exclusion of light cheerful material or even insightful material that is not anguished or threatening.

Helpful in avoiding such experiences is a reassuring guide. If your relative is conscious of your disapproval of his experimentation with psychedelic drugs, it is unlikely that he will turn to you for help. If he does, however, either in panic or in trust, remember that although drugs can "bring him down" from a bad trip, they are a last resort. Far better is simply talking reassuringly during those parts of his trip when he is into anxiety. If he is afraid about his dosage, he should be reassured that there is practically no lethal dose; if he is paranoid, the source of his suspicions should be explored gently and realistically with him; if he is fearful of a hallucination you might talk to him about the positive, creative side of what he is seeing, while at the same time reminding him that he is under the influence of a chemical that will wear off within twelve hours, taking the hallucinations along with it. Accompanying your relative on his trip removes the rare but highly publicized dangers of "thinking one is a bird and jumping out of a window," etc., and if you can remove your own fear and prejudice you may find it an expanding experience even if you have not injected the drug yourself. Bear in mind that the psychedelics, while not without serious risks, present the possibility, when used with judgment, of problem solving in a way that the opiates, barbiturates and "kick" drugs avoid. If you find that a relative has taken a psychedelic and confides to you that he is having a bad trip, or bummer, as it is popularly called, you can use the opportunity to guide him through the rest of his trip in a way that is permanently helpful to him. After all, it is this group of drugs that allow us "for a little while, to divest ourselves of those acquired assumptions and see the universe again with an innocent eye." As T. Huxley reminded us, we may, if we wish, "sit down in front of the facts like a child" or as Thomas Traherne, a seventeenth-century English mystic puts it, "to unlearn the dirty devices of the world and become as it were a little child again."

If talking through the experience is not helping nor is suggesting that your relative sit back and "enjoy it like watching a movie until it is over," then you may have to resort to a medication "down." If this must be used, first choice is Frenquel, an anti-hallucinatory drug without heavy sedative or tranquilizing properties. Second choice would be one of the sedatives, such as phenobarbital, Serax, Librium, or Valium. Although medically safe, this is an especially unpleasant way to come down from a psychedelic trip in that the phenothiazine causes the person to feel as though he were in a kind of physical straitjacket. If phenothiazines are the only resort, Thorazine may be given. Ask your doctor about dosage, but avoid taking the person to a hospital if possible, for it is likely that he will come down with the least anxiety if he remains in a familiar setting, and see that the chemical effects have gone and he is still "together" the next day.

The pattern of a user when he stops using his drug is described by John Frykman in this way:

1. *Shock*
2. *Emotional release*
3. *Depression*
4. *Physical symptoms*
5. *Guilt*
6. *Panic*

4 to 7 days

7. *Hostility*
8. *Beginning to return to normalcy*
9. *Gradual appearance of hope*
10. *Re-adjustment to reality*

Up to a year

A few comments on each stage (these could be worked out in much more detail):

1. *Shock:* very evident, almost a disbelief by the person that he has decided to "kick"; can be dramatically intensified if a serious health problem has developed from the drug use.

2. *Emotional release:* sometimes crying, expression of hostility, a feeling of "I've finally decided," etc.
3. *Depression:* almost universal as the person works through his problem; can repeat itself at several stages.
4. *Physical symptoms:* range from common phenomena like runny noses, aches and pains, to things like acting out the role of father or mother, assuming mannerisms of people who have been close in the drug scene, being obsessed with talking about the way it was, and, "If only this had never happened, I wouldn't have . . . "
5. *Guilt:* A wide variety of types—guilt in relationship to therapist, friends, self, family, society, etc.
6. *Panic:* "What am I doing? Where am I going?"; needing to go and get the fix, etc.
7. *Hostility:* can be displayed toward a variety of people, as well as toward the drug culture, straight culture, and the drug itself.
8. *Return:* this is a very difficult stage because it is where the life style really begins to change. A new way of living must be developed with regular death and bereavement: "The person is dead. I have to go on somehow." With drugs: "I can't depend on them any longer, even though I want to."
9. *Gradual appearance of hope:* this is one of the best signs as a person begins to see his way through. He starts to show other emotions besides grief—he laughs, talks more actively, talks about persons other than himself, expresses concern for them.
10. *Readjusts to reality:* the person has a new way of making it, a new life style. He no longer needs to be dependent on the drug.

"You need to remember that any of these phases which a person goes through can reappear, and that it is perfectly normal for these feelings of bereavement to last for a year or even a little longer. A person needs to go through these stages to preserve feelings of health, safety, sanity, etc.

"If you can understand that dependency feelings cause grief, no matter where those feelings appear, you can better understand the compulsive drug user. As you work with a person who exhibits dependence feelings, you should try to discourage him from establishing a new dependent relationship with you. You want him to know the relationship is dependable, but not dependent. You want to help the person develop ways of making decisions, solving problems, on his own. You strive to guide him to where he is able to make free choices about himself, where he is free to fail, free to succeed, free to cope with life itself."

Chapter 11
Alcoholics

Living with an alcoholic is a situation that is usually filled with rage and pain. Only when you have learned to view alcoholism as an illness rather than "bad" behavior can you manage to continue family functions without a daily series of scenes and quarrels that foster guilt and are utterly ineffective in terms of helping the problem.

If you are in a family or friendship or love relationship with an excessive drinker, either truly accept the situation and the person where he is at, or seek outside help immediately. No amount of lectures, nagging, bribes or manipulations will help reduce the intake of liquor and the output of frustration in the person with whom you are living. Help can come from any outside source, a doctor, social worker, rehabilitation group or counselor, but it should be objective; otherwise you will find yourself trapped in a cycle.

Don't be terrified of outside help because you are afraid to separate from your spouse or family member who is unable to stop drinking. If you have decided to leave, that separation may not be the catastrophe for him that you fear. Sometimes a great deal of solicitous care by a mothering and supportive person may actually work against his need and readiness to accept treatment. If you feel you can cope with the symptoms and want to stick around, you can be bolstered in this resolution by professionals who will respect your wish and extend help when and where it is needed.

If you are married to an alcoholic you may find your life punctuated by many separations and many reunions. You may be involved with someone like Ralph L., an utterly charming man who found it easy to attract women because of his physical appeal and excellent mind. When Nancy married Ralph all her friends were very jealous. He was a young writer with a promising reputation, a handsome face and exciting personality. Intelligent but rather ordinary-looking herself, Nancy was the daughter of an alcoholic and worried just a bit before the marriage about Ralph's casual and cheerful daily "nips." Still he was so charming about it, gave out such an aura of gaiety and never seemed in any way out of control or intoxicated, that she thought it only a controlled social drinking. It wasn't until they had been married for some time that she began to see Ralph's conflict. Lots of things he really wanted (or seemed to want) came hard to him, so hard that he had to bolster his confidence with booze. The booze had to be taken in increasing amounts because of the psychological addictive quality of alcohol, and after a while even the large amounts he consumed every day just weren't having the desired effect.

If the person in your family "drinks" but you are not really sure he is an alcoholic, you should know that four kinds of behavior separate the alcoholics from other drinkers. First, his use of alcohol is different from the usual drinking standards of the home, neighborhood, and job groups with which he is involved. Second, he cannot properly perform his role in those groups. Third, he is not able to stop drinking once he starts even though he knows it impairs his health. Fourth, his excessive use of alcohol causes him physical and emotional damage.

As Harrison Trice points out, "The first distinctive feature, deviation from drinking norms, varies from society to society . . . alcoholism is a different thing in France from what it is in America. The French, who experience little guilt or stigma with drinking, show physical rather than psychiatric symptoms of alcoholism. The middle-class Protestant American, on the other hand, shows emotional damage from excessive drinking as is evidenced in his guilt feelings, his lying to protect his drinking, and his deep resentment of those around him. Particularly characteristic of the alcoholic in the United States is his inability to control the amount of alcohol consumed. In France the typical alcoholic drinks constantly but does so at a controlled level."

In trying to find out what stage of alcoholism has been reached, you can classify the drinker into a few groups: "abstainers" who don't drink at all, "social" drinkers who drink moderately and may very occasionally get drunk, "excessive" drinkers who begin to have physical, personal, and social difficulties arising out of their need, and the "alcoholics" who are really suffering from a disease that can be given a medical diagnosis and requires a specific regimen of treatment like other physical diseases. We can consider a person a chronic alcoholic when his body has been physically damaged by booze so that the effects persist even when he is not drinking.

Neil Kessel and Henry Walton describe addiction to liquor as different from addiction to most dangerous drugs like cocaine, opium and heroin. Social indulgence makes the addiction more acceptable, and alcohol addicts don't need to go on increasing their intake in quite the same way that drug addicts do. The drug addict experiences a craving when he stops but the alcoholic may be able to abstain for long periods, especially if he is in a hospital. The term addiction is suitable, however, in this sense: all addicts are dependent upon the substances they take.

The World Health Organization's definition of alcoholics is "those excessive drinkers whose dependence on alcohol has reached such a degree that they show a noticeable mental disturbance or an interference with their mental and bodily health, their interpersonal relations and their smooth social and economic functioning. They therefore require treatment."

There are cliches about the families of alcoholics based on statistics, and statistics (as everyone who has worked in the area of mental health knows) are subject to the widest possible interpretations. The standard book on the subject will say that more than likely the wife of an alcoholic is frequently the daughter of an alcoholic. If you are the daughter of a heavy drinker, guard against looking for, in a mate, a revival of the relationship with your father. As an alcoholic's wife you may often admit being aware that your husband drank a lot at the time of your marriage, but that you hadn't realized the full implications of this. Of course lots of women marry heavy drinkers truly believing that they are going to be able to reform them.

You should also realize that you may have to manage the greatest part of the household responsibilities by yourself, make decisions, often go out to work in addition to raising the children. You may lose your sensitivity to the effect your constant belittling and critical tone has on your alcoholic mate and further inhibit his self-confidence by your immense capabilities. Someone on the outside looking in will hardly seem to notice your need for an adequate husband, you may seem to play all the roles so well yourself. In this fashion you unintentionally diminish him in his own eyes.

If your partner is alcoholic you may find the going very rough indeed. You will probably not have enough money to manage the household except by taking on extra responsibilities as a wage earner yourself. Booze is expensive, so that a large portion of your family income may go for liquor and bar tabs. Promises will be given and not kept, standards at home will go down and down and with them a measure of family pride.

Your husband or wife may no longer be dependable in terms of time and place. You cannot expect him home for regular meals; food is often wasted and you lose your enthusiasm. If there are children they cannot help but notice both the lowering of standards and the unpredictability of their parent. You will find yourself asking friends over less and less frequently because of the embarrassment if there is a long wait or if he arrives home drunk.

You may find him physically violent at times or feel repelled by his sexual advances, which seem to be determined more by the consumption of booze than real warmth or desire. You will probably miss the companionship of a less problematic marriage, putting more and more of your energy into the children in a way that is really an emotional pressure on them to fulfill the needs unfulfilled by your mate, rather than a natural surge of extra fun and enjoyment in their company.

After a while you may feel so resentful that you leave the situation. Families of alcoholics like Ralph L. mentioned previously tend to patterns of fight, bust up, return, try again, fight, bust up, return, try again. It's more common for a husband to leave an alcoholic wife than a wife to leave an alcoholic husband. Probably the reason women can handle such marriages for longer periods of time is that they can and do have mothering impulses toward their men, that drinking is more accepted socially in men than in women, that sometimes the women are financially dependent; and, because of social acceptance, women alcoholics are generally more disturbed in personality than men.

If you stay with your drinking husband you may be pushing down enormous feelings of rage toward him. You may not express it to him directly but use others in the family to do so, saying for example that "the children can't stand their father since he drinks" when actually this is your feeling.

A study of alcoholics and their families by Myers explains that "a competent mother can make up for most of the deficiencies resulting from the father's alcoholism. So pronounced are the capabilities of alcoholic's wives to sustain the roles proper to their husbands, that the children do not commonly suffer material privation." The effect upon the child of an alcoholic parent is considerably reduced if the other parent is able to provide a sympathetic explanation of the condition in terms of illness.

Despite this pessimistic view, not all marriages to alcoholics fail or are even in trouble. You can view the physical problems as similar to those of a person who has any chronic disease. Such marriages exist with great joy and elan despite the liquor addiction, predicated on a genuine mutual respect for the other person's present needs, whatever they are. In such a marriage a strong feeling exists that any decision to "dry out" or reduce liquor consumption has to come from the person who is doing the drinking, for his own reasons, not because he has been pressured or nagged into changing.

Sometimes psychiatry fails in that it doesn't take into account or rather invalidates and discredits the large number of mutual dependency marriages that work, not just in a dreary plodding way but in a way that provides some actual sparkle on both sides when the problems mesh.

Here for example is the rather atypical situation of Joel O., a writer who has a drinking problem. His wife Helen has been hospitalized for a schizophrenic episode and works hard to keep on top of this "vulnerability" to breakdown. The couple has fused their mutual difficulties into a relationship which has as its base a tender regard for each other's needs.

Listening to Helen discuss living with her husband is extremely helpful, especially to the judgmental person who believes that there is always one "sick" and one "caretaking" person in this kind of situation. She says, "I knew Joel had great will, we both knew it, but we needed professional help of some kind. Even before he dried out we had, despite the physical problem, a personally happy situation anyhow."

In investigating what made him want to stop drinking it seemed clear that in Joel's case it might have been Helen's tolerance, which was part of her belief that alcoholism is a physical problem although perhaps there are emotional results. "There was never any doubt," says Helen, "that it's not his fault. Though it may have started with problems, I have a feeling that he grew out of them and was left with only the physical addiction. After all, any time Joel got drunk (and that was very rare) it was an emotional situation. Usually he would drink all day to keep even."

When asked if now that he is on the wagon it is better for his friends not to have liquor around, Joel replies that "In somebody else's house it doesn't bother me. In my own house I couldn't take it. I tell friends that if they want wine or beer here I can manage that since I don't care too much for either, but I can't have a bottle of whiskey in my own home. Of course being on the wagon affects friendships; some friends who are still drinking heavily don't come around any more."

Helen describes part of going on the wagon in terms of Joel's changed eating habits. Now that he's dried out his physical craving is gone, she says, and it's just a desire, not a need. He drinks a great deal of coffee and can indulge in rich desserts. Sometimes it is hard for Helen to watch him eating things she cannot; sometimes Joel becomes envious of drinking going on and has to leave his favorite bar. When watching heavy drinking, he feels ambivalent, half the time thinking, "Did I ever act like that?" and half the time wishing he could again.

Helen feels that they are a special case. It is more usual for a couple to have been together and the drinking begun because of certain problems that they went through together. However, to think that alcoholism is a result of marital problems is the same kind of easy answer that says emotional illness is always a result of family problems or people hurting each other.

Joel feels it is more likely that the propensity is there before the problem. He says, "If alcohol works for you you'll use it for almost anything. The first thing that the lush does if anything hurts is to take a drink." That's why he puts little stock in drugs like antabuse (a daily tablet which makes unpleasant symptoms occur if liquor is taken within three days), for some people will die rather than not drink, and often when people take antabuse they will later take a drink anyhow, even knowing that they are going to experience unpleasant effects.

If the question of treatment comes up in your family it's important to remember that any course of treatment for drying out has to meet individual needs. Nothing can happen without the person's initial acceptance of the need for treatment. First he must realize that he actually is an alcoholic, and then he must see that he cannot change the process without some kind of help.

The next step involves general medical treatment of the actual physical havoc wrought by the booze inside the body. Such difficulties as gastritis (inflammation of the stomach), cirrhosis of the liver, and the nutritional lacks and disorders are treated by a combination regimen of diet and dietary supplements. Disorders of the nervous system respond more slowly and in some cases leave permanent after-effects.

Withdrawal symptoms can now be lessened through the use of tranquilizers. They make the occurrence of hallucinations or delirium tremens far less frequent now than they used to be but should be used carefully lest they become addictive too. Often it's a good idea to enter a hospital for a few days or weeks since it is easiest to stay off booze while getting help.

While psychiatry can help in some ways, a recovered alcoholic pointed out quite correctly that, "Nothing has delayed recovery for problem drinkers longer than the belief that knowing why they drink excessively will make them able to control it." If you have heart disease, all the information about the cause of your condition isn't going to change it, and knowing that you had a difficult childhood is interesting and may be helpful in many ways, but excessive drinking is not just emotional problems plus liquor, but a different situation altogether.

Because functioning is disturbed, if your family member is seeing a psychiatrist, make sure the doctor refuses to treat him unless he stops drinking, since what is needed is coping with the problem right away. Most capable psychiatrists send their patient to Alcoholics Anonymous for support during the treatment. Although some sophisticated drinkers are turned off by the evangelical and religious tone of AA, it has been and continues to be a tremendous help to many who wish to cut down on drinking. The organization also maintains groups for family members where you can compare notes, commiserate, and receive understanding for your role of living with an alcoholic who may be in one of many stages, either drying out, on the wagon, or unable to attempt either.

Antabuse can help some people who do not mind the idea of a medication that will cause acute physical discomfort on taking a drink. The alcoholic makes his decision about drinking in the morning when he takes his daily pill of antabuse. If he has a drink within three or five days he will have an unpleasant physical reaction, so that the idea of what will happen is intended as a deterrent to the idea of the potential pleasure of drinking. Antabuse is not in any way a cure. It has to be used carefully under a doctor's observation, and it in no way keeps the alcoholic from going back to drinking if nothing has changed in his motivation or in his life while he is taking it. However, it is a crutch to some while they are getting help of other kinds.

Doctors are in some agreement about physical disturbance

leading to propensity to alcoholism, but they don't understand just what it is. It is likely to be some kind of chemical or metabolic reaction, just as occurs in some kinds of what are called emotional illnesses. A former alcoholic now permanently on the wagon said that it is helpful for the person who lives with alcoholics to believe that "there is a sound physiological reason for my attempting to solve my problems through alcohol, for my inability to cope with my liquor, and my former inability to cope with my life without it."

You may be living with a person who says that he really does want to dry out, but is afraid to go into a hospital. Are there any ways that you can help him at home, assuming that is his decision and not one you have foisted on him through pressure?

You can see that he gets through the first day of drying out by being especially supportive. It is helpful to suggest that he shower and put on his most comfortable, clean and casual clothes. If the alcoholic in your family is a woman it is good for her initially to pay some attention to appearance. If dressing is usually interspersed with sips from a bottle, then suggest that the person sit down regularly and sip fruit juice, coffee, or water. These won't help the feeling, but they will help pass the time. If these liquids are taken in small quantities, a sip or so at a time, the stomach is not as likely to be upset. It is important to encourage the person to eat some solid food as the first step in changing the intake pattern, but this may take time.

If the person cannot cope with either dressing or eating after the first day, then he really needs to be hospitalized. While you are waiting you can help him relax by letting out his feelings with you as a concerned but not anxious listener. Let him yell if it hurts, or withdraw if this seems necessary. Try to avoid conflict and argument with him, but help him express his anger freely without feeling guilt.

Encourage him not to do anything that will put too much of a strain on him. Physical activity can help—buying a box of soft drinks, candy bars, and other items to stash away for that terrible moment in the middle of the night when an urge to drink comes over him.

Bear in mind that when the person who is trying to get on

the wagon becomes anxious about being able to really stay off booze, the best thing you can do is help him get interested and involved in something else for the next little while. Rather than worrying about futures, assure him that he should only think of the moment, that the next day, the next week, will take care of itself.

Eating regularly and frequently will help, as will eating sweets. Alcoholics usually can't bear sweets while they're drinking but take to them when on the wagon, for they provide a little of the sugar usually gotten from the liquor. Eventually the need for sweets lessens, but they can really get people over hurdles to begin with.

Help him to be in a position to exercise regularly without overdoing it. Stress or competitive situations should be avoided; we are talking here about the kind of exercise that is fun. See that he rests also, for fatigue is serious for the alcoholic.

Perhaps the most important suggestion for someone who drinks is this: "Practice doing it sober." For instance, if he "has attained a sense of accomplishment by tearing up two tickets to the theatre, hopping on a plane to Nassau or falling into bed with a stranger," let him practice doing each of these things sober. If not, he will drink again in order to get his kicks. The ability to experience failure or lack of skill yet trying again and succeeding is a great freedom from dependence on any substance.

In stressing for so long your role in helping the alcoholic in your family to go on the wagon, we may have neglected a point that has deep implications. For in many cases the drinking will not lessen, except for brief periods when your relative is motivated to get over the worst of his physical symptoms. If you are living with such a person no amount of "household tips" on how to keep him distracted with candy bars will help, for he is not ready to change, doesn't really want to, and may never really want to. If this is your situation the decision is up to you and it is a clear one. Can you "dig" the compulsion to drink in your partner to the point that you can go about your own life without feeling in the midst of tragedy? Can you accept the person with his drinking and the constant tactical problems it poses without provoking guilt, torments, and otherwise attempt to take all the fun (and who are we to deny that in some cases it may truly be fun) out of boozing? If you cannot accept the drinking of a drinking man who shows no inclination on his own to stop, then you cannot accept the man. Stay with him without recrimination, or leave him. Whether husband, wife or parent, your role can be supportive if it is his decision to stop, but it cannot be anything but punitive if you keep trying to remake a person living in the way that is his choice.

Some of the most delightful and talented people have been boozers; whatever their private agonies and hangups, their personalities had areas of sheer delight that must have made it worthwhile to live with them anyhow. Sometimes friends or relatives of a talented alcoholic must stand helplessly by while he goes so far into drinking that his body is destroyed. Such a person was the poet Dylan Thomas, fascinating when drunk as well as sober. It is painful that his brilliance came to such an early end, for his system could no longer take the enormous amounts of liquor poured into it and he died of "massive insult to the brain" while still comparatively young.

Scott Fitzgerald has immortalized the plight of the alcoholic in "Babylon Revisited," a touching yet bitter story of a man's attempt to pull himself out of the liquor haze in which he had lived for years and reclaim his child.

Alcoholism differs in no way from the other kinds of disturbances described in this book. It hits all kinds of people, it has multiple causes, and improvement in the symptoms come from many sources, the main one being a real spontaneous urge on the part of the alcoholic himself to change.

Like the other kinds of disturbances, sometimes it gets better and sometimes it does not, despite all the efforts of the person who lives with the drinker and wishes the difficulty just didn't exist. For families of alcoholics sometimes the person being on the wagon is like being "on the road," it may or may not be temporary, there's no way to be sure where it all will go.

An American folksinger, Buffy St. Marie, after a girlhood of segregation, expresses the limited yet totally worthwhile goal that can be hoped for by anyone tentatively taken back into the mainstream of life:

Don't ask why
don't ask how
don't ask forever.
We'll make a space
in the lives
that we planned
and there we'll stay
until it's time for you to go.

This feeling is the result of many years of experience with one person who was disturbed by his emotions in the way that alcoholics can be. As in all tests of endurance, values accrue, not all of them painful. Out of nature's differences, constitutional weakness, metabolic susceptibility, a certain meaning seems to emerge, sometimes benefiting the patient, sometimes the family, sometimes the community in which they live. A small success or a moment's breakthrough and everybody learns. Communication, won at such cost, opens our eyes to what we take for granted.

Chapter 12
The Mentally Retarded

Mrs. William L. of New York City is the mother of four children. Three of them are in the public school system; one is a retarded child. When Mrs. L. brought Doris for her original diagnosis, hope was held out to her that the child might eventually benefit from the new teaching methods within the city school system and eventually become eligible for a state program run by the Division of Vocational Rehabilitation. "In a sheltered workshop your daughter may be guided to a measure of self help, performing tasks for which she receives some recompense, secure in a feeling that she is a contributing member of her protected community."

Although this prediction proved over-optimistic for Mrs. L.'s daughter, whose defects were too all-inclusive for her to be helped within a public school system, it is one which holds in larger and larger measure for huge numbers of the group known as the mentally retarded. This is particularly so in the last few years; focus on this long-neglected group of children has begun to lead to enlarged and diversified programs within school systems throughout the nation.

For every child like this one there are today ten children like Robert O. of Great Neck, New York, whose diagnosis at three of retardation, educable level, has proved a challenge to the local school system that has been met with more than moderate success. At three Robert's muscular coordination was poor, his gait shambling. He went up and down stairs by putting the same foot forward each time. He knew only three words and had not yet achieved bladder control. Although no one of these characteristics would be considered significant in itself, the sum of them worried Mrs. O., who took Robert to a developmental clinic where careful examination of his general symptoms placed him clearly in the mentally retarded group, prognosis withheld until a later time when a more total assessment could be made of his plus and minus factors.

Eventually Robert was placed in a special class in the public school system in the community where he lived. There are eight children in that class; as the children (all with I.Q.'s of 50 or above) proceed through the elementary school, they are handled as an essentially ungraded class in which individuals are encouraged and diverted into different areas of trainability or educational achievement depending on not only their objective testing but the vital attributes of personality (docility or rebelliousness, friendliness or complicating emotional disturbance). Once in junior high school they are bused to a special class. Into this class are fed educable and trainable retarded children from surrounding areas within a forty-five-minute radius. As these children reach the limit of the schooling deemed suitable for their tailormade programs, the Division of Vocational Rehabilitation steps in, along with other public agencies, to work out sheltered programs that will take in the needs of the "whole" child, vocational, recreational, social, and educational, in a way that is not too far afield from the objective potential of each.

Dr. Milton Aisenson, Long Island pediatrician, points out that for every Robert O. maintained at home, either in the public school system or in private schools, there are hundreds more in small or large institutions where schooling is equally vital.

Parents of mentally retarded children who place them in institutions usually do so with a familial heartbreak equal to the pain and exhaustion of parents of seriously emotionally disturbed youngsters who make the decision for the same reasons, to protect the normality of other children in the family or simply to improve the prospects for learning in the handicapped child. Public schools are run in such diverse public institutions as Willowbrook on Staten Island, Letchworth Village in New York State, New York State Psychiatric Institute, and many residential centers throughout the country. Some of them maintain short term diagnostic centers; some of them facilities for education and training; others are lifetime residences where the mentally retarded are given an environment in which, ideally, other secondary difficulties such as emotional disturbance through undue pressuring are less likely to develop.

Before deciding how best to live with your mentally retarded relative, you need to look at some large questions with an open mind.

What exactly is the clinical concept called retardation? What causes it, and what is the scope of the problem? What kinds of children can be helped within the public school system and what kinds of children are so beyond the reach of book-learning and self-help that public school facilities simply do not have the time or personnel to take them on?

What can parents do to assist teachers in the special training of their handicapped youngsters? And last but clearly not least, when should parents finally accept the fact that their child may not be educable or trainable within the public school system that services their area?

In discussing the clinical aspect of retardation, Dr. Lena Hollingsworth compares mental capacities to looms. These looms are of various degrees of capacity for weaving complex and subtle patterns. A loom of simple capacity can go on as long as it lasts, weaving new patterns but not exceeding a given degree of complexity. The parent or teacher who realizes that on the "loom" which the child obtains through heredity, only *simple* patterns may be woven, is wise.

Doctors today feel that the question of what is retardation can best be answered by the definition and classification recently proposed by the American Association of Mental Deficiency, which states that:

> Mental retardation refers to sub-average general intellectual functioning which originates during the developmental period and is associated with impairment in adaptive behavior.

Important in this kind of definition is the fact that the attributes of mentally retarded persons cannot be reflected by any single kind of classification. Only deficiencies measured in the way the person adapts to real life plus measured intelligence of a certain level can determine retardation.

Mental retardation is not a disease but a group of symptoms which derive from many causes, some inborn, others determined later. For the most part it is shown in the preschool child by a lag in maturing, in the school-age child by a learning disability, and in the adolescent or adult by social inadequacy. In many cases all three areas of impairment are clear, and in all cases there is below-average intellectual functioning.

Stella Slaughter, a former director of the Division of Education of Exceptional Children of the University of Wisconsin, points out that, "It is only when a parent knows something about the degree of retardation of his child that he can wisely plan for his development and progress. For this reason a child suspected of retardation should be given an individual mental test at as early an age as he can respond in enough ways to make results translatable in terms of I.Q." Mrs. Slaughter explains that:

> Children with I.Q.s below 50 may not be expected to achieve any appreciable degree of academic success. However, there are many more mentally retarded children whose I.Q.s exceed 50, than those who fall below. The higher the I.Q. the greater the implied trainability. Most children with I.Q.s of 50 or 55 can eventually learn to read a little. Most with I.Q.s of 70 and 75 may be taught to read as well as the average third

or fourth grader, a few even better. Those between 50 and 75 can manipulate numbers to some extent; the larger proportion of them can learn to write legibly. The relatively more intelligent may acquire more knowledge in the field of social science, providing curricular choices and teaching methods are adapted to their needs.

Although even a conservative estimate identifies over five million retardates in the United States today, it is good to know that the trainable child (I.Q. roughly 30 to 50), excluded from most public schools in recent years, is now being trained in some public school classroom situations.

In looking for a class for your child it is advisable to try to select only one whose diagnosis indicates that his primary handicap is mental retardation at the trainable level. Children with an I.Q. of 30 or under cannot, even under optimum conditions, be helped to achieve even minimum self-care status within the public school system. Such children are treated more kindly by the gentlest, most warmly structured environment possible.

The problems you face with a mentally retarded child are enormous and complicated; however, much can be accomplished in the training and teaching of this member of a psychological "minority" group. As is the case with other minority groups, the mentally retarded are entitled to the aid and special concern of the community. As in all levels of education, the problem of funds is a critical one, and Federal participation is necessary. A pamphlet prepared by the United States Department of Health, Education and Welfare by Michael J. Begab says that:

> In a culture that places a premium on high intelligence, social status and prestige, the retarded child is apt to be regarded as a liability and a potential threat to family goals and aspirations. The disturbed feelings of parents that arise under these circumstances should, in most instances, be looked upon as normal reactions to an intensely frustrating, ego damaging experience. Community and professional understanding of this fact is a first step . . . but it is only a beginning. Unless skilled services are provided before these reactions become crystallized, the social milieu of the

> home will not only fail to promote, but will suppress development.

All this is a rather fancy way of saying that special facilities are of course necessary for our retarded. What few books say, however, and what few professionals have expressed in a way adequate to help families learn to live with their retarded members either in the home or in other situations with continued family contact, is this: parents of a mentally defective child are used to having their reactions scrutinized through a cloudy grey lens by everyone from the neighbors to social workers to the more highly trained professionals with whom they come in contact.

It is terribly easy for someone on the outside looking in to say, "Learn to accept the situation," but if there are other children in the family, there is a permanent tug of war between your urge to help your handicapped child live in the way that promises him the most happiness, and the deep needs of the other children which may be threatened by having the retarded child live at home.

A rare comment on this reality of life is made by Simon Olshansky, who says that:

> Most parents who have a mentally defective child suffer chronic sorrow throughout their lives regardless of whether the child is kept at home or is "put away" . . . many factors such as a parent's personality, ethnic group, religion and social class, influence the intensity of this sorrow. Although chronic sorrow may be experienced by some parents of minimally retarded children, this reaction is probably more clearly universal among parents whose children are severely or moderately retarded. The helping professions have somewhat belabored the tendency of the parent to deny the reality of his child's mental deficiency. Few workers have reported what is probably a more frequent occurrence, the parent's tendency to deny his chronic sorrow. This tendency is often reinforced by the professional helper's habit of viewing chronic sorrow as a *neurotic manifestation rather than as a natural and understandable response to a tragic fact.* All the parental reactions reported

in the literature, such as guilt, shame, and anger, may well be intertwined with chronic sorrow. Moreover, a parent's experiencing chronic sorrow does not preclude his deriving satisfaction and joy from his child's modest achievements in growth and development. . . .

When the parent is asked to "accept" mental deficiency, it is not clear just what he is being asked to do. The great stress professional workers tend to place on "acceptance" may suggest to the parent that he is expected to perceive his child from the point of view of the professional helper. This expectation may make him both resentful and resistant. . . . We have seen relatively few parents who did not recover enough, after the initial shock of discovery, to mobilize their efforts in behalf of the child. It is understandable that some parents move slowly and erratically toward recognition of the mental defect and toward meeting the child's special needs. Some of them even "regress" to the point of denying, at certain times, the reality of the child's defectiveness. On other occasions they become unduly optimistic about the child's potentialities. In our view, such regression may help the parent to tolerate better the terrible reality that confronts him each day.

Why does the professional worker become so impatient with the parent's slowness or occasional regression and why does he feel such a great sense of urgency to do something about it? After all, the parent has a lifetime in which to learn to deal with the needs and problems of a mentally defective child. In most cases one can ask what will be lost if the parent is unable for several years to view his child as mentally defective. . . .

Although chronic sorrow is *a natural, rather than a neurotic,* response to a tragic fact, some parents do respond neurotically to their child's handicap and may require treatment for their neurosis. Judging from our experience, however, the number of neurotic parents is small. It is regrettable that this small number of people has received so much professional attention that the tragedy of having a mentally defective child has been viewed less as a tragedy than as a psychiatric problem.

How can you deal with this grief reaction in a way that does not deny it, yet allows you to live with your problem in as cheerful a way as is possible?

The suggestions for dealing with emotionally disturbed parents of mentally ill children in Chapter 5 apply here also, yet there is a difference. The disturbed child can, except in certain cases of extreme psychosis, often outgrow his difficulties. Many kinds of emotional disorder in children are curable, many are temporary. The retarded child will become a retarded adolescent and a retarded adult, with a strong degree of predictability as to his lifelong capabilities and inadequacies. Your adjustment must be based not on hope for a changing situation, but on whatever alternative happiness areas can be nourished in your own lives, and the fullest exploitation of them possible.

Robert O.'s mother and father take some comfort in the fact that their son has been appraised as only mildly to moderately retarded, so that when he completes the schooling the county provides, the Division of Vocational Rehabilitation will be able to train him in electronics assembly and tool repair. After his training he will go into a sheltered workshop such as provided by Altro Health and Rehabilitation Services or, hopefully, be able to hold a minimum job in a small place run by an informed employer.

Doris L.'s mother and father can hold no such hope for their daughter. As the severity of her retardation began to show itself, they realized that her greatest goal would have to be self-help in her bodily needs and assistance in such simple tasks as dusting and sweeping at home. They take their comfort in knowing that her kind of difficulty is not expressed through anger, discontent, or destructive acts, and base their decision to keep her at home on these individual matters.

For both sets of parents, satisfaction and pleasure are most likely to be found in areas of activity outside the situation of their retarded children. If you have the lifelong responsibility of living with or providing for a retarded person, it is absolutely vital to divert a large measure of attention from the problem to some sort of self-expression, through work, social contacts, recreation, community interests, or other meaningful personal relationships, so that a somewhat smaller proportion of yourself is invested in the retarded person. If this sounds harsh, remember that in many cases a merciful situation prevails in that the most severely retarded often have little awareness of the extent of their handicap. You cannot justify neglect of human beings constitutionally damaged, but neither can you justify neglect of yourself to the point of a strained marriage, and other children who can be permanently injured by an over-investment of time, energy and worry in the retarded family member.

Bernard Barber and William Jenne have looked into some of what happens to the brothers and sisters of retarded children. In this investigation "83 boys and girls, aged 10–16, with a retarded sibling at home were asked to rank a series of life goals in terms of the importance of these goals to them. Mothers of the normal siblings provided information regarding frequency of interaction with the retarded child. Many siblings ranked devotion to a worthwhile cause and making a contribution to mankind as high. Perhaps feeling that they are serving a welfare function in the family provided the frequent interacters with motivation to achieve in a welfare profession. Frequent-interacting boys placed greater emphasis than non-interacting boys on success in business. For girls, however, the frequent interacters were less interested in success in business.

This study suggested that the sustained interaction with the retarded sibling came to be regarded as a duty by the normal siblings. In the performance of this duty, the normal sibling turned his life career toward the improvement of mankind or at least toward the achievement of goals which would require much dedication and sacrifice. Unlike the children who maintained sustained interaction with their siblings, however, the non-interactors were much more concerned with the life goals involving interpersonal relations.

The question of which retarded children and adults should continue to live at home and which should be placed in a special facility or institution is not simple. A reporter on a daily newspaper says that, "My parents kept my retarded brother at home until he was eighteen. I was ashamed to bring home friends; his habits were frightening as well as embarrassing, and they pressured him to achieve in a way that must have been agonizing for him as well as for me. My adolescence was colored by a feeling of tension and despite much later therapy I never became easy enough with men to contemplate marriage."

Important in such decisions is the kind of personality of your retarded family member. Is he or she pleasant, gentle and docile, or chronically upset, discontent with existing activity? Is he or she able to toilet and at least partially dress and feed himself, so that the sheer physical labor of caring for a person who grows larger and larger but remains a physically helpless infant is not a totally depressing physical drain on the rest of the family? Are the other children in the family secure enough in their own relationships not to be scared away from making friends by "shame" over the retarded person? Are you able to accept the presence of a retarded child or adult without constantly berating yourself for imagined guilt, or expending enormous energy in a heroic but usually doomed effort to remedy what nature did not provide?

All of these questions cannot be answered immediately. Some of them take time, sometimes the personality of an infant (though the actual diagnosis of retardation has been made) is not clear enough to assess either the positives or negatives. Often you cannot tell what the child is capable of until he has given it a try. Timing is also an individual matter; you should get all the help available from facilities listed in the back of this book.

It should be reassuring to know that "it has been reliably estimated that over 85 percent of mental retardation in this country is non-hereditary and that if every person with an intelligence quotient below 80 were prevented from having children, there would be no appreciable decrease of mental deficiency in future generations. Mental retardates who have demonstrated economic competence and social responsibility therefore have every right to marry and have progeny unless, in special cases, a geneticist finds adequate reasons to the contrary."

Sometimes you will find that a child first diagnosed as retarded is not really so, but this is the exception and often even when a later description of pseudo-retardation is given, for all practical purposes the problem remains much the same.

George Kisker points out that "the focusing of attention on

mental retardation has helped to correct a number of popular misconceptions. One is that true retardation is a mental disease and can be cured like many mental diseases. . . . Another is that such people are a menace and should be kept in institutions, that they are unteachable and a complete loss to society, and that they are readily recognizable."

If your child is not amenable to an education, there is a wide area of vocational training—even training for simple tasks—which some special public school programs have undertaken. Essentially he must be treated with special care and sensitivity. But that substantial educational progress *can* be made has been pointed out by numerous authors, medical people, and educators.

According to Max L. Hutt and Robert G. Gibby:

> The experience of the past decade has clearly revealed the fact that the retarded child can profit from any school experiences, provided they are adapted to his needs. There has been a decided increase in the instructional facilities available; in particular the number of special classes in public schools has shown a substantial growth. Due to the fact that the retarded child is usually "lost" in the regular class, it has been found necessary to establish special provisions for his educational care—to establish so-called "special classes" in which his needs are more adequately met.

Present ideas in teaching the mentally retarded have an interesting historical background which you should know. It is important, for many of the older approaches are still employed by different educators in public schools throughout the country. In the nineteenth century there was an emphasis upon improvement of the "imperfect" senses of mentally retarded children's sight, sound, touch and taste. This was called "the physiological method"; and, as perfected by Edward Sequin, it supplemented sensory training with certain academic skills, such as vocabulary and comprehension—which were usually taught from concrete examples. Maria Montessori, early in the twentieth century, developed a method of teaching the mentally retarded which parallels many present programs. Her approach was similar to her approach as to non-retarded children. She employed an attitude of permissiveness by allowing children to choose their own activity areas along with direction for self-help. John Dewey's theory was grafted onto various teaching programs. His concepts of "learning by doing" and "theme learning" were used, but there was an emphasis upon defects and individual instruction to compensate for these defects.

In the 1930's and '40's there were a number of methods employed, some of which are still used. "Occupational Education" stressed vocational training, guidance, and selective job placement. The method of Martins, Kirk and Johnson, still used today, was based on giving training goaled toward some eventual job that is realistic in view of the retarded person's life situation. It of course takes into consideration individual developmental needs. This program emphasized adjustment and occupational competence, integrating the retarded with "normal" children in non-academic activities.

More recently a program has been developed which combines a number of these techniques. The emphasis upon *training* includes development of self-help, social motor, academic, vocational and recreational skills. A sheltered school environment was used, with a curriculum geared toward the demands of ordinary living, and academic work was based on the concept of "learning for *survival* purposes." Among the important goals which this technique tried for were sensory improvements, cooperative behavior, future adjustment within a sheltered environment and limited employment.

On the elementary school level, a number of different approaches are currently employed in public elementary schools for educable mentally retarded children. These include the following:

Homogeneous Special Class: This type is for children with a narrow I.Q. range and some degree of integration with regular class students in general activities.

Heterogeneous Special Class: There is wide age and I.Q. range in this type. The program, usually of a highly segregated nature, is dependent upon the skill of the teacher for effectiveness. This program is usually organized in small school systems and the class size consists of about fifteen pupils.

"Two Track" Homogeneous Class: At each level classes are organized for upper-level educables (I.Q.'s 65–80) and lower-level educables (50–65). Limited to large, city school systems with many children in special classes.

The Special School: Children are transported to a center school for the mentally retarded, usually operated in large cities, or on a county level.

Other plans are: 1) Placement of the mentally retarded in small classes for regular students, with small teacher-student ratios, and 2) Placement of the mentally retarded in a special class for part of the day, and in a regular class for the rest of the day.

The type of public school program employed by a particular school depends upon the size of the facility, available funds, number and type (I.Q. range) of mentally retarded children in that or surrounding districts, and availability of qualified teachers. The curriculum used depends largely upon the type of program employed, and the orientation of the administrators responsible for program planning.

Although it is hard to reach conclusions dealing with the question of special versus regular classes for mentally retarded children, some studies are informative.

Kirk, in comparing the results of many such studies, listed a number of tentative conclusions. He found that there were no significant benefits from special-class programs for trainable mentally retarded children (I.Q.'s below 50), which were for the most part hastily conceived with a staff which had little prior training, but that education could have a positive effect upon intellectual growth of educable mentally retarded children. He found also that mentally retarded children generally read below their own mental-age-reading-grade expectancy, do better in arithmetic reasoning, learn at a much slower rate (than normals) in the areas of art and music, and, finally, are inferior to normal children in non-intellectual ability (possibly contradicting Sequin's early emphasis on the "physiological method" of training).

The overall effectiveness of a public school program for your retarded child depends upon such factors as sufficient funds, creative programming, sensitive and well-trained teachers, and the "knack" of exploring the full potential of the child. But whatever the measuring rod used, there have been positive results reported from various public schools throughout the country. Gerhart Saenger, in a follow-up study of a large number of pupils who had attended special classes for I.Q.'s between 40 and 50, found that two-thirds of the former pupils were living in the community, only 26 percent were institutionalized, 27 percent of those in the community worked for pay, and an additional 9 percent who had no job had formerly been employed.

Picking a school is not always a matter of free choice. In many cases you are lucky if there is any facility available at all, but where you *do* have a choice remember that essential personal characteristics for teachers of the mentally retarded should include genuine interest, "a high level of acceptance of the limited capacities of mentally retarded children to conform to the educational and social standards set by the school and community; intellectual curiosity about the learning characteristics of the mentally retarded; historical insight into the pioneer teaching techniques; a knowledge of organizations, associations, and community and Federal programs for the mentally retarded."

Look for teachers who can understand the characteristics of the mentally retarded child and his place in society; who can develop a *fundamental* curriculum through relating the broad personal and social needs of the mentally retarded; understand and apply pedagogical procedures based on an understanding of the known learning characteristics of the mentally retarded; and select, develop and use appropriate instructional materials and equipment in teaching mentally retarded children.

In living with a retarded person you are faced with the inescapable fact that disruption of the orderly learning process is one of the most serious disabilities that exists. Your relative's trouble may be *primary;* that is, there exists a specific learning disability. Or it may be *secondary* in that the disability is associated with a neurotic or psychotic disorder. There has been a new surge of interest and work on primary disabilities. In 1961 the President's Panel on Mental Retardation was set up and 1956 to 1963 saw a long-term project in operation by the American Association on Mental Deficiency. This project concluded that "most of the mental disorders that affect normally intelligent people may also affect the mentally retarded. Thus, the mentally retarded sometimes have acute transitory psychotic attacks, with episodes of excitement, depression, paranoid trends, or hallucinatory experiences. Such events are often brought on by life situations and are therefore often preventable and treatable."

In cases of mild retardation secondary to brain changes, it is possible to increase social capacity. Offering your relative affection, security, social recognition, achievement, and new experience is of great importance. Many retarded persons are more incapacitated by their emotional difficulties than by their intellectual impairments. The social training of the trainable retarded is of immense importance and is as significant as is educational training of whatever abilities and aptitudes they may happen to have. According to present estimates, 50 percent of those admitted to state schools can be returned to the community socially improved and sometimes ready to take on gainful employment. The problem of the treatment of the severely retarded, on the other hand, consists largely of physical care and custody, with simple training in self-help, if possible, and self-protection.

All this may be slim comfort to you who have faced the harsh admission that your child is retarded, and who want to try to keep him home. Although new methods of preventing some of these difficulties are at hand (a nutritional defect correctable by early diet has already been found to cause one form of retardation), there are still huge unexplained areas, and your doctor may have already said, "Expectations are futile; give up!"

Maximum acceptance of a birth defect or congenital condition is more likely when the child is less aware of his own problem. In such cases the logical decision is often to institutionalize for the sake of the other children, yourself and the child's own benefit. In other instances you may have a child who is close enough to normal intelligence to be painfully aware that he doesn't quite make it, that something about him is different from other children. This awareness is fraught with pain, for you and for him. You must learn to at least swallow the fact that in some ways your retarded child will, if he stays at home, still sometimes be scapegoated by other children, will always limp along behind, and will need constant props from you not to develop behavior disturbances on top of his retardation. Pity may color your judgment, especially when the child seems to identify so readily with characters like Anderson's Ugly Duckling who thought he "would have been thankful if only the ducks would have tolerated him among them—the poor ugly creature!" You can find it easier to live with this if you do not give way to totally unrealistic hopes but learn to take pleasure in the most minute of achievements.

You should be aware of the difference between mental retardation and mental deficiency. Usually mental "deficiency" refers to conditions in which there has been organic impairment or destruction of brain tissue, causing a true deficiency in quantity or quality of the brain cells which perform the usual functions of intelligence. These are essentially incurable. Mental "retardation" is a condition in which the total functioning of the mind is impaired, regardless of the cause. Social, economic, and cultural factors may be responsible for mental retardation as frequently as the better known biologic changes resulting from birth injury, prematurity, or metabolic disorders. Theoretically at least, the use of the term *mental retardation* implies that if the cause or causes can be found and suitable corrective measures applied, the degree of mental retardation can be lessened or some intellectual function return. So far, the factual picture is rarely that hopeful.

You may find it easier to accept raising a retarded child by applying to an organization for financial aid. In New York State, for example, two thousand dollars a year is available for private education of handicapped children, including those with emotional disturbance without physical problems. These funds are unrelated to family income and can help provide the child with special schooling which might otherwise be too expensive. To get information as to whether special funds exist in your own state, write directly to the superintendent of schools in your immediate area, asking for a referral. In cases where special public school classes do not exist, there is usually some provision for aid to parents in placing their child in a private facility, residential or day. Information concerning application for special help in the different states can be found at the end of this book.

You shouldn't decide to place a retarded charge in an institution without a conference with his doctor about all the questions involved. Separation may be easier to accept if you come to the conclusion that the difficulties at home are insurmountable; feelings of the other children, conflict between parents, inadequate help, your own state of mind. Although some experts advise that "the child should be kept in his own home unless serious family problems result from his presence," you cannot always do the impossible. It may help to accept his presence for the first years to know that "the better the care a retarded child has had in his own home in the early years the more likely it will be that he will be able to make a satisfactory adjustment in an institution if and when it becomes necessary. Emotional support and careful attention in infancy will be many times more effective than the same amount of effort would be in later years."

Parents of seriously retarded children can benefit greatly from the advice of artist Anita Steckel, mother of Dinah, now ten years old and seriously retarded and suffering from the not uncommon secondary condition of epilepsy. Ms. Steckel, whose daughter is being treated at Letchworth Village in New York, offers guidlines that may ease some of your pain if your child is being helped in an institution.

Ms. Steckel suggests that the most important thing for parents is to understand what, for their child, is a happy experience and learn to take pleasure in their child's pleasures. "Dinah throws kisses as I taught her long ago, and loves to 'kiss kiss' from a distance. She also kisses parts of the car or a magazine and makes the sound of kissing to people we pass on the road. Some people might see this as very sad, but it is not. It is wonderful because it shows her ability to find pleasure and affection in things and people she doesn't 'know.' It's wonderful that she can find joy in all these things.

"Another important fact to recognize is how your child's limitations release him or her from the usual growing pains of anxiety, frustration, aspiration, fear of failure and other fears. It is important to understand that your pain has nothing at all to do with your seriously retarded child's pain. When you can begin to understand that his pain is quite different from yours, that his little pleasures have nothing to do with what would give you pleasure, then there is a chance for you to accept your differences and diminish some of your pain caused by your comparisons with normality."

Do realize that your seriously retarded child's awareness

and memories are different from yours. "He does not know the meaning of such a complex thought as parent, sister, friend, so he does not feel deprived of what he cannot comprehend. The seriously retarded can therefore share affection easily, and attachments develop miraculously for those who are close at the time." Says Ms. Steckel, "Parents can be released from the terrifying fear that their retarded child (young or old) will wake in the night crying for them. Holidays such as Christmas and Thanksgiving cannot have the same meaning for your retarded child as they do for you. Remember this when you feel too much pain on those special days to visit your child."

Ms. Steckel adds, "My child likes to turn pages of magazines, but, feeling no need to identify pictures in them, she is as content to see the magazine upside down as right side up at this point. And she is exactly as happy turning the pages of a financial report or a news magazine as a 'gloriously illustrated' children's book. Once I realized this simple fact, I knew I didn't have to give one damn what 'other people' thought I *should* bring my daughter.

"You must learn to give up the usual parent ego and remember that when your child is in a home with others like him, protected from outside pressures and cruelties, with care and medical aid always available, he is receiving your devotion just as much as Mrs. Brown's child down the street.

"Some terrors of parents are real; for example, that your child is being neglected in an understaffed facility." Ms. Steckel urges such parents to write, call, and pressure all in power to grant more money for the best quality staff and treatment facilities for retardates. "Facilities should be continually checked to make sure the quality of care has not deteriorated, and that even after the death of individual parents the community will be parents to all our children.

"I saw two gentle smiling elderly retarded women swinging linked arms, walked along in a row with others to the dinner hall. Obviously together for quite a while, they were cheerful buddies. One dropped the other's hand and walked away a few yards while the other stopped and stared, curious at the interruption, as was I. Then we both smiled as we saw her kick an apple on the ground playfully as though it were a ball, just for fun, with great glee on her face. She then rejoined her friend and, swinging arms again, they continued down the road to dinner. Nothing I alone with my 'fat parent ego' could have given her would in any way have approached what the people at this institution have done for Dinah," continues Anita Steckel. "Of course you should not give up all ego simply because so much giving up as a parent has been called for in your case. Learn that you and your child are not one and you will have a chance to survive the pain. Try to be able to live full lives within your separate limits, secure among your different set of peers. I know my daughter will be one of the two who pulls away to kick the apple someday and rejoin her friend on her walk to the dinner hall, and I am content that she will know such joyful moments even as I feel the pain."

Through expressing rather than denying pain, you should try to find out exactly what potential the future holds for the child, bearing in mind that "properly treated, most persons who are only moderately retarded are capable of living reasonably happy lives. . . . The way a retarded child is treated may make all the difference between his being a complete drain on the emotional and financial resources of a family or community or being able to support himself with corresponding feelings of usefulness and satisfaction."

It isn't so many years ago that the attitude of many people to the mentally retarded was that expressed by William Faulkner in *The Sound and the Fury* when he wrote about a crowd that gathered about the severely retarded middle-aged "child" Benjamin Compson:

> "I bet you won't go up and tech him."
> "How come I won't?"
> "I bet you won't. I bet you skeered to."
> "He won't hurt folks. He jes a loony."
> "How come a loony won't hurt folks?"
> "Dat he won't. I teched him."
> "I bet you won't now."
> "Case Miss Dilsey's lookin."
> "You won't no ways."
> "He don't hurt folks. He jes a loony."

Perhaps, along with the lifelong sadness of living with a retarded member of your family, you can help yourselves as well as them by knowing that in most cases this attitude has changed, that among adults of sensitivity or awareness retardation no longer carries the old terrifying mocking connotations. Even more important, you can find some peace by seeing that some of his reactions are determined not by the way *you* would feel knowing your life was constricted, but by *his* actual feelings, which may be a kind of happiness, interest, or simple pleasure suitable to his mental age. When your demands do not exceed his reality, perhaps you can rejoice with him over the sight of a kitten, the taste of sweetened oatmeal, the sound of an airplane, or any pleasure at all that he perceives.

Chapter 13

Let My People Go: Caring for the Emotionally Disturbed at Home and in the Community

During the last fifty years the population of this country has doubled while the population of public mental hospitals has quadrupled. In 1966 an estimated twenty million Americans suffered from some form of mental illness, and as things stand now it is likely that one person in twelve will be hospitalized at some time during his life for a disturbance of this kind.

Remedying this situation by psychiatric care alone is like watering the lawn with a teacup. Despite heroic efforts on the part of the nation's 25,000 psychiatrists, and other professionally trained mental health workers, many hospitalized patients are still doomed to live out a segregated life with little active treatment. All our "advanced thinking" cannot provide—at least in the next twenty years—the personnel needed. For this reason alone thousands are deprived, by long-term institutionalization, of even the pleasures which might remain "around their illness." It is as tragic as it is ironic that lots of them aren't even getting the treatment that might justify this deprivation.

The advent of the tranquilizing drugs began to reverse the trend in 1959, but they haven't helped enough. There is only one way to send men, women, or children back to their families and communities. Not with faith that all their pain will ease, that the blind will lead the blind, but with knowledge of what to expect, both the limits and the positive side of their "difference." This knowledge must be carefully and responsibly diagnosed, widely distributed, and deeply felt.

People help people, and people hurt people. People with minor illnesses can live with people with little tolerance and it can be destructive. People with major illness can live with people who have been guided to real understanding of what it's all about, and it can be tolerable, and helpful.

Nobody can live with emotional disturbance without a stab of pain for the waste of it, the patient not able to "have fun" or "feel for others" or "do something well and feel content in the doing." Historically, the emotionally disturbed wear a crown of thorns; to those luckier people it seems as though they will sting on contact, or that their illness is contagious.

None of this is easy to put out of our minds, but when we understand the real nature of emotional disturbance we begin to see that not only is it practically necessary in this time of hospital shortage that as few people as possible be locked away, but that constructive steps toward their return are desirable. For them, for us, for the psychiatrists, and for our future, there are agonizing drawbacks to two worlds, one of "health" and the other of "disease," separated by high brick walls.

More patients will have to be cared for at home and more *should* be. Training is needed on three fronts: the family or community in which the patient is to live, the professional person needed to supervise this "return," and the patient himself.

Sometimes what *has* to be turns out to have an odd value. It should be a last resort to send our sick away. Most mental hospitals do the best they can with what they've got. In the best of them treatment is vigorous. All mental hospitals suffer from disadvantages that are bigger than money problems or personnel problems. They are "removed," they are "away" and they are "out." In-patients are often out-people, and if you have watched a husband, wife, parent, or child try to take the few steps back over that creaky rope ladder to home, you know what a delicate matter it is to weigh the advantages of sending your sick for help at a distance, against the abrasions of return. Emotionally disturbed people are "out of step." Write them out of the group with a program note to oneself to "think about it again next year—or in two—or five years" and you've got the kind of exclusion clause that might pertain to things but surely not to people. A book called *Asylums* by Erving Goffman gives you some idea of the problems involved.

There are situations with no alternatives to removal, such as acts of destruction against society or self. There are times when the nature of "home" is so hurting that the patient would be happier and safer in a mud bog under shell fire. But these are extremes.

Here is a huge hospital, away in the distance, taking a lot of time to visit, its patients as socially removed from the community it serves as a bellhop from an executive, a laundress from a college dean. Often it isn't even attached to one community since its special purpose is more expensive than one community can support. There live the patients, exposed to care which is excellent, mediocre, or dreadful. Already deprived by illness, they can be deprived further, for when in Rome they act like the Romans, but what is learned in "Central Painful" State Hospital may not reflect the values and attitudes with which they must cope when they return.

Anybody who breathes a sigh of relief when the mentally ill go marching off for "help" is just plain shortsighted. Those who are left become as deprived as those who go.

Child psychiatrist Dr. Sol Nichtern has pointed out what happens when you eliminate population extremes: a kind of creeping conformity in which everyone gets the idea that exclusion is the way to solve problems. The community takes on a new and narrower image, and the cxtremes of this image become the new oddballs, the next batch of "deviates." Then if a budget gets tightened, schools are overcrowded, these new extremes may be handled by shipping them out. The community becomes like an old maid set in her ways, bigoted, supersensitive to any deviation at all.

And what of the patient himself, sent into a situation in which there are fewer people to care for him than at home? One serious problem long-term institutional care creates is the habit of dependence on an authority. Though the institution when used appropriately can provide structured living for unstructured people and interrupt unhealthy reactions between the patient and family, it presents as many difficulties as it solves. One is the separation of the family from the problems of the patient, eliminating the need for you to help solve these problems. Once the person is removed, the family restructures itself and develops new patterns. Having adapted itself to a balance which is free of his problem, it may then be unable to adjust to the person who has changed. In other instances elimination of the patient permits the sick areas within the family to remain untouched. Sometimes keeping him within the family during treatment changes the whole relationship.

Disturbed people need to be treated, and ideally it is the right of every person with an emotional disturbance to get help. This can be psychotherapy, drugs, other therapy, anything that will keep him as comfortable and safe as possible while he goes through his trip.

This isn't always possible in hospitals, either because of doctor shortage, money shortage, or because the cause of the problem isn't clearly understood.

In trying to figure out how to cope with emotional disturbance, you cannot afford to neglect as a source of help the only group of which there is no shortage at all, families. There are enough families to go around—every sick person came from one. To consider families only as a possible cause of illness and not as a possible source of strength is like hunting for your glasses when they're on your nose. Families, like *all* volunteer mental health personnel, also need training, supervision, and controls. It isn't easy, especially since some of the chief reasons for wanting to send such members "away" are lack of communication, ignorance and shame. Living with a diabetic is acceptable to the community. He needs daily insulin; he is on a special diet: this can be described to neighbors with no trouble at all.

Few of the symptoms, restrictions, and treatment needed for the disturbed person, however, can be communicated to friends and neighbors without tension and stigma. Until this is overcome the job of living with emotional illness becomes a double one, caring for the patient and concealing his illness. That is why it seems so difficult to live with these difficulties.

Dr. Lewis Robbins says that it "is hard to distinguish sometimes between sick and obnoxious behavior. There is a big difference if someone is blind or physically crippled; he is not usually held responsible and elicits sympathy. . . . Each of us modifies his patterns of reactions and doesn't just give expression to them. Some of the symptoms of emotional illness are socially unacceptable, but there's more to it than that. Each of us has to control himself, and we are inclined to resent the person who doesn't. Tolerance doesn't yet exist when mental illness is concerned."

Despite these "islands" of unmentionable problems, the idea of doing the best we can at home should be considered. Recent revolutionary legislation has restored many of the civil rights of the emotionally disturbed, proper public information will help reduce the stigma, and a brave knowledgeable attitude on the part of families may prove to help the most.

We have surely made some progress since Freud introduced the idea that in these conditions there was no single end point or single beginning. This idea has led to something called community psychiatry where the ill are not socially segregated at all. According to this concept, psychiatric service, like medical service, is a privilege that we are all entitled to secure in the community.

Nobody knows how to live with emotional disturbance in *general;* even the most highly trained will find themselves drawn toward one type of manifestation, repelled by another. There are no rules that apply to all cases, and though you have to accept the classifications necessary for purposes of making what generalities *can* be made, not many *should* be. Causes vary, cases vary, symptoms vary, which makes it vital that the layman searching this book for guidelines not play, or be tempted to play, "doctor." "Nurse" is something else, and as you proceed from day to day, bear in mind your own limits.

An unorthodox yet helpful account of how one concerned parent attempted to communicate with a family member who had been diagnosed as chronic schizophrenic is recorded here as an example of the lengths to which a caretaking person may go in trying to establish better contact with her relative. Jean R., mother of a son who has presented problems literally from infancy, visited several people who had been on the staff of R. D. Laing's Kingsley Hall residence in London. At their suggestion she took seven LSD trips, all problem solving, all having elements of fright and danger, all having positive results that she later tried to reinforce with action so that they didn't fade away, and all contributing enormously to her knowledge of how to live with people who have symptoms which are labeled "crazy."

In describing the experience, Mrs. R. stated that she took LSD as a calculated risk for a special reason and felt that she was lucky. Most instructions for taking LSD with less hazard mention the importance of setting, having as a guide a person who can successfully negotiate and describe reality during the trip. They also mention the desirability of having only a few trusted people around, staying in a familiar or safe environment and staying away from situations which may be complicated or problematic.

During the first trip Mrs. R. experienced the familiar distortions of time, space, senses and body boundaries that resemble those distortions described by "schizophrenics" or "hysterics" or "paranoids." The trip helped her to better communicate with the person she chose as guide, a young man labeled as psychotic. Knowing that she was experiencing some of the sensations he lived with most of the time, and that she did this by choice because there were pleasant positive aspects to the experience, filled him with hopefulness about the possibility of his being acceptable *as he was.*

To accept the experience and the feelings, to let the emotionally disturbed person go through his "trip" with warm reassurance that the frightening part will pass, to make the mild supportive comment to focus attention on something else when the pain is too bad, is the role you can assume, whether or not you are a family member or friend of the disturbed person.

This is not to advocate an LSD trip as a way to cure all, cure part, or offer great insights. It is possibly dangerous and it might be fruitless. But it is one, if risky, way to remain open to better understanding of what emotional disturbance really involves.

When Bruno Bettelheim wrote as the title of his study of delinquents "Love is Not Enough," he used a word that has all but lost its common meaning. Sick, entwined, parasitic love is not enough; misplaced fearful permissiveness is not enough. Even mature, healthy love is sometimes not enough, as in cases of brain injury. Psychoses exist that can only be described as "of unknown cause," and sometimes socially damaging forces are so strong that one person's love is like a light sweater in a snowstorm. But *real* love, though it may not be enough, is often all the patient has. Therefore your concern, if guided toward the same goals as those of trained objective strangers, can be of enormous help.

A recent paper prepared by the American Psychiatric Association bears the alarming title "The Crisis in Mental Health Manpower." Apart from recommendations as to how to secure needed workers in the four core disciplines of psychiatry, psychology, social work and nursing, this White Paper states that "all in all, as the efforts to maintain patients in the community increase, the need increases for personnel other than in the core disciplines to participate in the care and rehabilitation of patients. . . . It may be that in time, under the pressures of the community mental health program, a wholly new kind of 'mental health technician' may evolve, competent to perform many kinds of operating tasks formerly performed by only the core professionals.

". . . One must also cast a plea for immediate action in the context of emerging needs and pressures on the four core disciplines to play administrative, leadership, and consultant roles in a vast range of new programs to meet social needs.

"There is the continuing program of how to supply services to citizens in sparsely populated states, Alaska, for example. Here again one must look to general practitioners, public health nurses, and many other persons to do the job in isolated communities. But the latter must have training, orientation and leadership and the resources of a central organization staffed by the four core disciplines if an adequate job is to be done and standards maintained."

The emergency measures suggested for Alaska may be the measures that are needed even in states where the highest concentration of psychiatrists is still inadequate to meet the needs of sick people. Every family is like an Alaskan family, remote, caught in a frozen sweep of ice when emotional disturbance strikes. Help may exist thirty miles from your house, but that thirty miles is enough to take that member who is ill out of your life and into a new one from which he may eventually be ejected, his manner stiff and rigid, not sure anymore what is his world. Help may exist five minutes away but you may be unable to afford it. Help in the form of trained psychiatric personnel may simply not be available at all. There is only one answer to the agonizing doctor shortage and that is training families. You are motivated to learn, just like the Alaskans, for your stake is great: the sick people are your own.

The Joint Commission on Chronic Illness in the United States published a study on *Care of the Long Term Patient,* in which many of the recommendations made are similar to the kind of program described in this book. Although it was prepared with the thought of chronic illness of *all* types, the principles described make clear sense in reference to the emotionally disturbed.

Most long-term patients can best be cared for at home during much of their illness and prefer care in that setting under supervision of their personal physician. In spite of this, community planning continues to underemphasize such care. Comparatively little effort has been made to organize and provide the means whereby physicians can obtain for their patients the variety of services required to meet the needs of long-term illness.

It is important that the patient's personal physician participate as continuously as possible in the medical care of each patient at all stages of illness. The physician determines the nature, time, and place for the patient's diagnostic work-up and therapeutic services. Physicians, therefore, must equip themselves with knowledge of new methods of treating long-term illness, learn to use other health professions in care of the patient, and become familiar with community resources that offer the various services the patient may require.

Planning to improve care of the long-term patient at home should be part of a community's general health care programs. Such planning must take into account the fact that for some patients care at home may precede, follow, or be interspersed with care in a hospital or other institution.

If, as is generally agreed, "the number of emotionally disturbed people in a community is so large that specialists can solve but a small proportion of the problems," then the time to help train families is now! Here are some areas in which families need help toward providing better home care for patients:

Ability to accept the patient's limitations.

Recognition and acceptance of a reasonable amount of expression of resentment.

Recognition that the patient has capacity for growth even within limited areas.

Ingenuity in providing activity through which the patient may constructively redirect his aggressive tendencies.

Ability to set reasonable limits for patients when indicated.

Ability to derive some satisfaction from helping the patient.

Ability to regard the patient as an individual with potentialities rather than regarding him in terms of a stereotyped concept of mental illness.

Ability to provide a supportive, encouraging emotional climate.

Respect and appreciation for a patient's differing concept of reality.

Acceptance of cultural, ethnic, and personality differences.

Ability to recognize the pressures within the patient and symptoms of increasing illness.

Ability to accept the patient's need for privacy and withdrawal.

Sheltered employment, with employers who have special understanding of the needs and capacities of the emotionally disturbed and a sympathetic interest in helping them to reach an optimum personal and work adjustment, should be provided for all patients who have the capability and desire. Adequate, continuing services to the employer and the patient throughout the placement are essential.

For patients living in their own homes, in foster homes, or by themselves, there should be specialized programs of occupational and recreational therapy for those who are unable to use community facilities, or in locations where no such facilities are available.

Other community resources, if they are adequate to meet the needs of all long-term patients, would also go far to meet the needs of the emotionally disturbed in home care. The availability or lack of these services may be the crucial factor in determining whether large numbers of patients can adjust in the community. We know that, if these services are provided by staff with sufficient understanding and skill, the emotionally disturbed can use them well.

Similar understanding is needed in the area of living with mental retardation. It is by now painfully obvious that misconceptions have subjected the mentally deficient to the same unfortunate stigma that the emotionally disturbed have suffered. Only gradually has it been recognized that a majority of the mentally retarded can make a contribution to society.

The facts are these: of the estimated total of 2,400,000 retarded individuals in the United States, about 75 percent are only mildly sub-normal, another 20 percent are moderately so, and only 5 percent are severe cases. This means that most are potentially capable of being taught to make some kind of social adaptation in appropriate circumstances. Many of the mildly handicapped can go further than this, and can be so trained that they can hold useful productive jobs.

Special institutions devote themselves to training, but fall far short of solving the problem. For one thing, institutions must of necessity be used to care for those who will never be able to live in a family or community. In the second place, institutions for the mentally handicapped usually have long waiting lists. Third, the growing realization that many long-term patients do not belong in institutions applies to the mentally handicapped as well as to others who are chronically ill. Ninety percent of the mentally retarded will spend most of their life in the community. By and large they are not getting care or training in any adequate fashion.

Though not all the mentally handicapped in the community are long-term patients, some are. In addition, all of them are subject to the chronic illness that attacks the general population, and physical defects are more than twice as frequent among the mentally deficient as the general population. Clearly intelligent planning for the retarded hinges on an accurate diagnosis of the degree of retardation for each patient. Such diagnosis is the only basis for the making of a plan for medical care; for a decision as to where the mentally handicapped person will live; for a realistic finding as to what kind of training or education will enable the patient to do best.

Unfortunately, too many of our mentally retarded do not have access to correct diagnosis. For many, the only member of the diagnostic team within reach is the physician. The same professional competencies required for a mental health clinic can be useful in diagnosing the mentally handicapped, but as we have seen, many areas are entirely without such clinic services. Even where psychiatrists and clinical psychologists are employed in mental health clinics they are likely to be so pressed by long waiting lists and the needs of the emotionally disturbed that they cannot give appropriate attention to the retarded.

The need for special education for the families of the mentally retarded has been amply demonstrated. It should be clear that the less severely retarded have proved their competence for citizenship and productive employment; many may be helped to contribute to family life and to participate in useful activity under sheltered conditions. It is some time since Dr. Karl Menninger pointed out that "America's future greatness is threatened unless life in many of her families is helped to become more healthy. Unlimited efforts should be spent on studies of the family to devise ways and means of strengthening it. Affection and understanding between parents and children are basic to mental health; the acceptance of responsibility and the sharing of activities lead to confidence and pride in the whole unit; the development of tolerance of the opinions, eccentricities, and peculiar techniques of relatives makes living and working with strangers more pleasant and effective."

In today's world it isn't easy to raise children blessed with a normal amount of resilience, "strong" children who can survive a typical amount of psychological and metabolic trauma. Civilization as we know it is as intrusive as a thunderstorm or an earthquake; something is always happening and often the event is a painful one. How much more difficult therefore to live with an adult or raise a child invested by natural temperament with "special problems," "supersensitive," and "weak."

Yet if you have cared for the emotionally disturbed or less severely retarded at home you can know the advantages, to society, to the patient, and to the family itself, when such care is given with knowledge and guidance. You understand and respond to such statements as this by the mother of a child who has been labeled schizophrenic since infancy. "Our child may need medicine for her lifetime. She will also need continued therapy, not unlike the efforts of a physical therapist to reeducate new muscles to take over the function of those atrophied by polio.

"Sometimes from an infirmity a tremendous gust toward achievement, of a development made possible by the narrowing of sights, results. We have come a long way with Nancy; in the past fifteen years improved methods of treatment have been found, other breakthroughs can be expected. We have watched her stumble through life, and words cannot describe our sadness at seeing her hurt. But she always picks herself up and tries again, and on this strength—which shines from her in a rare and touching way when the anxiety is reduced—we have *built,* for ourselves, for our other children who learn the lesson of persistence, and for her. The hope exists that, since she is a little better this year than last and a little better last year than the one before, she will get better. It is important that she live accepted by her parents, her brothers, perhaps the rest of the world as it begins to understand. She may make a contribution, she may find herself some happiness, she may just live, continually beset with problems.

"Yet we are not sorry we have Nancy with us. She has opened our eyes to our own priceless gift of easier communication and we are grateful that it is possible for her to be helped at home."

Epilogue

To be grown up in this culture and not do harm involves keeping our ears open to the people who have really different values, whether classified emotionally disturbed, rebellious adolescent, minority group, or old and senile. Taken together these voices of the "others" lead to an awareness of ourselves as balanced precariously over a chasm, one foot on the top of each mountain. Those of us who are successful at maintaining this balance are able to do two things: keep our authentic inner life ("to thine own self be true"), and negotiate the kind of outward reality-relationship, perhaps a job, that in some measure fulfills the needs and demands of the society in which we live. Our emotionally disturbed are people who can do one but not the other; they can satisfy either their own inner voices or the culture in which they live, but they cannot do both at the same time. It is this inability to balance which sets up their agony.

In trying to be true to ourselves we have to discover who we really are by tendency almost from birth, and relax in that. Yet not to put one foot back over the chasm between times is to be so frightened, so cut off from the broad flow of life which must involve communication with other kinds of values, that we come then, out of fear, to where our society is at. Those other people, the people on the opposite side of the chasm who perceive differently, experience differently, are "wrong." Not only are they wrong but they are "crazy." We can, if we are really insecure enough, give their craziness names, because names are reassuring. We can communicate, by our tone and often just by our gesture or a look, that those names imply something lesser, inferior, something that denotes shame. We call them schizophrenic, manic depressive, paranoid, and we sometimes do that not just because we are trying helpfully to classify those times in which certain people are overwhelmingly "disturbed by their emotions" and therefore truly need help, but because we are in terror that the differences of their perception during those times will threaten our own precarious self-image.

I started this book four years ago. I had just completed a book for the American Psychiatric Association in the course of which I interviewed many famous psychiatrists. For this one I used the medical model, based on the idea that emotional disturbance is an illness, subject to the same classification and diagnosis as physical illness.

For a long time I regretted organizing the book around this given. I regret it no longer; it is a helpful way to proceed if we do not take the word "illness" literally but think of it as existing in a different state, during which perceptions are altered, either temporarily or permanently. You can understand this if you think of the so-called "crazy" person as on a drug which makes him see and experience things differently. If he has perceived things differently once, either because of his physical makeup or sensitivity from birth or because he *is* on a drug (you can consider the chemical explanations for behavior almost as though a person is inwardly directed by a drug), that way of perceiving can come back again and again, triggered by any of the things mentioned by those who explain emotional disturbance by psychological or emotional reasons. For example, his problems will return if people around him put him in a double bind by indicating one thing and saying another, or invalidating his true feelings. His problem will return if the community or people who care about him fail to help him solve his reality problems (job training, a satisfying place to live, an authentic relationship).

For a while work on the book ceased, then it resumed. Along with the resumption of work went an enormous urge to search, explore and discover why certain things I had observed had happened, where the failure of communication exists that allowed people to be shut off and stigmatized from communities, and to emotionally crash and even suicide in the very facilities to which they have been sent to protect them against their pain.

Toward this exploration I have read and interviewed in every direction, but most of all I have continued close involvement and relationships with people considered by our society to be, in one way or another, emotionally disturbed. I have faced, with as much honesty as I could muster, the role of the caretaking person in sometimes producing—through confusion, unconscious anger, old attributions or lack of insight—an increase of symptoms in the person he loves. Since the beginning of the book I have played, at various times, with all six "models of madness" described by Dr. Osmond in a little paper that tried to bring order into the jungle of theories on causation about emotional disturbance. I started out, in fact, using the term "mental illness," words I later removed, feeling not, as Thomas Szasz says, that it is exactly a myth, but it is an already stigmatized and contemptuous way to describe differences in perception and functioning.

For a long time causation troubled me. How, I wondered, could I possibly explain how to live more authentically and helpfully with family members or friends who are emotionally upset, without knowing the cause of the unpleasantness? Laing and Esterson and Don Jackson's studies of families of schizophrenics worried me greatly for a long time, because if, as was claimed, some families use other family members to resolve their own problems, displacing them on to the "sick" one who becomes therefore the unconscious scapegoat of unconsciously destructive caretaking family members, then how could these unwitting victimizers rally round to help, especially through such an impersonal experience as reading a book?

Today I feel more comfortable with the direction this book has taken. It becomes more and more clear that emotional disturbance probably has multiple causes. Certain people are more sensitive to certain stimuli, based on personality from birth, biogenetic makeup, reaction to chemicals, reaction to social injustice, art, other people, and every conceivable influence from the world outside and the body and mind within. Whatever these causes, however plagued by a low threshold for pain, an ungainly or unattractive body, a withering of certain senses and an exaggeration of others, I believe that every human being has the right to a life filled with the events of dynamic existence in the world. Trying to find the true nature of their confusion behind their symptoms can only help us to live with them in the learning or expanding sense. We must stay open enough to see that sometimes inadvertently our needs gone underground may conflict with theirs, or even that our need is for them to be sick and that we need help ourselves to no longer make this happen.

Using the "dirty" words of psychiatry—schizophrenia, manic depression, alcoholism—we can communicate the kind of difference that exists, yet clean up the words, take the sting out of them by recognizing the hairline difference between those people whose problems have been given a name, and us whose problems are still nameless.

We can freely and honestly express our feelings about that member of the family for whom life seems to be so perennially hard, who is always having such a rough time of one kind or another, and encourage, with all the sympathy at our disposal, that he keep trying to make it in the world, with his handicap (which could be seen by society as occasionally beautiful and visionary). We can influence enough people in our own building, our own neighborhood, our own community, to no longer regard these words as stigmatized, or derogatory, so that eventually the goal might be that our emotionally disturbed friend or relative can say, "It's a little hard for me to see it your way. Explain it to me. I'm schizophrenic and I sometimes see things differently," in just the way that a person can say in today's society, "I'm blind. Please help me cross the street," or, "I'm hard of hearing, please talk louder."

And finally, we can recognize our own lack of power over a final outcome and accept (after all forms of help have been made available and we ourselves have been made available) the person where he is at. Trying to teach is one thing; imposing one's own values on a person who experiences life differently is the quickest way of feeling that the effort has been a failure.

A child who has had emotional problems from infancy has reached adulthood. A boy asks her to marry him and she says yes, insisting that this occur although they have known each other only a short while. The boy has problems too and the parents cross their fingers and hope that perhaps the self-confidence that comes from really being wanted by a peer will help them both. Two weeks later the girl runs away with another boy, the young groom gets an annulment and the marriage is over. Over the telephone the mother asks the daughter if she doesn't feel sad about its ending so soon. "Oh, no," the girl replies, "it was a wonderful wedding."

Nobody, unless there is no alternative, should be deprived of major life experiences. That those experiences may seem to be shallow and chancy is a judgment of ours based on our feeling that length of time is one of the conditions of intensity. Yet a happy moment is fixed forever as a happy moment, and in the midst of our pain at what we, as persons who care, simply cannot and may never be able to do, we should rejoice that the person we worry about can enjoy the moment, seize the day.

Glossary

"Mental illness" as described in standard practice (the American Psychiatric Association terms) is divided into broad categories each of which is associated with a cluster of symptoms. There is much overlapping between the different categories and there are very few clear cases.

Recent diagnostic thinking takes the view that mental disorders fall into three main groups.

A. Disorders caused by impairment of brain tissue
B. Mental deficiency
C. Disorders of psychogenic origin

Here a word of warning; it is important to remember that in the area of disorders of psychogenic origin (commonly known as manic depressive illness, the schizophrenias, etc.) the specific descriptions, though useful as a communication device between doctors, are highly controversial. For that reason, rather than going too specifically into the details of classification, we present here a general glance at these categories. If your doctor feels it will be helpful you may want to write to the American Psychiatric Association in Washington for their booklet on nomenclature. Usually, however, more harm than good is done by your attempts at self-diagnosis or diagnosis of a relative through such information.

Temporary Brain Impairment

Some mental illnesses of physical origin may be of a temporary nature. Certain distinct signs of these illnesses are hallucinations, illusions, and delusions. If a patient is suffering from a temporary brain disorder, he may appear to act in this fashion:

> For minutes, hours or days he may not know where he is, may misidentify nurse or doctor, misinterpret what is being said, and hear sounds nobody else can hear, such as beating of drums, shooting, rattling, footsteps, or muffled voices. He may see faces appear and disappear on the walls, or see water around him and believe he is at a beach or in a swamp, and he may react accordingly by yelling, crying, and trying to get out of bed.

Such illness as rheumatism or influenza may cause this condition and it is probable that when the fever of other illness subsides, so may the relative's mental disturbance. Another cause of temporary mental disturbance may be intoxication, either through alcohol, drugs, or poison.

Improper body functioning, due to vitamin deficiency or diabetes, may lead to emotional disorders of varying seriousness. The Vitamin B deficiency called pellagra causes emotional symptoms unlike most emotional disturbances. Pellagra, because of its physical effects, can cause death when the disease goes unchecked.

The human body, like any machine with complex parts, will break down if it is overused and overtaxed while beset with physical illness. William B., a pharmacist who undertook the sole ownership of a busy suburban drugstore, suddenly increased his weekly working hours from forty to sixty-five. Within three months his wife and family noticed that he had become extremely nervous and irritable even to the extent of falsely accusing his wife of being unfaithful and trying to poison him to collect on his life insurance policy. When he was finally taken to the family doctor he was found to have the beginnings of diabetes. There was also a noticeable deficiency of certain necessary vitamins. The prescription: certain medications and a long vacation—even if it meant selling the business. William, frightened by his doctor's diagnosis, followed all the advice. The result was a marked improvement in both his physical and mental condition.

Glandular Imbalance

Improper functioning of glands can have a direct effect on behavior and mental processes. An overactive thyroid gland will make an individual over-alert, restless and sleepless. Other signs which might indicate that your relative's unusual behavior is a result of a glandular disturbance of some kind include the shakes, wide staring eyes, problems of memory.

Brain Damage

Brain damage caused by a blow or internal growth may have serious effects on a person's mental functioning. If the blow is particularly hard or causes internal bleeding the damage may be permanent. If the blow is mild or moderate, it may produce a temporary mental disorder. Your relative may be dazed for a short time or in a deep coma lasting several weeks. During this period he may be restless and delusional and will often hallucinate. He does not realize where he is, misinterprets what is going on around him, has mood swings between irritability and depression, hostile outbreaks and elation. He may eat normally and attend to his toilet needs, but he has difficulty in retaining what his senses tell him.

A number of other physical causes of mental disorders of a temporary or acute nature are circulatory disturbances and convulsions.

Permanent Brain Damage

Before discussing permanent brain disorders, it may be helpful to look at certain characteristics common to all of them. The basic effect is a marked change in personality. A cheerful person may become moody and depressed, while a sharp-witted, intelligent one may become dull and forgetful. He may begin to see or hear strange things and become terrified of any number of events which previously never bothered him. Since the range of disorder is enormous, the patient may suffer from nothing more than a mild peculiarity such as a newly acquired habit of interrupting others' conversations. On the other hand his disorder can result in a totally helpless condition.

Infectious diseases may cause permanent as well as temporary mental disorders. Perhaps the most striking example is syphilis of the brain. If the condition is left untreated, you will see a steady decline of the patient's ability to function in the everyday world.

Intoxication from alcohol, drugs, or gas may also result in a permanent or chronic change. This condition occurs when the dosage is so extensive that the tissue of the brain is destroyed. The condition is always much more serious where there is constant repetitious damage to brain tissue.

Advanced age brings with it many mental disorders caused by damage to the brain. It is shocking to find that a once hearty parent now cannot take care of his own bodily needs or remember what happened the day before. A brain tumor may affect your parent's entire personality and result in permanent brain damage which can lead to death if its growth cannot be checked. The first symptom may be the onset of severe headaches. Later the personality may collapse entirely; the patient may lose use of his smell, sight, and hearing. He may be unable to remember the most fundamental facts of his daily life.

Dr. Karl A. Menninger provides a vivid description of the effects of a brain tumor on a fifty-two-year-old minister. The minister,

> . . . began to complain of severe headaches, which occurred from two to three times a week. About the middle of April it was noted that his sermons were incoherent, and that he stumbled through them, but always in an unconcerned manner.
>
> Fired from his position he then went on a road trip. His condition apparently got progressively worse, and people noticed a sharp change in his personality.
>
> His memory now failed markedly; his attention, interest, and ability to concentrate were also impaired. He was unable to remember details; speech was slow and dragging, so that he became unable to carry on a conversation; he would break off suddenly and did not seem to realize what he was saying. He developed peculiar mannerisms, such as kicking with his right foot, or tapping on objects with his right forefinger. He read signs over and over again. During the month prior to his examination at the clinic he would sit around uninterested; he was careless about his habits and dress, soiled his clothes, and on one occasion urinated into his slipper, pouring the urine out of the window, much to his own amusement, but to the chagrin of his wife. . . .

Epilepsy, with its accompanying seizures or convulsions, may or may not result in permanent mental impairment. The epileptic may be susceptible to attacks at any time during the day or night, and subject to sharp, violent swings of mood. Epileptics can learn to live with their disorder and for that reason there is often much hope for them and their families.

> In a small southeastern college town, a burly, thirty-six-year-old man named Carl was known to all as an epileptic. Delivering newspapers on his bicycle each day, every so often he would go off into one of his "fits." Often townspeople would see Carl in this condition and help him

inside to their home or store for a brief rest, or a calm, reassuring talk. After his "rest," Carl would continue on his paper route as if nothing had happened. This went on for at least eleven years.

Mental Deficiency

The mental disorders caused by physical factors described above do not include one symptom which may be present in a chronic or permanent condition: mental deficiency and retardation. What is the difference between a mentally deficient person and a person with average or above-average intelligence?

Take the T. brothers, Lewis, Leo and Phillip. Lewis, aged 22, and Leo, aged 24, have both graduated from college and have jobs. Lewis, a bachelor, works as a salesman. He has a variety of interests ranging from politics to women. Leo is married and is attending law school at night while working at an office job during the day. The third T. brother, aged 19, in contrast to both Lewis and Leo, never graduated from high school. He was a slow learner as a child, and never could keep up with the rest of his class in public school. When he was eleven years old, Phillip was given a battery of tests by the school psychologist. At that time it was determined that Phillip had a "mental age" of 8 years; and it was suggested to Mr. and Mrs. T. that Phillip be placed in the special class for "slow learners," where he would take non-academic subjects like wood shop and auto-mechanics.

This didn't quite work out, for Phillip found it difficult to follow even the simplest instructions. His attention drifted and he failed in this program also. When he was sixteen, Phillip quit school and got a job as a day laborer. The job lasted three weeks and there then followed a series of menial jobs, none of which he could hold. After failing the Army intelligence test, Phillip began staying home in his bedroom day after day. Today, Phillip rarely goes outside the house and has become a virtual prisoner of his inadequate brain.

The range of "average" I.Q. scores is 90 to 110 and there are three labeled categories of mental deficiency based on I.Q. scores. These include: Mild Mental Deficiency, an I.Q. range of 71 to 80; Moderate Mental Deficiency, an I.Q. range of 51 to 70; and Severe Mental Deficiency, an I.Q. range of below 50. Persons in this range need complete custodial care.

A striking picture of a person with a severe mental deficiency is presented by William Faulkner in his novel, *The Sound and the Fury.* The character, named Benjy, is a thirty-three-year-old man with the intelligence of a seven-year-old. He is cared for by his family and is unable to communicate his thoughts and feelings to anyone. Benjy's life is portrayed as being both pathetic and confusing, for he neither understands nor adjusts to the strange, fearful world around him.

If a person has a low I.Q. we usually consider it one sign of mental deficiency. However, I.Q. test scores should not be considered the ultimate basis for determining his capabilities since there are other important indications in determining whether or not he will be able to lead a productive life. Two of them are *motivation* and *proper training.*

Adequate communication (especially the ability to speak and write in a manner that is understood by others) is a sign of at least an average intelligence. If you notice that your relative has a great deal of trouble in communicating his thoughts and feelings, this may be one sign that he is mentally deficient.

There are a number of disorders, usually observable at birth, which either cause, or are associated with, this condition. They include: cretinism, mongoloidism, microcephalitis, and hydrocephalitis. Because these four kinds of problems cause peculiar body deformities they are easily observable.

Cretinism, caused by a thyroid deficiency, results in an unusual physical appearance. The cretin has a large head placed on a short, stubby neck. The cretin's eyes are half-shut, and his eyelids are swollen. He has a large, protruding abdomen, scanty hair, and short, pudgy arms and legs. Finally the cretin suffers from mental deficiency. His intelligence is clearly below average.

A *mongoloid* can always be identified at birth. The back of the head of a mongoloid baby is flattened. He has a comparatively large, fissured tongue, and he is relatively underweight. The mongoloid either has very poor speech or cannot speak at all. He is always mentally retarded.

The *microcephalic* has a much smaller head than the average person. His head is shaped like a cone, and his forehead recedes. There is no protuberance on the back of the head as there is with the average person. The microcephalic's I.Q. usually ranges from 30 to 50.

The *hydrocephalic,* on the other hand, has a huge head which contains an abnormal amount of brain fluid. In this condition the mental effects vary from person to person.

Disorders of Psychogenic Origin

The mental disorders described to this point have clearly identifiable physical bases in common. Emotional disorders which are not physical in origin are harder to identify. These include certain kinds of psychoses, less serious but sometimes crippling disorders called neuroses, and somewhat different conditions called personality disorders.

Dr. Daniel Blain, a past president of the American Psychiatric Association, was recently asked his opinion of the meaning of the term "psychosis." According to Dr. Blain, "We are speaking, essentially, of the development of *unreality,* and a departure from reality—whether it's in terms of a hallucination, or a delusion, or warping of interpretation of phenomenon so as to suggest bad judgment. The person who has a psychotic condition is really out of control . . ." Remember that this evaluation should be quantitative in terms of just how long and how seriously a person's "out of control" behavior interferes with his reasonably happy functioning in the world or his chosen subculture.

Psychoses which are not easily explainable by physical causes are called psychogenic in origin, that is, they seem to originate in the mind, with no one clear cause.

> Peter L., age 22, grew up in a small North Carolina town. His mother was committed to the State Mental Hospital shortly after Peter's birth.

Peter's father, a sober, somber man of 52, attempted to raise a family of three children with the help of his sister. Mr. L. administered frequent beatings to his children.

Peter, a quiet boy throughout high school with interests in electronics and photography, maintained an A average and was able to win a scholarship to college. In college Peter led a quiet, simple life. Aside from a part-time job operating a movie projector on weekends, Peter had no other outside interests, and he never managed to make friends or go out on dates.

One morning in his sophomore year, during a physics lecture, Peter suddenly rose from his seat and began to scream. He ran out of the lecture hall and locked himself into his dormitory room for the rest of the day. A few days later, Peter was referred to the college infirmary by his dormitory floor advisor after other students brought the incident to the attention of the advisor. However, Peter did not go for an appointment. He instead returned to a class lecture and took his accustomed seat. This time during the lecture Peter arose silently and began undressing in front of the rest of the class. When students attempted to stop him, Peter began hitting and kicking them. When the students finally subdued Peter they took him back to his dormitory room. Peter lay on his bed and stared up at the ceiling for many hours until school authorities, acting on complaints from students, professors, and the dormitory floor advisor, had him taken to the State Mental Hospital, not far from the college. After four months there, when asked about his work, Peter said, "Oh, I'm designing the world's most powerful microphone. A microphone so strong it can even hear protozoa."

When the staff doctor described Peter's condition as a "complete breakdown," he was referring to what we may also call a psychosis. The best known of these psychoses are called manic depressive reaction and the schizophrenias.

A major difficulty in specifically describing these illnesses is that such identification based on general symptoms can be a form of name-calling with dangerous results. A person too quickly labeled can begin to conform to the role of patient (sometimes thankfully) rather than dealing with the actualities of his symptoms and how he can eventually come to terms with his world. Nor is it helpful for even a well-meaning parent or friend to attempt self-diagnosis of psychosis or even neurosis.

Involutional Illness

When adults reach late middle age they must face certain painful events. Their child raising years are over and with them a sense of youth, sexual enjoyment, and future goals. Occasionally, the time they anticipate seems now filled with frustration and shrunken expectations.

The result of these changes may lead some people to feel a great deal of self-pity. When changes brought on during middle age are accompanied by a feeling of frustrated hopelessness, a problem called involutional psychosis may exist.

Neurosis

Members of your family may do strange things which, although not completely irrational, nevertheless make them unhappy. They may be very sad for long periods or have violent aversions to certain ordinary events, be extremely anxious most of the time or follow ritualistic patterns of behavior. If this is the case, they may be suffering from a neurosis.

You may have used the word "neurosis" or "neurotic" in conversation to describe a person who has gotten on your nerves, or who acts in a peculiar manner, for it is difficult to define precisely.

Robert M. White, a professor of clinical psychology at Harvard, says that "Neurosis can be considered a kind of maladjustment in the common meaning of the word, but it can be distinguished from lesser maladjustments by qualities that owe their being to a fundamental struggle with anxiety." White describes neurotic tendencies as an excessive need for affection, attention-seeking devices, a need for power, and a stifling of feelings.

We are all confronted with daily problems and situations which lead to stress. Sometimes we become nervous and anxious. However, we can usually keep this anxiety under some sort of check so that when the crisis or stress has passed we can return to a more relaxed state.

Neuroses may be classified as *anxiety reaction, phobias, conversion reaction, dissociative reaction, compulsive reaction,* or *depressive reaction.*

Personality Disorders

Kisker points out that personality disorders cover a wide area, and include such disturbances as *personality pattern disturbance, inadequate personality, schizoid personality, cyclothymic personality,* the *passive-dependent personality* or *passive-aggressive personality, immature personality, sociopathic personality, antisocial reaction, sexual deviation,* and *severe addiction.*

Transient Stress Disorders

Reactions to certain conditions of stress may lead to temporary and minor personality disturbances, for a person may in some way alter under the pressure of such occurrences as earthquakes, fires, war and loss of a beloved person.

What seems to be a neurotic or psychotic condition in a family member may sometimes be just a problem of adjustment to a temporary stress situation.

We must all go through a series of adjustments as we pass through various stages of our lives. Infancy, childhood, adolescence, adulthood, and old age—all have certain obstacles that must be hurdled, but sometimes the transition from one stage to another is not a smooth one, and a family member may react in a disturbed, confused, or strange manner such as this report by Kisker:

> "She worried constantly about the effect of prenatal impressions on the baby," reported a physician about a thirty-year-old mother-to-be.

> She had heard many stories about such influences; one, for example, about a child born without legs because the mother, shortly after conception, had witnessed an accident in which a child's legs were amputated. . . . Although she knew it was foolish to believe such superstitions she dared not act counter to their import. Fear of dying at childbirth, fear lest the baby die or be born "imperfect," dominated her thinking.

Sometimes the condition passes by itself when the stress is gone. At other times the difficulty becomes so severe that real help and understanding are required to bring a person back to the state in which he was before the situation developed.

A family is divorcing and the eight-year-old daughter begins to wet her bed, is silent and withdrawn in the daytime and stares into space in school. When questioned she answers only that everything is "okay," but after a few weeks the mother finds the child waking at frequent intervals during the night, padding around the house silently, unable to sleep.

Fire destroys the house and possessions of a young couple and the pregnant wife miscarries in her seventh month, losing the premature child. She seems to make a sensible adjustment, helping reconstruct a life for them in a new place, but six weeks later she is overcome by spells of stuttering, has an urge to "sleep away the day," finds it hard to do even simple household chores, and develops a smell phobia in the course of which she walks around their apartment whenever she is awake, checking to see that there are no lit matches or cigarette butts and that the stove is turned off. These symptoms continue for several months, increasing to the point where much of her time is spent sleeping or checking to see if there is danger.

A fifty-year-old man is fired from a high executive job at a firm where he has spent the last sixteen years. His efforts to get a similar job at another firm prove fruitless and he is forced to accept a subordinate position at an inferior place. He begins to drink heavily, quarrels with his wife and children and moves to a furnished room where he becomes seclusive, cooking inadequate meals for himself as though he were poverty stricken, unwilling to even go to a movie because of unrealistic economic fears.

A mother of two is hospitalized for cancer and happens to overhear two visitors who think she is asleep discussing the nature of her illness. She becomes hysterical, seems to adjust after warmly sympathetic talks with her doctor, her husband and a capable social worker. A week later she starts "hearing voices" telling her that the illness will be cured, that things will get better.

All these incidents are simple examples of not unusual reactions to temporary or permanent stress situations. In some cases psychotherapy and "the help of friends" will lessen the pain to the point that the symptoms will recede and the person go back to his former ways. In other cases the blow may be so severe that adjustment is not completely possible. All stress situations lower a person's normal defenses, but in most cases if the pain is caused by an outside event, helping the patient acknowledge his grief will produce an outpouring of pent-up emotions and reduce the seemingly emotionally disturbed behavior.

How can you recognize when a transient situation stress has pushed your family member into the kind of disturbance that cannot be dealt with that easily? The answer is simply: try simple measures first. If true sympathy, a peaceful regime which includes rest, good food, planned recreation, doesn't help at all, and the person has been helped to ventilate all emotions, maybe more heroic measures will be needed. Recognize first, however, his right to his symptoms and expression of pain. Except in the case of terminal illness where denial may be a self-protective device, the later adjustment is bound to be a better one if all the feelings have been expressed.

Suggested Reading

The suggested reading list has been made up of material which the author has at first hand experienced as especially helpful in at least one of the many areas which make up this book. A strong attempt has been made to suggest paperback editions whenever available and most of the books have been checked for availability. Many of the books are recent and in some cases controversial, but standard classics have not been neglected.

Understanding Human Nature. Alfred Adler, Fawcett, N.Y.

Wayward Youth. Aichhorn, Viking Press, N.Y.

When Disaster Strikes, American National Red Cross, Washington, D. C., 1968.

Design For Therapy. Conference Held at Mayflower Hotel, Washington, D.C., 1955, available through American Psychiatric Association, Washington, D.C.

The Radical Therapist. Jerome Angel, Ballantine Books, N.Y.

How to Help Older Folk—A Guide for You and Your Family. Arthur, Lippincott, Philadelphia.

Handbook of Community Psychiatry. Bellak, Grune and Stratton, N.Y.

Parents Not Guilty of Their Children's Neuroses. Bergler, Liveright, N.Y.

A Layman's Guide to Psychiatry and Psychoanalysis. Berne, Grove Press, N.Y.

Recreational Trends in North American Hospitals. Blain and Vosburgh, American Psychiatric Association, Washington, D.C.

Child Care and the Growth of Lives. John Bowly, Penguin Books, London.

A Two Year Old Goes to Hospital. Bowly, Robertson and Rosenbluth, The Psychoanalytic Study of the Child, Vol. 11, International Universities Press, N.Y., 1953.

Vocational Services for Psychiatric Clinic Patients. Bozeman, Harvard University Press, Cambridge, Mass.

The Layman's Guide to Psychiatry. Brussel, Barnes and Noble, N.Y.

Alice's Adventures in Wonderland. Lewis Carroll, The Annotated Alice, Meridian Books, World Publishing, Cleveland.

Murder, Madness and the Law. Cohen, Coffin and Frank, World Publishing Co., N.Y., 1962.

The Death of the Family. David Cooper, Random House, N.Y.

Psychiatry and Anti-Psychiatry. David Cooper, Random House, N.Y.

Schizophrenia and the Family. Lidz Fleck Cornelson, International Universities Press, N.Y.

Crime and Punishment, Dostoievsky, Harmondsworth, Penguin Books, London.

The Cry for Help. Farberow and Schneidman, editors, McGraw-Hill, N.Y.

Residential Treatment Centers for Emotionally Disturbed Children. Published by the Federal Security Agency, Dept. of Health, Education and Welfare, Children's Bureau, available through U.S. Gov. Printing Office, Supt. of Documents, Washington, D.C.

Introduction to Psychiatric Occupational Therapy. Fidler and Fidler, Macmillan, N.Y.

The Psychoanalytic Reader. Robert Fliess, editor, International Universities Press, N.Y.

Patterns of Sexual Behavior. Clellan Ford and Frank Beach, Harper and Row, N.Y.

Psychoanalytic Principles in Casework with Children. Fraiberg, Family Service Association of America, N.Y., 1955.

Volunteer Work with Psychiatric Patients. Frank, reprint by the National Association for Mental Health, N.Y.

Psychoanalysis for Teachers and Parents. Anna Freud, Beacon Press, London.

The Art of Loving. Erich Fromm, Harper Colophon Books, N.Y.

A New Connection, John Frykman, Scrimshaw Press, San Francisco.

Asylums. E. Goffman, Anchor Books, Doubleday, N.Y.

Wanted: Your Magic. Gray, National Association for Mental Health, N.Y., 1954.

Sex Offenses, The Problems, Causes, and Prevention. Guttmacher, W. W. Norton, N.Y.

The Power Tactics of Jesus Christ and Other Essays, Jay Haley, Discus Avon Books, N.Y.

Psychiatric Aide Education. Hall, Menninger Clinic Monograph Series No. 9, Grune and Stratton, N.Y.

Culture Against Man. Jules Henry, Random House, N.Y.

Women in Marital Conflict. Hollis, Family Service Association of America, N.Y., 1949.

The Practice of Mental Nursing. Houliston, Williams and Wilkins, Boston.

The Therapeutic Community. M. Jones, Basic Books, N.Y.

Sexual Behavior in the Human Female. Kinsey, Pocket Books, Simon & Schuster, N.Y.

Sexual Behavior in the Human Male. Kinsey, Pocket Books, Simon & Schuster, N.Y.

The Divided Self. Ronald Laing, Penguin Books, N.Y.

The Politics of Experience and the Bird of Paradise. Laing, Penguin Press, N.Y. Pantheon.

Politics of the Family. Ronald Laing, Penguin Books, Toronto.

The Self and Others. Ronald Laing, Penguin Books, N.Y.

Sanity, Madness, and the Family. Laing and Esterson, Tavistock, London.

New Light on Epilepsy and Migraine. Lennox, Harper and Row, N.Y., 1946.

Psychotherapy in Medical Practice. M. Levine, Macmillan, N.Y.

Maternal Overprotection. David Levy, W. W. Norton and Co.

Gift from the Sea. Anne Lindbergh, Random House, N.Y.

The Mentally Disabled and the Law, The Report of the American Bar Foundation on the Rights of the Mentally Ill. Lindeman and McIntyre, editors, University of Chicago Press, Chicago, 1961.

The Addict and the Law. Lindesmith, Alfred.

Man's Search for Himself. Rollo May, New American Library, N.Y.

The Human Mind. Karl Menninger, Literary Guild of America, N.Y.

Love Against Hate. Karl Menninger, Harcourt, Brace and Jovanovitch, N.Y.

Man Against Himself. Karl Menninger, Harcourt, Brace and Jovanovitch, N.Y.

The Vital Balance. Karl Menninger, Viking Press, N.Y.

Psychiatrist to a Troubled World. William Menninger, Viking Press, N.Y.

You and Psychiatry. William Menninger and Munro Leaf, Charles Scribner's Sons, N.Y.

Growing with Music, A Program for the Mentally Retarded. Miller, *Exceptional Children* 20:305, 1954.

Handbook for Psychiatric Aides. National Association for Mental Health, N.Y.

Mental Health Publications and Audio Visual Aids. National Association for Mental Health, N.Y.

Psychiatric Clinics and Other Resources in the United States Directory, 1952. National Association for Mental Health, N.Y.

When You Grow Older. Plawton and Stewart, Public Affairs Pamphlet No. 131, U.S. Gov. Printing Office, Washington, D.C.

Music Therapy. Podolsky, Philosophical Library, N.Y., 1954.

How Psychiatry Helps. Polatin and Philtine, editors, Collier Books, N.Y.

Family Care of Mental Patients. Pollock Utica State Hospitals Press, Utica, N.Y., 1956.

The Teacher and Mental Health. Public Health Service Publication No. 385, U.S. Gov. Printing Office, Washington, D.C.

Catalogue of Mental Health Pamphlets and Other Reprints. Public Health Service Pamphlets No. 19, U.S. Gov. Printing Office, Washington 25, D.C.

Client Centered Therapy. Carl Rogers, Houghton Mifflin, Boston.

The Three Christs of Ypsilanti. Milton Rokeach, Vintage Books, Random House, N.Y.

Cooking, A Therapy for the Mentally Ill. Rosemeier, *J. Am. Dietetic Assoc.* 30:470, 1954.

Direct Analysis. J. Rosen, Grune and Stratton, N.Y.

The New Group Therapies. Henrick Ruiteneek, Discus Avon Books, N.Y.

An Introduction to Physical Methods of Treatment in Psychiatry. Sargant and Slater, Williams and Wilkins, Baltimore.

Clues to Suicide. Schneidman and Farberow, editors, McGraw-Hill, N.Y.

Rehabilitation of Mental Hospital Patients. Schwartz, Public Health Monograph 17, U.S. Gov. Printing Office, Washington, D.C.

A Way to the Soul of the Mentally Ill. Schwing, International Universities Press, N.Y.

The Attendant's Guide. E. M. Stern, National Association for Mental Health, N.Y.

The Mental Hospital, A Guide for the Citizen. Edith Stern, National Association for Mental Health, N.Y., 1947.

Mental Illness, A Guide for the Family. Edith Stern, National Association for Mental Health, N.Y.

The Manufacture of Madness. Thomas Szasz, Dell Publishing Co., N.Y.

The Myth of Mental Illness. Thomas Szasz, Delta Books, N.Y.

Music in Hospitals. Van De Wall, Russell Sage Foundation, N.Y.

Veterans Administration Information Bulletin, Dept. of Medicine and Surgery, available through Office of Chief Medical Director Veterans Administration, Washington, D.C. 20025, 1954.

Constructive Programs for the Mental Health of the Elderly. Zeman, distributed as a pamphlet by the National Association for Mental Health, N.Y.

Where to Look for Help

The most recent list of facilities for the emotionally disturbed is the Mental Health Directory (1971) put out by the National Institute of Mental Health. It can be secured through:

Superintendent of Documents
Government Printing Office
Washington, D.C. 20402 $3.75

Lists of facilities for addicts and alcoholics can be secured through the National Institute of Mental Health in Washington which maintains a Drug Addiction Program and Alcoholism Prevention Center.

All states, with the exception of Kentucky, Montana, Nebraska, and Vermont, have a State Mental Hygiene Society that conducts clinics. States with the largest number of clinics and psychiatric centers are California, Illinois, Maine (which has a huge number of adult psychiatric but no child guidance clinics), Maryland, New Jersey, New York, Ohio, Pennsylvania, and Virginia.

If you want to know about psychiatric resources, you can write to any of the following organizations:

Alabama Assn. for Mental Health, Inc.
901 South Eighteenth Street
Birmingham, Alabama 35205

Alaska Mental Health Assn.
1020 I Street
Anchorage, Alaska 99501

Arizona Assn. for Mental Health, Inc.
341 West McDowell Road
Phoenix, Arizona 85003

The Arkansas Assn. for Mental Health, Inc.
424 East 6th Street
Little Rock, Arkansas 72202

California Assn. for Mental Health
901 "H" Street, Suite 212
Sacramento, California 95814

Colorado Assn. for Mental Health, Inc.
1375 Delaware Street
Denver, Colorado 80204

Connecticut Assn. for Mental Health, Inc.
123 Tremont Street
Hartford, Connecticut 06105

Mental Health Assn. of Delaware, Inc.
701 Shipley Street
Wilmington, Delaware 19801

District of Columbia Mental Health Assn., Inc.
3000 Connecticut Ave., N.W.
Suite 100
Washington, D.C. 20008

Mental Health Assn. of Florida, Inc.
Suite 207, Myrick Bldg.
132 E. Colonial Drive
Orlando, Florida 32801

The Georgia Assn. for Mental Health, Inc.
230 Peachtree Street, N.W.
Suite 214
Altanta, Georgia 30303

The Mental Health Assn. of Hawaii
200 North Vineyard, Room 101
Honolulu, Hawaii 96817

Idaho Mental Health Assn.
311 North 10th Street
Boise, Idaho 83702

Illinois Assn. for Mental Health, Inc.
710 Reisch Bldg.—Lincoln Square
Springfield, Illinois 62701

The Mental Health Assn. in Indiana
1433 N. Meridian St.
Indianapolis, Indiana 46202

The Iowa Assn. for Mental Health, Inc.
521 14th Street
Des Moines, Iowa 50309

Kansas Assn. for Mental Health, Inc.
4015 West 21st Street
Topeka, Kansas 66604

Kentucky Assn. for Mental Health, Inc.
Suite 104, 310 West Liberty Street
Louisville, Kentucky 40202

Louisiana Assn. for Mental Health
1528 Jackson Avenue
New Orleans, Louisiana 70130

Maryland Assn. for Mental Health, Inc.
325 East 25th Street
Baltimore, Maryland 21218

The Massachusetts Assn. for Mental Health, Inc.
38 Chauncey Street, Room 801
Boston, Massachusetts 02111

Michigan Society for Mental Health, Inc.
27208 Southfield Road
Lathrup Village, Michigan 48075

Minnesota Assn. for Mental Health, Inc.
45-10 W. 77th Street
Room 100
Minneapolis, Minnesota 55435

Mississippi Assn. for Mental Health, Inc.
902-904 Standard Life Bldg.
Box 2081
Jackson, Mississippi 39205

Missouri Assn. for Mental Health
411 Madison Street
Jefferson City, Missouri 65101

Montana Assn. for Mental Health
Box 88—214 Main Ave., N.
Choteau, Montana 59422

Nevada Assn. for Mental Health
2018 E. Charleston Boulevard
Las Vegas, Nevada 89104

The New Jersey Assn. for Mental Health, Inc.
60 South Fullerton Avenue
Montclair, New Jersey 07042

The New York State Assn. for Mental Health, Inc.
90 State Street
Albany, New York 12207

North Carolina Mental Health Assn.
425 North Boylan Avenue
Raleigh, North Carolina 27603

North Dakota Mental Health Assn.
P.O. Box 160
202½ N. Third Street
Bismarck, North Dakota 58501

Mental Health Federation, Inc.
(Ohio Division)
M-59 The Neil House Hotel
Columbus, Ohio 43215

The Oklahoma Assn. for Mental Health, Inc.
3113 Classen Boulevard
Oklahoma City, Oklahoma 73118

Mental Health Assn. of Oregon
718 W. Burnside Street, Rm. 301
Portland, Oregon 97209

Pennsylvania Mental Health, Inc.
1601 Walnut Street
Philadelphia, Pennsylvania 19103

Rhode Island Assn. for Mental Health, Inc.
333 Grotto Avenue
Providence, Rhode Island 02906

South Carolina Mental Health Assn.
1823 Gadsden Street
Columbia, South Carolina 29201

South Dakota Mental Health Assn.
101½ S. Pierre Street, Box 355
Pierre, South Dakota 57501

Tennessee Mental Health Assn.
1717 West End Building, Suite 421
Nashville, Tennessee 37203

Texas Assn. for Mental Health
Suite 107, Lantern Lane
Austin, Texas 78731

Utah Assn. for Mental Health
211 East 3rd South, Suite 202
Salt Lake City, Utah 84111

Virginia Assn. for Mental Health
#2 North First Street
Richmond, Virginia 23219

The West Virginia Assn. for Mental Health, Inc.
815 Quarrier Street
318 Morrison Building
Charleston, West Virginia 25301

Wisconsin Association for Mental Health
119 East Mifflin
P.O. Box 1486
Madison, Wisconsin 53701

American Psychiatric Association
1700 18th St., N.W.
Washington, D.C. 20009
Gives list of board-certified psychiatrists.

American Psychoanalytic Association Inc.
1 East 57 Street
N.Y., N.Y. 10022

National Association for Mental Health Inc.
Washington, D.C.

National Epilepsy League Inc.
208 N. Wells Street
Chicago 6, Ill.

American Epilepsy Society
Baylor University
College of Medicine
Houston, Texas 77025

Gamblers Anonymous
P.O. Box 17173
Los Angeles, Calif. 90017

Alcoholics Anonymous
133 East 39 Street
N.Y., N.Y. 10016

National Association for Retarded Children
386 Park Ave. South
N.Y., N.Y. 10017

Family Protection League of the U.S.A.
4143 Moody Street
Corona, Calif. 91720

Narcotics Anonymous care of The Salvation Army
120 West 14 Street
N.Y., N.Y. 10011

Family Service Association of America
44 East 23 Street
N.Y., N.Y. 10010